CONTEMPORARY GRANDPARENTIN

D0401448

Changing family relationships in global contexts

Edited by Sara Arber and Virpi Timonen

Dublin, 14 June, 2012

For Norah –

With thanks for excellent company in Copenhagen & hoping to meet you again in the near future.

Best wishes –

Virpi

First published in Great Britain in 2012 by

The Policy Press
University of Bristol
Fourth Floor
Beacon House
Queen's Road
Bristol BS8 1QU
UK
t: +44 (0)117 331 4054
f: +44 (0)117 331 4093
tpp-info@bristol.ac.uk
www.policypress.co.uk

North American office:
The Policy Press
c/o The University of Chicago Press
1427 East 60th Street
Chicago, IL 60637, USA
t: +1 773 702 7700
f: +1 773 702 9756
sales@press.uchicago.edu • www.press.uchicago.edu

British Library Cataloguing in Publication Data
A catalogue record for this book is available from the British Library.

Library of Congress Cataloging-in-Publication Data
A catalog record for this book has been requested.

ISBN 978 1 84742 967 4 paperback
ISBN 978 1 84742 968 1 hardcover

Cover design by Qube Design Associates, Bristol.
Front cover: image kindly supplied by istock
Printed and bound in Great Britain by TJ International,
Padstow
The Policy Press uses environmentally responsible print
partners.

For my grandson, Marcus Hugh,
and any future grandchildren
Sara Arber

For the sanity-saving grandparents
– Liisa, Viljo, Mary and Páid –
of my sanity-eroding,
yet world-beating daughters,
Suvi and Anja
Virpi Timonen

Contents

List of tables and figures

Tables

Figures

Notes on contributors

Sara Arber is Professor of Sociology and co-director of the Centre for Research on Ageing and Gender at the University of Surrey, UK. She is past president of the British Sociological Association, and of the International Sociological Association Research Committee on Sociology of Aging (RC11). Sara's research interests include gender and ageing, class and gender inequalities in health, and sociology of sleep. Her books include *The myth of generational conflict: Family and state in ageing societies* (Routledge, 2000, with Claudine Attias-Donfut) and *Gender and ageing: Changing roles and relationships* (Open University Press, 2003, with Kate Davidson and Jay Ginn).

Lindsey Baker is a lecturer in the Leonard Davis School of Gerontology at the University of Southern California, USA. Lindsey's research interests focus on the exchange of space, time and financial transfers between generations, particularly within the grandparent–grandchild relationship. She has published primarily on the influence of raising grandchildren on the health and wellbeing of older adults in *Journal of Marriage and the Family*, *Journal of Gerontology: Social Sciences*, *Journal of Family Issues* and other leading peer-reviewed journals.

Rita Borges Neves is a researcher at the Centre for Research in the Social Sciences at the University of Minho, Portugal and a research associate at the Institute of Psychiatry of King's College London, UK. She has been involved in several research projects regarding ageing, including the Survey of Health, Ageing and Retirement in Europe (SHARE). Rita is interested in social inequalities in health, productive activities, wellbeing and ageing, and lectures in sociology of health.

Lynda Clarke is head of the Department of Population Studies at the London School of Hygiene and Tropical Medicine, UK. She specialises in family demography, particularly family change, health and policy. Previously, she undertook social research at the Thomas Coram Research Institute, the Office for National Statistics and the Family Policy Studies Centre as Director of Family Demography, including a national study of grandparenthood. Currently, Lynda is collaborating in international studies in South Africa of fathers and of youth health services, adolescent sexual health and the impact of imprisonment on men and their families in the US and Britain.

Alice Delerue Matos is Assistant Professor in sociology and demography at the University of Minho, Portugal and Research Coordinator of the Population, Family and Health Research Group at the Research Centre for the Social Sciences. Alice's research interests include the sociology of ageing, family intergenerational relationships and class and gender inequalities of the older population. She has coordinated several research projects, and currently shares the coordination of the Portuguese research team of SHARE. She has authored and co-authored national and international publications on ageing.

Martha Doyle is a research fellow in the Social Policy and Ageing Research Centre in Trinity College Dublin, Ireland. Her research interests include the political representation of older people, the analysis of community care and supports for older people, migrant care workers and research methods that aim to foster the social inclusion and participation of older people.

Gunhild O. Hagestad is senior researcher at NOVA (Norwegian Social Research) and professor emerita of sociology. She has held faculty positions at several universities in the US, and at the University of Oslo and University of Agder, Norway. Her main interests are intergenerational relations and life-course patterns in ageing societies, and she has been part of several UN consultancies on population ageing. Gunhild has participated in two major EU-funded projects, one of them on grandparenthood, and she has been part of numerous other international research teams. She is the author of more than 100 publications in nine languages.

Madonna Harrington Meyer is Meredith Professor for teaching excellence, professor of sociology, and senior research associate at the Center for Policy Research at Syracuse University, US. She is author of articles on ageing, healthcare and gender. Her book with Pamela Herd, *Market friendly or family friendly? The state and gender inequality in old age* (Russell Sage, 2007) was awarded the Gerontological Society of America's Kalish Publication Award. She is editor of *Care work: Gender, labor, and the welfare state* (Routledge, 2000), and winner of the National Council of Family Relations' Jessie Bernard Outstanding Contribution to Feminist Scholarship award.

Katharina Herlofson is a researcher at Norwegian Social Research, Oslo. Her interests include gender and intergenerational ties in a comparative perspective. She has participated in EU-funded international research projects (OASIS and Multilinks) and is currently a co-investigator for the Norwegian Life Course, Ageing and Generation Panel Study. Among her recent publications are an article on population and family structures in ageing societies (with Gunhild Hagestad) in *Demographic Research* (2011) and an article on family obligations and welfare state regimes (with Svein Olav Daatland and Ivar Lima) in *Ageing and Society* (2011).

Oliver Huxhold received his PhD in psychology from the Free University Berlin in 2007. He is now a senior researcher at the German Centre of Gerontology (DZA) in Berlin, Germany. Oliver's current research interests are on developmental dynamics over the life course and quantitative research methods. He has published articles on a variety of topics, including age differences in intra-individual changes in cognition and motor performance, effects of different social support functions, and influences of socioeconomic status on health trajectories across the lifespan.

Lisanne S.F. Ko is a research fellow in the Sau Po Center on Ageing at the University of Hong Kong and has previously held faculty positions in medical and social science faculties in several universities in Hong Kong. Her main research interests include the ageing experience of older adults, health service utilisation and urban development. She has extensive research experience in areas of ageing: active ageing, housing for older persons, social and healthcare services for older people, long-term care services for older people, poverty among older adults, financial sustainability, reverse mortgage, ageing education, colonisation and indigenous medicines, and urbanisation and gentrification.

Katharina Mahne is a researcher at the German Centre of Gerontology (DZA) in Berlin, Germany, and is involved in the German Ageing Survey (DEAS). Her research focus is on the interrelation of social structure and intergenerational relations in later life. Katharina is currently completing her doctoral dissertation in the field of grandparenthood. Her publications include *Grandparenthood: A common aspiration for later life? On the subjective importance of the grandparent role in Germany* (forthcoming, Advances in Life Course Research, with Andreas Motel-Klingebiel).

Jennifer Mason is Professor of Sociology at the University of Manchester, UK, where she is also co-director of the Morgan Centre for the Study of Relationships and Personal Life. Her research interests include family, personal life, relationships and research methodologies. In recent years she has collaborated with colleagues in projects on a range of topics including family resemblances, inter/ generational dynamics and critical associations. She directed two of the ESRC National Centre for Research Methods 'Nodes' – Real Life Methods (2005-08) and Realities (2008-11). Her books include *Passing on: Kinship and inheritance in England* (Routledge, 2000, with Janet Finch), *Qualitative researching* (Sage Publications, 2002) and *Understanding social research: Thinking creatively about method* (Sage Publications, 2011, with Angela Dale).

Vanessa May is Lecturer in sociology at the University of Manchester, UK, and a member of the Morgan Centre for the Study of Relationships and Personal Life. Her research interests include lone motherhood, post-divorce parenting, intergenerational relationships, the self, belonging, narrative analysis, biographical methods and mixed methods. She is author of a forthcoming book, *Connecting self and society: Belonging in a changing world* (Palgrave Macmillan).

Merril Silverstein is Professor of Gerontology and Sociology at the University of Southern California. His research focuses on ageing within the context of family life. He has authored over 100 publications, including the books *Intergenerational relations across time and place* (Springer, 2005), *Handbook of theories of aging* (Second edition, Springer, 2009), and *From generation to generation: Continuity and discontinuity in aging families* (John Hopkins University Press, 2011). He is principal investigator of the Longitudinal Study of Generations, a project that has tracked multigenerational families over four decades, and a longitudinal study of ageing in rural China. He currently serves as Editor-in-Chief of the *Journal of Gerontology: Social Sciences.*

Shirley Hsiao-Li Sun has a PhD in sociology from New York University. She is an Assistant Professor of Sociology at the Nanyang Technological University in Singapore, and the assistant editor for the *Journal of Chinese Overseas* (BRILL). Her research interests include citizenship and immigration, family, social inequalities, public policy, population studies, and science and technology. Her articles appear in several international peer-reviewed journals including *Citizenship Studies*, *Social & Public Policy Review*, *Journal of Workplace rights*, *Journal of*

Comparative Family Studies, and *Childhood.* She is author of *Population policy and reproduction in Singapore: Making future citizens* (Routledge, 2012).

Anna Tarrant was recently awarded her PhD in human geography and is Senior Teaching Associate in geography at the Lancaster Environment Centre, Lancaster University, UK. She has published on grandparent identities using a relational perspective and also male identities in relation to the intersections of gender and ageing in *Area* and *Geography Compass.*

Virpi Timonen is Associate Professor of Social Policy and Ageing at Trinity College Dublin, Ireland. She has published on home care policies, migrant care workers, grandparenting in divorced families and participation of older adults in care settings and communities in *Ageing & Society, Journal of Aging Studies, Journal of Family Issues, Research on Aging, Journal of Social Policy* and several other leading international journals. Virpi has authored five books, including *Ageing societies: A comparative introduction* (Open University Press, 2008). She is a co-investigator in the Irish Longitudinal Study of Ageing, TILDA, and chairs the TILDA Translational Research and Policy Implementation sub-committee.

ONE

A new look at grandparenting

Virpi Timonen and Sara Arber

An ageing world contains growing numbers of grandparents, who share longer lifespans with, on average, smaller numbers of grandchildren. The scope for grandparenting is therefore widening, and grandparenting is taking on new forms as the social and economic contexts of family relationships evolve. Diversity in grandparenting also arises from grandparents' own choices regarding engagement with grandchildren. Time is ripe for a new look at grandparenting.

This chapter provides an overview of the main themes, arguments and frameworks that research on grandparents has yielded, highlighting how this book addresses lacunae in the literature and engages with new or poorly understood aspects of grandparenthood. It introduces concepts and theoretical frameworks that will be advanced within *Contemporary grandparenting*, and provides an overview of how the chapters in this book link together to further our understanding of contemporary grandparenting in diverse welfare state and cultural contexts.[1]

While grandparenthood is widely acknowledged as being of great and growing importance in contemporary societies, it has remained inadequately theorised. This is not surprising because the demographic, socioeconomic, family and social policy contexts that frame and shape grandparenthood have changed radically in recent decades, and continue to evolve. The sub-title of the book emphasises that grandparenting is embedded within 'changing family relationships'. *Contemporary grandparenting* also seeks to provide new insights into how grandparents themselves exert an influence on the grandparent role, hence departing from earlier characterisations that have tended to pay little attention to grandparents' agency. Changing family, economic and social contexts, and some grandparents' ability to shape their role within these contexts, mean that grandparenting today is very different from grandparenting some decades ago.

Adopting a gendered perspective is fundamental when studying the practices of grandparents. The term 'grandparenting' often in reality reflects care and support provided by grandmothers. However, it is important to consider the ways in which women and men 'perform' grandparenting in different societal and family contexts, and how cultural and social changes shape the gendered nature of grandparenting. It is critical to consider the nature of triadic grandparent–adult child–grandchild relationships, and how these are manifest in 'family practices' (Morgan, 2011). A complex nexus of gendered interrelationships across three generations pertains: not only the gender of the grandparent, but also the gender of the grandchild, and the gendered roles of the middle generation, influence grandparenting practices.

To understand contemporary grandparenting, both macro and micro perspectives are necessary. The macro–micro distinction is reflected in the division of chapters into two parts: Part One is more macro-focused, while Part Two is predominantly micro-focused. However, we stress that micro and macro levels of analysis ought to be in dialogue, since one always influences the other. Grandparents' responses to economic, societal and family transformations are discussed in Part One. Chapters in Part One address both structures (especially welfare states and social policies) and limits that arise from within family contexts (socioeconomic circumstances, geographical distances and so on). Part Two focuses on 'identities' and 'agency', which are clearly micro-level constructs, but powerfully shaped by macro structures such as social policies pertaining to care and families. Both Part One and Part Two discuss a wide variety of societal contexts. The inclusion of a variety of countries serves to highlight the fact that while grandparenting is a universal phenomenon, its forms and intensity and the lived experience of grandparenting differ markedly between societal and cultural contexts.

Demographics of grandparenting

Thanks to greater longevity, grandparenting now takes place over much longer periods of time than in the past (Uhlenberg, 1996). There has been an increase in the number of grandparents, who are typically grandparenting for two or more decades, into the adult lifespan of their grandchildren. In many developed countries, approximately 80 per cent of older persons are grandparents (Connidis, 2010). The age at which the majority of adults become grandparents (of at least one grandchild) has declined until recently in most developed countries (according to Dench and Ogg, 2002, this was 54 in the UK at the turn of the millennium), but is now increasing due to higher ages of childbearing among more recent cohorts (Chambers et al, 2009).

The combination of greater longevity and lower fertility has given rise to 'beanpole families' with several 'vertical' but fewer 'horizontal' family relationships (Harper, 2005). From the grandchild's perspective, having one or more surviving grandparents, even well into adulthood, is becoming increasingly common. Three-quarters of 30-year-olds in the United States have at least one surviving grandparent (Uhlenberg and Kirby, 1998). Lower fertility rates translate into fewer grandchildren per surviving grandparent. The extended period of shared lifetime, but smaller number of grandchildren, create longer and potentially stronger bonds between the two 'non-adjacent' generations (Connidis, 2010). Today's grandparents are also on average healthier and wealthier than in the past, yielding more scope, in principle, for their active engagement with grandchildren.

Children are more likely to have grandmothers than grandfathers, and share longer spans of their lives with grandmothers. This is because women in most societies outlive men by approximately five years (Arber and Ginn, 2005), as well as the cultural norms that men tend to be older than women when they marry. However, western countries have witnessed greater gains in longevity for men than women over recent years, resulting in convergence in male and female life expectancies and hence older people spending longer living as married couples (Arber et al, 2003). Thus, grandchildren are now likely to share more of their lives with a grandparent couple, and fewer years with a 'single' grandparent, typically their grandmother. The sequencing of motherhood and grandmotherhood has become clearer, so that women generally do not have to divide their attention between their own young children and adult children's young children. However, some repartnered men experience a second fatherhood at a time when their children from an earlier relationship have become parents themselves. It is important to consider how the gender and marital status of grandparents intersect and influence the nature of their relationships with grandchildren, for example the nature of relationships between divorced or widowed grandfathers and their grandchildren, compared with married grandfathers and their grandchildren.

In short, falling fertility rates and increases in survival have brought about an increased 'supply' of grandparents in tandem with a decreased 'supply' of grandchildren in the developed world. As a result, more older adults are grandparents to, on average, fewer children, for longer periods of time than in the past. This has paved the way to possible qualitative changes in grandparent–grandchild relationships; these qualitative changes remain poorly understood. Alongside demographic shifts, international and rural–urban migration influences grandparenting and intergenerational relations across global contexts (Izuhara, 2010), with consequences that are examined in several chapters in this book.

Earlier frameworks for research on grandparenthood

A common theme connecting both earlier and more recent research on grandparenting pertains to the 'function' of grandparents as 'supporters', 'savers' or 'rescuers' of the younger generations (see von Hentig, 1946; Hagestad, 2006). Research in the 1940s and 1950s focused on the solidarity of grandparents towards their adult children and grandchildren in the context of post-world war economic and social challenges (Szinovacz, 1998). Although emphasis on the nuclear family and 'generational independence' shifted the focus away from grandparents in family research in the 1950s and 1960s, there were some notable exceptions such as Townsend's (1957) classic study of *The family life of old people* in London. Townsend showed that many grandmothers were heavily involved in rearing their grandchildren, with some providing care to successive cohorts of young children for four or five decades. The grandmother–adult daughter bond was a particularly significant conduit to functional solidarity (practical help and support) in the working-class urban community studied by Townsend.

Intergenerational solidarity, conflict and ambivalence

Townsend's research can be seen as a forerunner of the widely applied theoretical framework of 'intergenerational solidarity' put forward by Bengtson and colleagues (Bengtson and Roberts, 1991; for a succinct summary, see Katz and Lowenstein, 2010). In brief, the framework comprises structural solidarity (geographical distance), associational solidarity (frequency of contact), affectual solidarity (sentiments towards family members), functional solidarity (giving and receiving practical support within families), consensual solidarity (agreement over attitudes and key issues) and normative solidarity (valuing of family cohesion), but is also able to accommodate conflict (lack of solidarity). Later research showed that older people also experience 'ambivalence' (that is, both negative and positive sentiments) regarding their relationship with adult children (Luescher and Pillemer, 1998). Ambivalence also extends to the grandparenting role, reflected for instance in the expectation that grandparents adhere both to the 'norm of non-interference' (Troll and Bengtson, 1979) and the 'norm of obligation', to provide support when needed by the younger generations.

As well as functional or practical support provided by grandparents (Mancini and Bliezner, 1989), researchers have studied the role of grandparents in transmitting knowledge and values to younger generations (Kennedy, 1992) and providing a sense of family heritage and stability (Kornhaber, 1996). Research has demonstrated grandparental influence on grandchildren's core moral values (King, 2003) and religious practices and orientation (Copen and Silverstein, 2007). These 'functions' are all somewhat backward-looking – grandparents bringing something of the past to the present – whereas elements of contemporary grandparenting may be more forward-looking and responsive to present-day needs and challenges.

Intergenerational transfers and welfare state provisions

A key area of research relevant to solidarity between generations focuses on intergenerational transfers, namely the redistribution of resources within an extended family structure, incorporating both intra-household and inter-household exchanges (Soldo and Hill, 1993; Izuhara, 2010). In many societies, family support acts as the key social protection mechanism that provides informal insurance for social risks such as inability to earn an income, for instance due to unemployment or old age. Extensive research has examined the interaction between public and private transfers, and the extent to which the provision of intergenerational family support 'complements' or 'substitutes' for the state provisions of income and care (Arber and Attias-Donfut, 2000). Most evidence suggests that state transfers and services complement, rather than 'crowd out', informal (family) care of older people (Motel-Klingebiel et al, 2005). However, where state transfers to older adults are very low, filial obligations towards ageing parents tend to be higher than in countries where pensions and care services have enabled a greater degree of independence for older people (Sun, 2002).

These bodies of research focus either on the balance sheet of transfers of care and money between generations (the extent of intergenerational reciprocity within families), or on the transfers provided by the public (welfare) sector compared with intra-family transfers (state versus family inputs). Neither of these foci explicitly addresses the realities of grandparenting in different welfare state contexts that provide varying levels of childcare support, or in contexts where there is a lack of reciprocity across intergenerational relationships. 'Downward' transfers from grandparents to younger generations have gained greater salience with social and economic changes over recent decades. Older family members are an increasingly important source of financial, instrumental and emotional support for their families due to major social and economic shifts, including the rise of dual-earner families, increased marital breakdown and lone parenthood (Bengtson, 2001; Izuhara, 2010).

Grandparents as 'child savers' or 'mother savers'

A dominant research strand in the US has focused on families where grandparents (typically grandmothers) come to 'rescue' the grandchildren ('child savers'), whereas recent (mostly European) literature has focused on grandmothers caring for grandchildren in order to enable mothers to participate in the labour market ('mother savers') (see Chapters Two and Three in this book).

'Child savers' are grandparents who are the sole or primary caregivers of their grandchildren, under circumstances where the middle generation is severely challenged or incapacitated in their parenting roles (for instance imprisoned, suffering from mental illness, addicted to drugs). 'Child savers' typically reside in 'skipped-generation' households where the middle generation is absent all or most of the time. They are the sole or primary carers of their grandchildren, and have in many cases been appointed as legal custodians of their grandchildren. The number of custodial grandparents increased strongly in the US in the 1980s and 1990s (Hayslip and Kaminsky, 2005), especially in inner-city African American communities, as a result of drug use, HIV/AIDS, incarceration and partnership instability in the middle generation, but also because of child welfare policies that emphasised care within families. In the late 1990s, more than one in ten grandparents in the US had had primary responsibility for raising a grandchild at some point, often for a period of several years (Minkler, 1999). The vast majority of US grandparents who provide such extensive grandchild care are women, are disproportionately likely to be Hispanic or African American, and are economically disadvantaged (Fuller-Thomson and Minkler, 2001). Full-time custodial grandparents in the US have been shown to experience high levels of stress and clinical depression (Minkler et al, 1997; Bowers and Myers, 1999); this may be partly attributable to cumulative disadvantages among them (Goodman and Silverstein, 2002; Hughes et al, 2007; Baker and Silverstein, 2008). While the research focus has to date been on 'child-saving' grandparents in the US, Oduaran and Oduaran (2010) analyse the challenges faced by 'child-saving' grandparents in Sub-Saharan Africa (see also Oppong, 2006).

Notwithstanding the importance of custodial grandparenting, the majority of grandparents provide some care to, and have regular or occasional contact with, non-co-resident grandchildren. However, there has been less research on these 'typical' grandparents than on grandparents in the relatively rare (for most contexts) situation of 'skipped-generation' households. Approximately 40-60 per cent of grandparents provide at least occasional childcare to young grandchildren across the US and Europe (Attias-Donfut et al, 2005; Hughes et al, 2007). Within this group, those grandparents who are involved in regular, extensive provision of childcare in order to enable the child's mother to work outside the home have been referred to as 'mother savers'. Where divorce or separation occurs in the middle generation, grandparents often become heavily involved in support provision, especially if the separating couple has young children (Bengtson, 2001). Chapters in Part One of this book examine grandparents supporting the everyday lives of the middle generation, especially working mothers and dual-earner families, in coping with the pressures of work and raising a family in different societal and cultural contexts.

Typologies of grandparenting styles

Alongside the study of the 'function' of grandparents in younger family members' lives, another branch of research has sought to identify different 'types' or 'styles' of grandparents. The typology of Neugarten and Weinstein (1964) includes grandparents who are 'formal', 'fun-seekers', 'distant', 'surrogate parents' and 'reservoirs of family wisdom'. Cherlin and Furstenberg (1985) challenged this categorisation and argued that grandparenting styles do not remain static from the birth of the grandchild into adolescence and then adulthood. Rather, grandparent styles should be examined within a life-course perspective. Cherlin and Furstenberg (1985) proposed five styles of grandparenting, namely detached, passive, supportive, authoritative and influential. 'Detached' grandparents tended to be older and geographically distant from their grandchildren, while 'influential' grandparents had almost daily contact with their grandchildren. Later, Cherlin and Furstenberg (1992) simplified the classification, proposing 'remote', 'companionate' and 'involved' types. However, these categorisations are not well suited to examining possible differences in how a grandparent relates to different grandchildren, and also overlook the possibility that grandchildren may exert an influence on the nature of the relationship.

Gender, generation and grandparenting

Earlier research on grandparenthood has had a strong social psychological focus and the dominance of US literature is notable, with the result that the impact of broader family systems and cultural contexts on grandparenting practices has received inadequate attention. Grandparenting styles (discussed earlier) should not be treated exclusively as characteristics of the grandparents themselves, because they reflect broader family relations and contextual factors. For instance, Mueller and colleagues (2002) contend that influential and supportive grandparents are more common in close-knit family systems because the opportunity structures facilitate greater intergenerational involvement. Hagestad (2006) has argued that attempts to understand grandparenting must depart from the dyadic approach (that considers only the relationship between a grandparent and a grandchild) and take a three-generational perspective, that is, to seek an understanding of the characteristics and needs of grandparents, parents *and* grandchildren. The following subsections give an overview of research on each of these three generations separately; however, we emphasise the importance of seeing the generations as dynamic and interlinked, and of retaining a close focus on the impact of gender.

Grandparents' gender and other characteristics

Women are in most societies socialised to act as 'kin-keepers' (Roberto et al, 2001; Monserud, 2008), and hence are more likely than men to be emotionally close to their children and grandchildren, and more likely to become key figures in young grandchildren's lives (Hagestad, 1985; Uhlenberg and Hammill, 1998; Mills et al, 2001). The grandparent's gender may influence the subjective importance of the role. Somary and Stricker (1998) found that regardless of the frequency of interaction, grandmothers derived greater satisfaction than grandfathers from their grandparent role. Roberto and colleagues (2001, p 409) argue that, 'given traditional gender roles and the prevalence of "kin-keeping" among women, it is not surprising that there is a tendency to focus research on grandmothers'; this has nonetheless resulted in 'feminisation' of grandparenthood literature and limited understanding of grandfathering. Few studies to date have focused on the role of grandfathers (Kivett, 1985, 1991; Roberto et al, 2001; Mann, 2007).

Uhlenberg and Hammill (1998) showed that married grandparents are most likely to maintain frequent contact with their grandchildren, followed by widowed, remarried and divorced grandparents. Differences between married and other marital statuses are greater for grandfathers than for grandmothers; divorced grandfathers tend to have the lowest levels of contact with grandchildren (Tomassini et al, 2004). Other grandparent characteristics that have been argued to matter are personality, health and employment status (Troll, 1985), although the impact of employment status remains poorly understood. Health affects the grandparent–grandchild relationship, as grandparents with better physical and mental health tend to be more actively engaged with their grandchildren (Hodgson, 1992).

Silverstein and Long (1998) used the Longitudinal Study of Generations, which comprises data on 300 three-generation Californian families since 1971, to examine changes in grandparent–grandchild relationships over a 23-year period. They found that emotional intimacy was not constant and that older grandparents expressed higher levels of affection towards their grandchildren than younger grandparents. Alongside grandparents' age, the timing of entry into the grandparental role is a significant influence (Troll, 1985), especially if the grandparent experiences this role as 'off-time' (for example, too soon in his or her life course).

The middle generation

Grandparents and grandchildren are commonly thought of as 'dyads' (one grandparent in relation to one grandchild). However, the relationship between these two 'non-adjacent' generations has been shown to be mediated by the 'intermediate' or 'middle' generation – the grandparent's adult child and his/her partner or spouse who act as the relational 'bridge' between grandparents and grandchildren (Johnson and Barer, 1987; Hodgson, 1992; King and Elder, 1995; Fingerman, 2004; Monserud, 2008). The quality of the middle generation's relationship with their own parents and parents-in-law exerts a powerful influence on the quality of grandparent–grandchild relationships. Thus, the grandparent–grandchild relationship has been characterised as 'mediated' (Gladstone, 1989) or even as 'derived' (Johnson, 1998, p 188). According to Johnson (1985, p 91), grandparents are 'constrained by the mandate on the autonomy and privacy of the nuclear family in each generation' and have to shape their contact with grandchildren in accordance with 'the wishes of their children and children-in-law'. However, previous research has paid little attention to the consequences of longer duration of grandparent–grandchild relationships that extend into the grandchild's adulthood, and the impact of modern communications technologies in facilitating contact, both of which potentially erode the significance of mediation by the middle generation.

A crucial aspect of the middle generation's influence on the grandparent–grandchild relationship is *lineage*, namely whether the grandchildren are the offspring of sons (paternal) or daughters (maternal), which is fundamentally connected to gender. In western societies, a marked 'matrilineal bias' has been identified, manifest in more frequent interaction and provision of support between adult daughters and their parents (especially mothers – the maternal grandmothers), which is reflected in closer bonds between grandparents and the children of daughters (Hagestad, 1985; Eisenberg, 1988; Somary and Stricker, 1998; Brannen et al, 2000; Chan and Elder, 2000). Eisenberg's (1988) survey of young adult grandchildren in the US found that even when controlling for geographical distance, relationships with maternal grandmothers were still rated as the most important of all grandparental relationships by grandchildren. Chan and Elder (2000) attributed the 'matrilineal bias' to the strength of relationships between mothers and daughters. While their research found that a father's closer ties with his parents improved the strength of the paternal grandparent–grandchild relationship, the overall 'matrilineal advantage' remained. However, we know less about the role of paternal grandparents, especially in patrilineal cultures such as China (Ikels, 1998).

Family crises can accentuate the mediated character of the grandparent–grandchild relationship. For instance, where the middle generation is divorced or separated, the grandparent's access to grandchildren may be dependent on the custodial parent's willingness to allow such access, a problem that is more commonly faced by paternal grandparents (King, 2003; Amato and Cheadle, 2005). Within 'intact' family contexts also, grandparental care and support to grandchildren often takes place alongside, or through, the assistance that grandparents provide to their adult children.

The influence of other family and kin members (such as siblings and the other set of grandparents) on grandparenting remains poorly understood, despite exhortations to study grandparenting within broader family contexts (Szinovacz, 1998); empirical research continues to be segmented by relational type (Silverstein and Giarrusso, 2010).

Grandchild characteristics

Of the three generations, (young) grandchildren have to date been accorded least influence in theoretical frameworks, largely because they are rarely included in studies of grandparenting. The children of one adult child are often referred to as a 'set' of grandchildren. Uhlenberg and Hammill (1998) have argued that the more grandchild sets a grandparent has, the greater the likelihood of infrequent contact with grandchildren; nonetheless, those who have multiple sets of grandchildren are more likely to be in frequent contact with at least one set than those with only one set of grandchildren. This in turn is linked to the lower likelihood of those with fewer grandchild sets living in close geographical proximity to any grandchild(ren).

Silverstein and Long (1998) have shown that older grandchildren see their grandparents less frequently. Older grandparents also see their grandchildren less frequently – but this may be due to poorer health status rather than age *per se*. However, the quality of relationships does not necessarily decline as grandparents and grandchildren age and is more dependent on the foundations set by earlier grandparental involvement (Lawton et al, 1994). Finch (1989) argues that the relationship between grandparents and older grandchildren is not symmetrical, as it tends to be more important for the grandparents (the 'generational stake' hypothesis).

Mueller and colleagues (2002, p 364) suggest that as a grandchild enters adolescence, the nature of the relationship becomes more elusive and voluntary and is 'characterized by deeper communication, mutual exchange, guidance and support'. Findings from a US study of adolescents by Dellmann-Jenkins et al (1987) suggest that, while the onset of adolescence may change grandparent–grandchild relationships, most changes are positive and that interaction and recreational activities with grandparents are still seen as important. A Canadian qualitative study that adopted a life-history approach with grandparent–adult grandchild dyads found that the bond can grow and become more meaningful with the passage of time, with both grandparents and grandchildren indicating satisfaction with their relationship and the importance of mutual support and respect (Kemp, 2005). Some researchers have suggested that grandmothers may remain more emotionally involved with adolescent granddaughters than grandsons, exerting more influence on the former (King and Elder, 1995; Mueller et al, 2002). Nonetheless, we still know very little about grandchildren's agency, and about the bi-directional influences within grandparent–grandchild relationships.

Geographical distance and the grandparent–grandchild relationship

There is some debate on the extent to which relationship quality drives geographical distance between family members or vice versa (for example, whether family members move further away because they do not get along, or become less close due to geographical distance). Geographical distance has been shown to be associated with the frequency of contact between grandparents and younger family members, and also with affective solidarity; those who live closer to their grandchildren interact with them more frequently, and also tend to feel closer to them, on average, than geographically distant grandparents (Kivett, 1985, 1991; Hodgson, 1992; Cooney and Smith, 1996; Uhlenberg and Hammill, 1998). Cherlin and Furstenberg (1992, p 117) make the striking statement that 'distance, distance, distance' is the most important determinant of frequency of contact between grandparents and grandchildren. However, more recent research by Ferguson (2004, p 12) concludes that 'although distance predicts frequency of contact, it might not be closely related to the quality of the grandchild–grandparent relationship that can be maintained by exchanges of email, letters and telephone calls'.

Influences of societal and cultural contexts on grandparenting

Our review of earlier research shows that grandparents have been typically studied in one context, at one point in time, with a focus on the frequency of interaction, perceived closeness and intergenerational transfers. The picture that emerges is of grandparenting as strongly gendered, bounded by lineage, shaped by the wishes and needs of the middle generation, and oriented to 'saving' or 'rescuing' younger family members. The single best example of this orientation is the large literature on custodial grandparents (grandmothers) in African American communities in the United States, discussed earlier.

Macro-level influences on the nature of grandparenting have remained poorly understood because few comparative studies have been carried out, and because many studies have been insufficiently attuned to the impact of context. We therefore need to tease out more carefully the impact of societal context on grandparenting; previous comparative studies have failed to give a nuanced picture of the cultural and contextual influences on grandparenting. In view of this, Silverstein and Giarrrusso (2010, p 1053) encourage the interrogation of 'cultural frames that the elderly and their relatives use to negotiate the gap between expectations and behaviours regarding help and support, tensions between dependence and autonomy, residential decisions, and resource allocation strategies in aging families'.

Chapters in Part One of this book outline how grandparenting has changed in response to economic and family transformations in different societal and cultural contexts. Two of the chapters are comparative in approach, analysing data across two or more societal contexts, while three chapters are single-country studies that are highly attuned to the impact of societal context and cultural norms in shaping changing grandparenting practices.

Katharina Herlofson and Gunhild Hagestad (Chapter Two) highlight how welfare state structures (familialistic or de-familialised social policies) shape grandparental involvement and roles. They investigate differences in the extent and intensity of grandparents' involvement in the care of their grandchildren across European countries, drawing on the Survey of Health, Ageing and Retirement in Europe (SHARE) and Norwegian data. A North-South gradient is observed, with the highest proportions reporting some involvement in the Nordic countries, France and the Netherlands, and lowest in the Mediterranean countries. Herlofson and Hagestad distinguish between occasional and regular care, a distinction that yields a pattern of greater intensity of grandparental childcare in Southern Europe and lower intensity in Northern Europe. The authors advance the explanation that availability of formal childcare in some countries means that grandparental care is rarely very intensive but small amounts of it may be needed by dual-earner families, especially in times of crisis (hence grandparents as 'family savers'). In the Mediterranean countries, grandparental care when needed tends to be very intensive due to the absence of formal childcare options (hence grandparents as 'mother savers'). The welfare state context (availability of parental leave and public childcare) therefore powerfully shapes how grandparenting roles are defined and enacted.

Compared with the European countries discussed in Chapter Two, China presents a very different cultural, welfare state and economic context. China has experienced rapid economic growth and urbanisation within a very short period of time. In Chapter Three, Lindsey Baker and Merril Silverstein argue that, due to rural–urban migration of the middle generation, grandparental care of young children has been part of a deliberate family strategy aimed at maximising family resources (hence grandparents being characterised as 'family maximisers'). Grandparenting in 'skipped-generation' households in rural China therefore stands in marked contrast to that in 'skipped-generation' households in the United States; grandparental surrogate parenting in China is not a crisis response (as it usually is in the US) but rather a deliberate input into enhancing the extended family's economic prosperity. Unlike in the US, custodial grandparents in China have better psychological wellbeing than comparable grandparents who do not live in 'skipped-generation' households, demonstrating the importance of understanding the influence of the societal context, and the divergent routes into, and implications of, custodial grandparenting in different societies.

The strong focus on custodial grandparenting has overshadowed research on other important dimensions of grandparenting in the US. As Madonna Harrington Meyer demonstrates in Chapter Four, the US provides an excellent case study of a country where women's labour market participation has been relatively high for a long period of time, with most mothers and also many grandmothers in paid employment outside the home, despite little state support for formal childcare provision. Harrington Meyer studied grandmothers who were providing significant grandchild care, while also being constrained by their own paid employment – hence 'juggling'. The assumption that grandmothers are easily available to provide extensive childcare is outdated and, in practice, very problematic in the US and other countries where the cohorts of working mothers are ageing and becoming working grandmothers. Harrington Meyer shows that balancing work and care of grandchildren places great demands on working grandmothers, many of whom also look after ageing parents. Many also give extensive financial assistance to their indebted adult children.

Hong Kong represents a rapidly modernised society. The ideal of three-generational co-residence persists but has declined in prevalence (and also been somewhat modified); patrilocal co-residence now ideally takes place in the son's house, his ability to purchase a home being a signifier of his social and economic status. Lisanne Ko (in Chapter Five) illustrates how the traditional cultural ideal of co-residence of grandparents, together with the increased labour market participation of women, has led to grandparents performing major functional supportive roles for the middle generation and their grandchildren. She discusses how support provision by grandparents often gives rise to ambivalence, as grandparents who display extensive functional solidarity simultaneously experience conflict and feelings of resentment towards members of the middle generation. Ko suggests that such feelings of ambivalence may be particularly acute for grandfathers whose status in families has declined dramatically.

Western cultures discourage 'interference' by grandparents (norm of non-interference), but there are other contexts where extensive involvement of grandparents in bringing up grandchildren (including instructing them on morals and values, and disciplining them) is still widely expected. In Chapter Six, Shirley Sun discusses the Singapore context that has witnessed a recent emergence of dual-breadwinner families, and where strong expectations of intergenerational solidarity (especially normative, consensual and functional solidarity) prevail. Despite their own paid employment and trends away from co-residence, many grandparents become heavily involved in the care of young grandchildren in order to facilitate both parents' employment. However, young adults are often concerned about overburdening their parents, the ability of their parents to prepare their grandchildren for a competitive labour market through stimulating early education, and the tensions and anxieties of three-generational co-residence. Feelings of ambivalence may also arise for grandparents. Some families are in a position to restructure the intergenerational 'contract' by involving foreign domestic workers as paid helpers alongside grandparents who are less engaged in practical support provision, but grandparents continue to play an important role in transmitting values to grandchildren (acting as 'moral guardians').

Chapters in Part One therefore raise questions around structure and agency; both, of course, matter, but we need to investigate possible shifts and differences in the 'weight' of each. It appears that some grandparents may be in a position to exercise a lot of choice over the extent and nature of their grandparenting, whereas in other cases grandparenting is strongly shaped by structures (for instance, the middle generations' employment status and the availability or lack of affordable formal childcare). Chapters in this book point to significant gender and socioeconomic differences in grandparents' scope to exercise agency (for example, regarding their level of involvement in grandchild care), and these warrant further investigation.

Grandparenting norms, identities and agency

In contrast to the relative paucity of research on grandparenting within the macro-social context of welfare states, a long-standing body of research has explored micro-level experiences of grandparenting, and the impact on grandparents' wellbeing. As discussed earlier, this literature has analysed what grandparents think of their role, and how they experience it, and contains some indications that role perceptions are often imbued with ambivalence. For instance, Ferguson (2004, p 5) found that 'committed grandparents [heavily involved in childcare duties] often expressed reservations about the extent of their involvement'.

Generational changes (such as the ageing of the 'baby boomers', who are healthier, wealthier and more oriented to leisure activities than previous generations) are likely to impact on how grandparenthood is enacted. The current ideals of 'active' and 'successful' ageing point in the direction of self-actualisation and personal choices around leisure-time use, which may not be straightforwardly compatible with extensive provision of grandchild care. Alongside paid employment, grandparents' social lives, voluntary work, leisure interests and options may also shape frequency and nature of involvement with grandchildren. However, the literature has to date paid little attention to how grandparents themselves are constructing their identities and exercising agency in ways that cannot be fully understood in the light of lineage, the influence of the middle generation or intergenerational solidarity. Chapters in Part Two of this book focus on grandparent identities and practices, and how grandparents use their agency to shape these.

Key concepts examined are the norms of non-interference and of obligation – the expectation that grandparents offer help and support to younger generations without interfering in their decisions regarding, for instance, the upbringing of children. Vanessa May, Jennifer Mason and Lynda Clarke (Chapter Seven) examine the tensions both between and within these norms. Their analysis of 'normative talk' about grandparenting shows extremely strong consensus over the norms of 'not interfering' and 'being there' in the UK. However, the norm of non-interference is not easily aligned with ideas around 'good parenting', giving rise to 'the paradox of parenting' (where grandparents generally desist from interfering with their adult children's parenting despite wishing to instruct them). Another competing ideal concerns the value of personal independence and self-determination for grandparents. Grandparents who are heavily involved in looking after grandchildren may not be able to actualise the increasingly prevalent ideal of self-actualisation, a key facet of 'active ageing', giving rise to the paradox of self-determination.

Virpi Timonen and Martha Doyle (Chapter Eight) present new theorising on grandparental agency in situations where the middle generation is divorced or separated. The parents of divorced or separated adult children in their study were called on to provide a range of support (financial, childcare, co-residence) to the middle and grandchild generations. Many grandparents sought to draw boundaries around involvement in this support provision; some developed complex long-term strategies to optimise their level of contact with their grandchildren. The authors argue that these behaviours are manifestations of grandparental agency, which has to date been overshadowed by conceptualisations and theoretical frameworks that present grandparents as confined by the powerful structural constraints of lineage, middle-generation influence, and norms of non-interference and obligation (to support younger generations).

The changing nature of masculinities is influencing the practices of grandfathering. These include both the new generations of grandfathers who took a greater role in their own children's care, and grandfathers who draw on new channels such as information technology to communicate with their grandchildren. In Chapter Nine, Anna Tarrant discusses how forms of grandfathering are importantly influenced by intergenerational relationships in the UK. The room that men have to develop and enact their grandfathering identities and practices is shaped by their family context, especially the middle generation that can sometimes impart new (grand)fathering norms to the older generation (paternal grandfathers may be more exposed and open to this influence via their sons). Gender, intergenerational relationships and men's family circumstances (especially divorce) intersect and have outcomes that restrict or facilitate men's performance of their grandfather identities. Grandfathers may use new technologies to communicate with older grandchildren, which may lessen the influence of the middle generation.

Changing social norms have led to more informal and equal relationships between many grandparents and their grandchildren. Under-researched areas include grandchildren's influence on grandparents, and the longer-lasting relationships with older/adult grandchildren that become possible with increased life expectancies and are very different from interaction with young grandchildren. Two chapters investigate the much longer relationships that can be sustained by grandparents and grandchildren due to increasing life expectancy. In the Portuguese context, Alice Delerue Matos and Rita Borges Neves (Chapter Ten) argue that influence between emotionally and geographically close grandparents and their older grandchildren is reciprocal. Adolescent grandchildren help grandparents interpret societal changes, encourage social engagement, instil greater environmental awareness and healthier eating habits, and strengthen their ties with other family members such as parents. Older grandchildren assume diverse styles while 'acting' as grandchildren. Chapter Ten also argues that the middle generation plays little role in mediating close older grandchild–grandparent relationships.

Through analysis of grandparent, older grandchild and middle-generation characteristics, Katharina Mahne and Oliver Huxhold (Chapter Eleven) show the importance of all three generations in shaping contact between the two 'non-adjacent' generations. In the context of both grandparental employment and divorce suppressing contact frequency, Mahne and Huxhold's findings on the emotional bonds between grandparents and older grandchildren are noteworthy: affective solidarity appears to counteract the negative effects of an adult child's union dissolution and step-grandparenthood. Grandparents who experience an emotionally close relationship with their grandchild are more likely to maintain their frequency of interaction despite disrupting family events. The chapter also marshals evidence of intergenerational transmission of family interaction patterns: relationships between parents and their adult children prepare the ground for the relations between grandparents and grandchildren.

Within the broad norms of obligation and non-interference (discussed in Chapter Seven), the picture that emerges is of grandparents who are not always restricted or oriented by traditional norms arising from gender and lineage, or the wishes of the middle generation. Rather, chapters in Part Two show grandparents to be a diverse group within which some grandparents break gender stereotypes, develop strategies to circumvent or attenuate the influence of the middle generation, and are open to being influenced by their older grandchildren.

Conclusion

As a result of social, economic and demographic changes, framed by a wide variety of welfare state and cultural contexts, the role of grandparents in 21st-century families is more multidimensional, complex and dynamic than it has been in earlier periods in history. The chapters in this book provide analyses of grandparenting in a wide range of different contexts. They show that while grandparents are a heterogeneous group within each context, important differences persist between welfare states and cultures in how grandparenting is construed and enacted. The chapters in this volume bear witness to the evolving nature of grandparenting, in response both to external demands and needs and to grandparents' own choices.

Note
[1] *Contemporary grandparenting* is primarily based on revised versions of papers presented at the International Sociological Association (ISA) conference in Gothenburg, Sweden (July 2010) in two sessions on grandparenting, organised by Sara Arber and Virpi Timonen (in the ISA Research Committee on Ageing, RC11). Two additional chapters (by May and colleagues, and Timonen and Doyle) complement the chapters developed from the Gothenburg conference presentations.

References

Amato, P. and Cheadle, J. (2005) 'The long reach of divorce: divorce and child well-being across three generations', *Journal of Marriage and Family*, vol 67, no 1, pp 191-206.

Arber, S. and Attias-Donfut, C. (eds) (2000) *The myth of generational conflict: The family and state in ageing societies*, London: Routledge.

Arber, S. and Ginn, J. (2005) 'Gender dimensions of the age shift', in M. Johnson (ed) *The Cambridge handbook of age and ageing*, Cambridge: Cambridge University Press, pp 527-37.

Arber, S., Davidson, K. and Ginn, J. (eds) (2003) *Gender and ageing: Changing roles and relationships*, Maidenhead: Open University Press.

Attias-Donfut, C., Ogg, J. and Wolf, F.C. (2005) 'European patterns of intergenerational financial and time transfers', *European Journal of Ageing*, vol 2, no 3, pp 161-73.

Baker, L. and Silverstein, M. (2008) 'Preventive health behaviours among grandmothers raising grandchildren', *Journals of Gerontology: Social Sciences*, vol 63B, no 5, pp S304-S311.

Bengtson, V. (2001) 'Beyond the nuclear family: the increasing importance of multigenerational bonds', *Journal of Marriage and Family*, vol 63, no 1, pp 1-16.

Bengtson, V.L. and Roberts, R.E. (1991) 'Intergenerational solidarity in aging families: an example of formal theory construction', *Journal of Marriage and Family*, vol 53, no 4, pp 856-70.

Bowers, B.F. and Myers, B.J. (1999) 'Grandmothers providing care for grandchildren: consequences of various levels of caregiving', *Family Relations*, vol 48, no 3, pp 303-11.

Brannen, J., Heptinstall, E. and Bhopal, K. (2000) *Connecting children: Care and family life in later childhood*, London: Routledge.

Chambers, P., Allan, G., Phillipson, C. and Ray, M. (2009) *Family practices in later life*, Bristol: The Policy Press.

Chan, C.G. and Elder, G.H. (2000) 'Matrilineal advantage in grandchild–grandparent relations', *The Gerontologist*, vol 40, no 2, pp 179-90.

Cherlin, A. and Furstenberg, F.A. (1985) 'Styles and strategies of grandparenting', in V.L. Bengston and J.F. Robertson (eds) *Grandparenthood*, Beverly Hills, CA: Sage Publications.

Cherlin, A.J. and Furstenberg, F.F. (1992) *The new American grandparent*, Cambridge, MA: Harvard University Press.

Connidis, I. (2010) *Family ties and aging* (2nd edn), Los Angeles, CA: Pine Forge Press.

Cooney, T. and Smith, L. (1996) 'Young adults' relations with grandparents following recent parental divorce', *Journal of Gerontology: Social Sciences*, vol 51B, no 2, pp S91-5.

Copen, C. and Silverstein, M. (2007) 'The transmission of religious beliefs across generations: do grandparents matter?', *Journal of Comparative Family Studies*, vol 38, no 5, pp 497-510.

Dellmann-Jenkins, M., Papalia, D. and Lopez, M. (1987) 'Teenagers' reported interaction with grandparents: exploring the extent of alienation', *Journal of Family and Economic Issues*, vol 8, no 3-4, pp 35-46.

Dench, G. and Ogg, J. (2002) *Grandparenting in Britain: A baseline study* (2nd edn), London: Institute of Community Studies.

Eisenberg, A.R. (1988) 'Grandchildren's perspectives on relationships with grandparents: the influence of gender across generation', *Sex Roles*, vol 19, no 3-4, pp 205-17.

Ferguson, N. (with Douglas, G., Lowe, N., Murch, M. and Robinson, M.) (2004) *Grandparenting in divorced families*, Bristol: The Policy Press.

Finch, J. (1989) *Family obligations and social change*, Cambridge: Polity Press.

Fingerman, K.L. (2004) 'The role of offspring and in-laws in grandparents' ties to their grandchildren', *Journal of Family Issues*, vol 25, no 8, pp 1026-49.

Fuller-Thomson, E. and Minkler, M. (2001) 'American grandparents providing extensive child care to their grandchildren', *The Gerontologist*, vol 41, no 2, pp 201-9.

Gladstone, J.W. (1989) 'Grandmother–grandchild contact: the mediating influence of the middle generation following marriage breakdown and remarriage', *Canadian Journal on Aging*, vol 8, no 4, pp 355-65.

Goodman, C. and Silverstein, M. (2002) 'Grandmothers raising grandchildren: family structure and wellbeing in culturally diverse families', *The Gerontologist*, vol 42, no 5, pp 676-89.

Hagestad, G.O. (1985) 'Continuity and connectedness', in V.L. Bengston and J.F. Robertson (eds) *Grandparenthood*, Beverly Hills, CA: Sage Publications.

Hagestad, G.O. (2006) 'Transfers between grandparents and grandchildren: the importance of taking a three-generation perspective', *Zeitschrift für Familienforschung*, vol 18, no 3, pp 315-32.

Harper, S. (2005) 'Grandparenthood', in M.L. Johnson (ed) *The Cambridge handbook of age and ageing*, Cambridge: Cambridge University Press, pp 422-8.

Hayslip, B. and Kaminski, P.L. (2005) 'Grandparents raising their grandchildren: a review of the literature and suggestions for practice', *The Gerontologist*, vol 45, no 2, pp 262-9.

Hodgson, L.G. (1992) 'Adult grandchildren and their grandparents: the enduring bond', *International Journal of Aging and Human Development*, vol 34, no 3, pp 209-25.

Hughes, M.E, Waite, L.J, LaPierre, T.A. and Luo, Y. (2007) 'All in the family: the impact of caring for grandchildren on grandparents' health', *Journal of Gerontology: Social Sciences*, vol 62B, no 2, pp S108-S119.

Ikels, C. (1998) 'Grandparenthood in cross-cultural perspective', in M. Szinovacz (ed) *Handbook on grandparenthood*, Westport, CT: Greenwood Press, pp 40-52.

Izuhara, M. (ed) (2010) *Ageing and intergenerational relations: Family reciprocity from a global perspective*, Bristol: The Policy Press.

Johnson, C.L. (1985) 'Grandparenting options in divorcing families: an anthropological perspective', in V.L. Bengtson and J.F. Robertson (eds) *Grandparenthood*, Beverly Hills, CA: Sage Publications, pp 81-96.

Johnson, C.L. (1998) 'Effects of adult children's divorce on grandparenthood', in M.E. Szinovacz (ed) *Handbook on grandparenthood*, Westport, CT: Greenwood Press, pp 184-99.

Johnson, C.L. and Barer, B.M. (1987) 'Marital instability and the changing kinship networks of grandparents', *The Gerontologist*, vol 27, no 3, pp 330-5.

Katz, R. and Lowenstein, A. (2010) 'Theoretical perspectives on intergenerational solidarity, conflict and ambivalence', in M. Izuhara (ed) *Ageing and intergenerational relations: Family reciprocity from a global perspective*, Bristol: The Policy Press, pp 29-56.

Kemp, C.L. (2005) 'Dimensions of grandparent–adult grandchild relationships: from family ties to intergenerational friendships', *Canadian Journal of Aging*, vol 24, no 2, pp 161-77.

Kennedy, G. (1992) 'Quality in grandparent/grandchild relationships', *International Journal of Aging and Human Development*, vol 35, no 2, pp 83-98.

King, V. (2003) 'The legacy of a grandparent's divorce: consequences for ties between grandparents and grandchildren', *Journal of Marriage and Family*, vol 65, no 1, pp 70-83.

King, V. and Elder, G.H. (1995) 'How American children view their grandparents: linked lives across three rural generations', *Journal of Marriage and Family*, vol 57, no 1, pp 165-78.

Kivett, V. (1985) 'Grandfathers and grandchildren: patterns of association, helping, and psychological closeness', *Family Relations*, vol 34, no 4, pp 565-71.

Kivett, V. (1991) 'The grandparent–grandchild connection', *Marriage and Family Review*, vol 16, no 3, pp 267-90.

Kornhaber, A. (1996) *Contemporary grandparenting*, London: Sage Publications.

Lawton, R, Silverstein, M. and Bengtson, V. (1994) 'Solidarity between generations in families', in V.L. Bengtson and R.A. Harootyan (eds) *Intergenerational linkages: Hidden connections in American society*, New York, NY: Springer, pp 19-42.

Luescher, K. and Pillemer, K. (1998) 'Intergenerational ambivalence: a new approach to the study of parent–child relations in later life', *Journal of Marriage and Family*, vol 60, no 2, pp 413-45.

Mancini, J.A. and Bliezner, R. (1989) 'Aging parents and adult children: research themes in intergenerational relations', *Journal of Marriage and Family*, vol 51, no 2, pp 275-90.

Mann, R. (2007) 'Out of the shadows? Grandfatherhood, age and masculinities', *Journal of Aging Studies*, vol 21, no 4, pp 281-91.

Mills, T., Wakeman, M. and Fea, C. (2001) 'Adult grandchildren's perceptions of emotional closeness and consensus with their maternal and paternal grandparents', *Journal of Family Issues*, vol 22, no 5, pp 427-55.

Minkler, M. (1999) 'Intergenerational households headed by grandparents: contexts, realities and implications for policy', *Journal of Aging Studies*, vol 13, no 2, pp 199-218.

Minkler, M., Fuller-Thomson, E., Miller, D. and Driver, D. (1997) 'Depression in grandparents raising grandchildren: results of a national longitudinal study', *Archives of Family Medicine*, vol 6, no 5, pp 445-52.

Morgan, D.H.J. (2011) *Rethinking family practices*, Basingstoke: Palgrave Macmillan.

Monserud, M. (2008) 'Intergenerational relationships and affectual solidarity between grandparents and young adults', *Journal of Marriage and Family*, vol 70, no 1, pp 182-95.

Motel-Klingebiel, A., Tesch-Roemer, C. and von Kondratowitz, H.-J. (2005) 'Welfare states do not crowd out the family: evidence for mixed responsibility from comparative analyses', *Ageing & Society*, vol 25, no 6, pp 863-82.

Mueller, M.M., Wilhelm, B. and Elder, G.H. (2002) 'Variations in grandparenting', *Research on Aging*, vol 24, no 3, pp 360-88.

Neugarten, B. and Weinstein, K.T.J. (1964) 'The changing American grandparent', *Journal of Marriage and Family*, vol 26, no 2, pp 199-204.

Oduaran, A. and Oduaran, C. (2010) 'Grandparents and HIV and AIDS in Sub-Saharan Africa', in M. Izuhara (ed) *Ageing and intergenerational relations: Family reciprocity from a global perspective*, Bristol: The Policy Press, pp 95-110.

Oppong, C. (2006) 'Familial roles and social transformations: older men and women in Sub-Saharan Africa', *Research on Aging*, vol 28, no 6, pp 654-68.

Roberto, K., Allen, K.R. and Blieszner, R. (2001) 'Grandfathers' perceptions and expectations of relationships with their adult grandchildren', *Journal of Family Issues*, vol 22, no 4, pp 407-26.

Silverstein, M. and Giarrusso, R. (2010) 'Aging and family life: a decade review', *Journal of Marriage and Family*, vol 72, no 5, pp 1039-58.

Silverstein, M. and Long, J.D. (1998) 'Trajectories of grandparents' perceived solidarity with adult grandchildren: a growth curve analysis over 23 years', *Journal of Marriage and Family*, vol 60, no 4, pp 912-23.

Soldo, B. and Hill, M.S. (1993) 'Intergenerational transfers: economic, demographic, and social perspectives', in G.L. Lawton (ed) *Annual review of gerontology and geriatrics: Focus on kinship, aging, and social change*, New York, NY: Springer.

Somary, K. and Stricker, G. (1998) 'Becoming a grandparent: a longitudinal study of expectations and early experiences as a function of sex and lineage', *The Gerontologist*, vol 38, no 1, pp 53-61.

Sun, R. (2002) 'Old age support in contemporary urban China from both parents' and children's perspectives', *Research on Aging*, vol 29, no 3, pp 410-35.

Szinovacz, M.E. (ed) (1998) *Handbook on grandparenthood*, Westport, CT: Greenwood Press.

Tomassini, C., Kalogirou, S., Grundy, E., Fokkema, T., Martikainen, P., Broese van Groenou, M. and Karisto, A. (2004) 'Contacts between elderly parents and their children in four European countries: current patterns and future prospects', *European Journal of Ageing*, vol 1, no 1, pp 54-63.

Townsend, P. (1957) *The family life of old people*, London: Routledge.

Troll, L. (1985) 'The contingencies of grandparenting', in V.L. Bengston and J.F. Robertson (eds) *Grandparenthood*, Beverly Hills, CA: Sage Publications, pp 135-49.

Troll, L. and Bengtson, L. (1979) 'Generations in the family', in W. Burr, R. Hill, F. Nye and I. Reiss (eds) *Contemporary theories about the family*, New York, NY: Free Press.

Uhlenberg, P. (1996) 'Mortality decline in the twentieth century and supply of kin over the life course', *The Gerontologist*, vol 36, no 5, pp 681-5.

Uhlenberg, P. and Hammill, B.G. (1998) 'Frequency of grandparent contact with grandchild sets: Six factors that make a difference', *The Gerontologist*, vol 38, no 3, pp 276-85.

Uhlenberg, P. and Kirby, J.B. (1998) 'Grandparenthood over time: historical and demographic trends', in M. Szinovacz (ed) *Handbook on grandparenthood*, Westport, CT: Greenwood Press, pp 23-39.

von Hentig, H. (1946) 'The sociological function of the grandmother', *Social Forces*, vol 24, no 2, pp 389-92.

Part One
Grandparents responding to economic and family transformations

TWO

Transformations in the role of grandparents across welfare states

Katharina Herlofson and Gunhild O. Hagestad

Introduction: the many images of modern grandparenthood

In many European countries, grandparenthood is now receiving a great deal of media attention. Reporters want to know if we as social scientists observe new patterns in grandparenting, and they ask what we know about grandparent roles. It is not easy to provide simple answers, but we often respond that grandparents must be seen in several types of societal contexts: cultural, demographic and structural. In considering structural conditions, it is essential that we examine laws and social policies. As sociologists, we are convinced that considerations of contemporary grandparenthood, to a much greater extent than has been the case so far, must be based on a macro perspective, with a focus on how societal context shapes expectations and behaviour. Until the last decade or so, there had been no major comparative studies of grandparents across western societies.

In this chapter, we concentrate on two aspects of societal contexts: demography and social policy. Up until quite recently, culture was most commonly the focus of researchers, and many publications during the second half of the 20th century stressed that there were no clear cultural guidelines for modern grandparenting. Most past work on grandparenthood in late-modern, urbanised societies has taken a social-psychological, micro perspective, discussing variations in perceptions of grandparenthood and grandparent behaviour across different family contexts. The main unit considered has been the grandparent–grandchild dyad. It has been common to start from an underlying premise that we are dealing with what Burgess (1960) called 'a roleless role' or what Rosow (1976) described as a 'tenuous role': a social status that does not have clear expectations linked to it. Consequently, it is argued, individuals within families need to negotiate and develop their own styles of grandparenting, depending on personal circumstances and preferences (Neugarten and Weinstein, 1964; Robertson, 1977; Kivnick, 1983; Bengtson, 1985; Cherlin and Furstenberg, 1985). In the 1980s, the second author of this chapter also concluded that in a given society, there are no common role definitions for grandparents (Hagestad, 1985). Today, she is ready to abandon this view, even though it is still common to encounter contradictory images of grandparents, both within and across countries.

In North America, we find stark contrasts in contemporary images of grandparents. On the one hand, two well-known American social scientists conclude that in well-functioning families, grandparents are redundant (Elder and Conger, 2000). On the other hand, there is an abundant literature on grandparents who take over parental responsibilities, raising their grandchildren in family contexts without functioning parents in the middle generation, due to drug or alcohol abuse, mental or physical illness, incarceration and poverty (Burton 1992; Minkler and Roe, 1993; Jendrek, 1994; Cox, 2000; Hayslip and Goldberg-Glen, 2000; Goodman and Silverstein, 2002). The number of children in the United States living in grandparent-headed households without the parent generation present ('skipped-generation' households) increased significantly during the 1990s and their grandparents often act as 'surrogate parents' (Burton, 1992; Minkler and Roe, 1996; Szinovacz et al, 1999; Uhlenberg and Cheuk, 2010). In the 1990s, the cover of a major American news magazine went one step further and named them 'child savers'. Similar observations are also found for Sub-Saharan Africa, where AIDS has caused family losses and disruption (UNICEF/UNAIDS, 2004; Oppong, 2006), as well as for rural Asian and African areas, where the middle generation migrate to urban areas to find work, leaving their children behind to be cared for by grandparents (Schröder-Butterfill, 2004; Silverstein et al, 2006; Knodel et al, 2010; Uhlenberg and Cheuk, 2010). Baker and Silverstein (in Chapter Three) examine the impact of migration of the middle generation on the wellbeing of grandparents in 'skipped-generation' households in rural China and the US.

Descriptions of grandparents as child savers or as socially redundant are rarely found in European research. What we primarily see in this literature is a discussion of grandparents as providers of informal childcare on an occasional or a more regular basis (Wheelock and Jones, 2002; Gray, 2005; Leira et al, 2005; Tobío, 2007; Lewis et al, 2008; Hank and Buber, 2009; Koslowski, 2009; Dimova and Wolff, 2011; Arpino et al, 2010; Svensson-Dianellou et al, 2010; Aassve et al, 2011;

Igel and Szydlik, 2011). Colleagues in southern Europe (for example, Tobío, 2007) describe grandparents, especially maternal grandmothers, as what we might call 'mother savers'. By being there as care providers for grandchildren on a daily basis, they enable women to combine motherhood and employment. In northern Europe, especially in the Nordic countries, grandparents seem to be more of a back-up support, ready to step in when needed, but usually not on a regular or frequent basis (Hagestad and Herlofson, 2009; Hank and Buber, 2009; Igel and Szydlik, 2011). In our own country, Norway, it is a common perception that individuals in late middle age and early old age are too busy to be actively engaged in the role of grandparent. It is believed that they prefer to live the good life in sunny southern European climates, rather than investing time and energy in grandchildren at home. What research shows, however, is that many young parents say they would not make it without the support from their own parents in times of need (Hagestad, 2006). Here, as in other Nordic welfare states, grandparents may be described as 'family savers'.

The focus of the chapter

In this chapter, we examine perceptions of the grandparent role and reports of grandparental behaviour in different European societies. Do we see the contours of 'mother savers' and 'family savers'? To illustrate, we use data from two recent Norwegian studies: the Norwegian Life course, Ageing and Generation study (NorLAG), wave 1, 2002-03 (n = 5,589 aged 40-79), and the Norwegian Grandparent Study (NorGRAND), 2005 (n = 959 parents of 10- to 12-year-olds with own parents still living).[1] For a European perspective, we compare the Norwegian findings with results from the 2004 baseline study of the Survey of Health, Ageing and Retirement in Europe (SHARE) (n = 31,115, aged 50+).[2] After describing commonalities and differences across countries, we turn to a discussion of how social policies might shape perceptions of grandparent roles and behaviours. Are there indications that contrasts in role patterns reflect different policy contexts? First, however, it is important to provide a brief sketch of recent demographic change that is a major force in an ongoing transformation of grandparent roles. We need to recognise that altered mortality and fertility patterns have created a new context for ties between children, parents and grandparents.

The demography of grandparenthood

One reason why there is currently quite intense media interest in grandparents may be the fact that members of the large post-war baby boom are experiencing life with grandchildren (and some of them are clearly journalists and reporters). The wider demographic context of grandparenthood has changed significantly over the past century. Declining adult mortality has produced striking historical increases in the 'supply' of grandparents (Uhlenberg, 1996, 2005; Szinovacz, 1998a; Hoff, 2007; Uhlenberg and Cheuk, 2010). Based on United States census figures, Uhlenberg (2005) estimates that the proportion of ten-year-olds with all four grandparents living increased seven-fold over the 20th century, from 6% to 41%. Norwegian data show a remarkably similar figure: 40% of children aged 10-12 have all four grandparents living (Hagestad, 2006). At the same time, lowered fertility has reduced competition for grandparental attention, because 'top-heavy' generational structures have altered grandparent:grandchild ratios. In addition, contemporary fertility patterns mean that there is clearer sequencing of parenthood and grandparenthood, especially in the lives of women. Very few have children and grandchildren who are similar ages – a situation that was fairly common in early 20th-century families (but see discussion on simultaneous fathering and grandfathering by divorced men in Chapter Nine).

Uhlenberg (2005) also points out that it is important to consider the number of grandchild sets. Children of one adult child constitute a set. Uhlenberg estimates that in 2000, about one half of American women aged 60-64 had one or two sets of grandchildren. Our own estimate based on data from 2007-08 shows that this is the case for 57% of Norwegian women in their sixties, which is quite similar to the US figure. Here, it is important to recognise that findings will vary greatly, depending on whether one includes all women in a certain age group, or only those who are grandparents. Looking at the same Norwegian data, we find that more than three out of four grandmothers aged 60-69 have one or two sets of grandchildren.

Finally, reduced adult mortality makes it necessary to view grandparenthood in the context of several interdependent generations. By the time grandchildren arrive, most women in the West are in the 'empty-nest' phase; they are typically middle aged, healthy and vigorous. In many societies, people in middle age and the third age are also relatively affluent. All these changes mean that grandparents have a new potential for being a significant presence in the lives of children and grandchildren (Attias-Donfut and Segalen, 2002). Researchers

---

must be mindful of the powerful new continuity in parent–child ties, and the possibility that much grandparenting is done through continued parenting by providing financial support, practical help and encouragement to adult children (Hagestad, 2006), what Gutmann (1987) refers to as being an 'emeritus parent'.

Several earlier studies on grandparenthood have documented the centrality of grandmothers and in particular maternal grandmothers (Matthews and Sprey, 1985; Eisenberg, 1988; Kennedy, 1990; Dubas, 2001). Explanations commonly include discussions of women's kin-keeping role and the centrality of the mother–daughter bond. It is, however, important to *also* recognise the role of demography for this 'matrifocal' pattern: the mother's mother is generally the youngest, and is therefore the grandparent sharing most years, on average, with grandchildren (Hagestad, 1985, 2006; Spitze and Ward, 1998; Keck and Saraceno, 2008). Our analysis of data from NorGRAND revealed that 87% of the 10- to 12-year-olds had a maternal grandmother and 66% had a paternal grandfather living. Among those still living, maternal grandmothers were on average almost four-and-a-half years younger than paternal grandfathers (Herlofson and Hagestad, 2011).

The new demographic picture should compel us to recognise that a given intergenerational tie, such as that between grandparent and grandchild, is often embedded in a complex web of interconnected, vertical links. And yet, the conclusion reached in Szinovacz' (1998b) review of late 20th-century knowledge is still relevant: 'Neglecting the multiple linkages among grandparents, grandchildren, and the middle generation (the grandchildren's parents) constitutes a serious limitation of current research and theorizing' (p 258).

Is there a grandparenthood role? Surprising Norwegian findings

Vital, active and resourceful grandparents with a limited number of grandchildren may provide important support to families with young children. But are grandparents prepared to help out? Do parents of young children expect their own parents to do so? Given strong themes in past work on contemporary grandparenthood, and the pervasiveness of myths, we were quite surprised by findings from the two Norwegian studies: NorLAG and NorGRAND. In both surveys, respondents were given a set of Likert-type items about what grandparents *should* do, indicating their views on normative expectations. Here we focus on three of the items: grandparents should be available to grandchildren in cases of difficulty (such as illness or divorce); grandparents should provide encouragement to adult children in their role as parents; and grandparents should contribute to the economic security of adult children and their families. The results (Table 2.1) surprised us.

As Table 2.1 shows, there is remarkable consensus about grandparent roles among Norwegian parents and grandparents. Almost all agree (strongly agree or agree) that grandparents' duty is to be there for grandchildren in cases of difficulty (97% of the grandmothers and mothers) (for a discussion on the similarly striking prevalence of the norm of 'being there' in the UK context, see Chapter Seven). About nine out of 10 feel that grandparents should provide encouragement and support to their children in the parenting role. Again, the figures for grandmothers and mothers are identical (91%). Fewer agree that grandparents should contribute towards grandchildren's economic

Table 2.1: Role expectations among Norwegian grandparents and parents, by gender (%)

Percentage who agree or strongly agree that grandparents should:	Grandparents (NorLAG)		Parents (NorGRAND)	
	Men	Women	Men	Women
be available to grandchildren in crisis (for example, illness, divorce)	94%	97%	91%	97%
provide encouragement to children in role as parents	89%	91%	82%	91%
contribute to financial security of children and their families	48%	34%	32%	25%
(n =)	871	1,094	393	549

Sources: NorLAG, wave 1, 2002-03 (only respondents who are grandparents are included here); NorGRAND, 2005 (parents of 10- to 12-year-olds).

Table 2.2: Role enactment in Norway: frequency of grandmothers and grandfathers looking after grandchildren (%)

	Grandfathers	Grandmothers
Daily	4	5
Weekly	24	31
Monthly	28	27
More seldom	38	33
Never	6	4
Total	100%	100%
(n =)	879	1,101

Source: NorLAG, wave 1, 2002-03

security. Whereas gender differences among grandparents are almost absent in agreement regarding availability ('being there' in cases of difficulties) and in encouragement (support adult children in the parenting role), grandfathers are more likely than grandmothers to agree that a grandparent's duty is to contribute financially (48% of the grandfathers versus 34% of the grandmothers). Among parents, gender differences are somewhat more marked. Whereas more mothers than fathers agree that grandparents should be available (97% versus 91%) and provide encouragement (91% versus 82%), more fathers than mothers agree on the financial responsibility of grandparents (32% and 25% respectively).

We then turned to questions about actual role behaviours, and again we were surprised at the findings. In the NorLAG study, grandparents were asked how often they look after grandchildren. Table 2.2 shows that 63% of the grandmothers and 56% of the grandfathers reported that they take care of grandchildren monthly or more often. Very few said they look after grandchildren on a daily basis (4–5%) or never (6% of grandfathers and 4% of grandmothers).

Comparative data on role expectations and role enactment in European societies

The results presented above made us quite curious to find out how Norwegian grandparenthood appears in a comparative perspective. To our knowledge, only two datasets include information that makes it possible to study the role of grandparents across welfare states: the Generations and Gender Survey (GGS) and SHARE. The GGS does not include data on role expectations, only role enactment (see Aassve et al, 2011 for an analysis of grandchild care using GGS data). SHARE, on the other hand, contains several questions that are almost identical to those posed in the Norwegian research, and was therefore the most suitable dataset for comparisons. As NorLAG includes persons aged 40 to 79 and SHARE covers the population aged 50 and older, the figures overleaf are based on analyses of 50- to 79-year-olds (grandparents) in both studies.

Should grandparents be there for grandchildren in cases of difficulty? Should they contribute towards the economic security of grandchildren and their families? As illustrated in Figure 2.1, a large proportion of European grandparents *strongly* agree that grandparents should be there for grandchildren in cases of difficulty. We find southern European grandparents most inclined to strongly agree with this item, but also many Nordic grandparents see this as a central grandparental responsibility. In fact, the highest proportion of grandparents expressing strong agreement is found in Norway (around two thirds of grandfathers and nearly 80% of grandmothers strongly agree). The lowest figures are found in Continental European countries: 35–40% in Germany and Austria; around 30% in the Netherlands.

Figure 2.1: Percentage of grandparents (aged 50-79) who *strongly* agree that a grandparent's duty is to be there for grandchildren in cases of difficulty, by country and gender

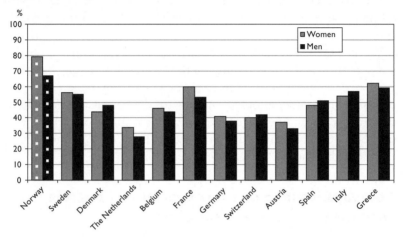

Sources: NorLAG, wave 1, 2002-03 (n = 1,965); SHARE, wave 1, release 2.5.0, 2004 (n = 10,751, weighted).

As for contributing towards the economic security of grandchildren, more grandparents in southern Europe strongly agree that this is a grandparent's duty (30-35%), compared with grandparents in more northern countries (Figure 2.2). On this item, grandparents in Germany and Switzerland are very similar to grandparents in two of the Nordic countries (Norway and Sweden). The countries with the lowest proportions strongly agreeing that grandparents should contribute financially are Denmark, the Netherlands and Austria (5-10%).

There are only small differences between grandmothers and grandfathers in role expectations, and as the two figures illustrate, there are no clear patterns across the various European countries. Grandmothers, more than grandfathers, tend to strongly agree that grandparents should be there in cases of difficulty (in eight of the 12 countries, Figure 2.1), whereas grandfathers, more than grandmothers, tend to strongly agree that they should contribute towards grandchildren's economic security (also in eight of the 12 countries, Figure 2.2). The only country where gender differences are statistically significant for both items turns out to be Norway.

Figure 2.2: Percentage of grandparents (aged 50-79) who **strongly** agree that a grandparent's duty is to contribute towards the economic security of their grandchildren, by country and gender

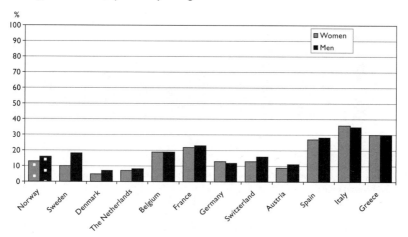

Sources: NorLAG, wave 1, 2002-03 (n = 1,860); SHARE, wave 1, release 2.5.0, 2004 (n = 10,717, weighted).

To what extent do grandparents look after grandchildren? As we saw (in Table 2.2), a majority of both grandmothers and grandfathers in Norway report taking care of grandchildren at least once a month, but very few provide this type of help on a daily basis. What does the pattern look like in other parts of Europe (Figures 2.3 and 2.4)?

Contrary to what many might expect, a larger proportion of Scandinavian grandparents are involved in grandchild care compared with grandparents in southern Europe (Figure 2.3). In Scandinavia, as well as in the Netherlands and Belgium, 55-60% report taking care of grandchildren 'regularly' or 'occasionally' during the past 12 months. In Continental and southern Europe, on the other hand, less than 50% are engaged in grandchild care. France is the only exception, with a pattern more similar to the Nordic than the southern and Continental European pattern. The highest proportions of grandparents involved in grandchild care are found in Denmark and the Netherlands, where around two thirds of grandmothers and circa 60% of grandfathers report taking care of grandchildren at least occasionally. Italy, on the other hand, has the lowest proportions, with about half of grandmothers and 36% of grandfathers involved.

Figure 2.3: Percentage of grandparents (aged 50-79) who look after grandchildren 'regularly' or 'occasionally' (past 12 months), by country and gender

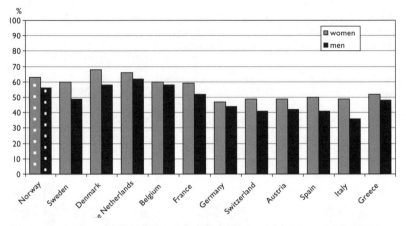

Sources: NorLAG, wave 1, 2002-03 (n = 1,980); SHARE, wave 1, release 2.5.0, 2004 (n = 13,442, weighted).

If we only consider regular, *daily* care, the picture is almost turned upside down. Among grandparents who report looking after grandchildren regularly or occasionally (past 12 months), very few in Scandinavia and the Netherlands do so on a daily basis (5% or less) (Figure 2.4). Somewhat larger proportions of grandparents involved in looking after grandchildren in Germany and Austria are engaged in such frequent grandchild care (close to 20%). In the Mediterranean countries on the other hand, between 40% (Spain and Greece) and 50% (Italy) of the grandparents who report any grandchild care seem to act more or less as full-time care providers. Figure 2.4 only includes grandparents who are involved in grandchild care on a frequent or occasional basis. If *all* grandparents are considered, including those who state they never look after grandchildren, the figures would be somewhat different and the country differences not quite as stark. Still, about 20% of all Italian and Greek grandparents provide grandchild care on a daily basis, compared with 1-2% of grandparents in Denmark and the Netherlands.

As the figures illustrate, differences between grandmothers and grandfathers are somewhat greater for role enactment than for role expectations. In all countries, a larger proportion of grandmothers report being involved in grandchild care. Among grandparents providing grandchild care, the proportions looking after grandchildren on a daily basis are similar for grandmothers and grandfathers in many countries. When considering *all* grandparents, gender differences in

Figure 2.4: Percentage of grandparents (aged 50-79) who provide daily (or almost daily) grandchild care among grandparents who look after grandchildren at least occasionally (past 12 months), by country and gender

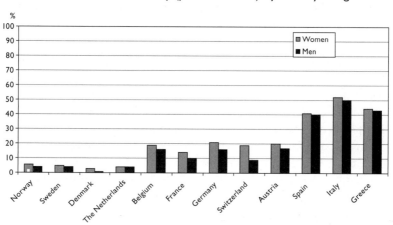

Sources: NorLAG, wave 1, 2002-03 (n = 1,698); SHARE, wave 1, release 2.5.0, 2004 (n = 8,063 weighted).

provision of daily care are somewhat greater, particularly in countries where such frequent care is common (Spain and Italy).

The rather small differences between grandmothers and grandfathers in grandchild care shown in Figures 2.4 and 2.5 may give a misleading picture of how married grandparents provide care. Grandfathers who report frequent grandchild care may more or less 'tag along' when their wives, the grandmothers, take care of grandchildren. Findings from a Norwegian study of parents with young children (under 12) showed a clear pattern: he (the grandfather) provided care if she (the grandmother) did, whereas she was much more likely to independently take caring responsibilities for grandchildren (Hagestad and Herlofson, 2009).

Grandparental roles in the context of wider family responsibilities

Responsibilities towards family members in a given society are shaped by cultural expectations, laws and social policies. In several debates about European patterns of normative family obligations, a north–south axis has been drawn. This can be observed in discussions of individualisation and 'the second demographic transition' (Lesthaeghe, 1983; van de Kaa, 1987; Surkyn and Lesthaeghe, 2004), as well as in debates about contrasts between welfare regimes, such as those triggered by Esping-Andersen's (1990, 1999) typologies (Anttonen and Sipilä, 1996; Leitner,

2003; Hagestad and Herlofson, 2007; Kalmijn and Saraceno, 2008; Haberkern and Szydlik, 2010).

Most of the debate concerning cultural expectations about family responsibility has focused on care for ageing family members. It has been far more common to study attitudes towards upward intergenerational support (from adult children to parents, so-called *filial* responsibility) than the other way around, from parents to adult children or from grandparents to grandchildren. Results from comparative studies of filial responsibility show a clear north–south gradient, with the southern European countries being considerably more supportive of this type of family responsibility norm than is the case in the north (Daatland and Herlofson, 2003; Kalmijn and Saraceno, 2008). In a recent publication, Daatland and colleagues (2011) include parental responsibility and add Eastern European countries. They find country differences to be less marked for parental than for filial norms, but the ordering of countries remains the same – expectations increase in intensity as we move from the north and west to the south and east. In a comparative European study of grandparents caring for grandchildren, Hank and Buber (2009) show how expectations about grandchild care (namely, "Grandparents' duty is to help grandchildren's parents in looking after young grandchildren"), as expressed by grandparents themselves, is far higher in the Mediterranean countries, France and Germany, than in Denmark and the Netherlands. Even among Danish and Dutch grandparents who reported caring for grandchildren at least weekly, less than 50% agreed that taking care of grandchildren is a grandparent's responsibility. This is in sharp contrast to Germany, France, Italy and Spain where more than 80% of grandparents who provided at least weekly grandchild care regarded it as a responsibility. In Greece, the figure was 95%.

As for laws about family responsibility, in some countries there are no legal obligations between parents and adult children, nor between grandparents and grandchildren (the Scandinavian countries and UK). In others, laws not only include a mutual responsibility between parents and adult children, but also grandparents' obligation to support grandchildren (southern Europe and Germany), as is shown in a recent overview by Saraceno and Keck (2008).

Typically, policies regarding care for children and care for old people, what Hagestad (2008) refers to as the 'book-end generations', are studied separately. It represents a major break-through when, as has happened in recent years, several European authors argue that exactly because of generational interconnectedness, we must consider policies regarding care for the young and the old *together* (Anttonen and Sipilä,

1996; Leitner, 2003; Anttonen et al, 2003; Saraceno and Keck, 2010). Part of this work presents typologies for grouping nations according to how they handle support and care for both 'book-ends', for example by ordering them on an underlying dimension of degree of familialism or extent of public services and transfers to children *and* old people (Leitner, 2003; Saraceno and Keck, 2008, 2010).

Building on Esping-Andersen's (1999) concepts, Saraceno and Keck (2008, 2010) outline four different types of policy regimes. A *de-familialised* regime is, as described by Esping-Andersen, one that lessens family responsibilities and dependencies by offering both care services and financial transfers. A *familialistic* regime, on the other hand, is one that lacks public alternatives to family care and support. Both Leitner (2003) and Saraceno and Keck (2010) stress the varieties of familialism, and the latter two authors propose a variant they call *supported familialism* (when families are financially compensated for meeting their caring responsibilities), as well as a type they label *optional familialism*. The latter is found in countries where families have a choice between de-familialisation (services) and supported familialism (financial compensation, or cash-for-care). What is stressed in both publications is that countries cluster differently depending on which care policies are considered – child care or elder care. Norway, for example, is characterised by high de-familialisation in elder care (comparatively high levels of institutional care and home care), whereas care for children can be considered a mix of optional familialism (parents have an option between daycare and cash-for-care when children are one to two years of age) and supported familialism (long parental leaves). The Scandinavian countries and France have comparatively high public childcare coverage rates for children under three and long, paid parental leaves; whereas the Mediterranean countries and Germany have low coverage rates and shorter parental leaves (Saraceno, 2011).

As pointed out by several authors, nations' different institutional care arrangements are often reflected in expectations about family responsibility (Daatland and Herlofson, 2003; Kalmijn and Saraceno, 2008; Haberkern and Szydlik, 2010). Filial obligation norms are usually found to have stronger support in familialistic welfare states than in those characterised by de-familialisation. As we showed earlier, the same is the case for expectations regarding grandparents' contributions to the economic security of grandchildren. Whether grandparents should 'be there' for grandchildren in cases of difficulties shows a different pattern. High proportions of grandparents in southern Europe do indeed strongly agree with this role expectation, but so do northern European grandparents. When actual grandchild care is considered, larger shares of grandparents in the north are involved 'regularly' or 'occasionally' compared to grandparents in the south, but the frequency of the care is much lower in the north than in the south. This brings us to the issue of substitution and complementarity.

The substitution versus complementarity debate revisited

Discussions of north–south contrasts and considerations of the interplay between families and public services have commonly used the concepts of *substitution* versus *complementarity* or *crowding out* versus *crowding in*. The substitution thesis states that there is an inverse relationship between service provision and extent of family care, arguing that when public service levels are high, family care is low or absent, and vice versa (Lingsom, 1997). This has also been referred to as a 'crowding-out' situation (Künemund and Rein, 1999; Motel-Klingebiel et al, 2005). However, most research in this field shows that complementarity between families and services is the most common arrangement, rather than a clear substitution. Depending on the type of welfare state, different kinds and degrees of complementarity exist. In some countries, families have the main responsibility and are supplemented by services; in others, services cover most of the needs and families have a complementary role.

To date, the substitution–complementarity debate has mostly concentrated on care for the old (Daatland and Herlofson, 2001; Motel-Klingebiel et al, 2005; Ogg and Renaut, 2006; Brandt et al, 2009). The arguments set forth in these discussions are, however, also applicable to considerations of young children and their families, as pointed out in recent publications on child care and grandparenting (Raeymaeckers et al, 2008; Hank and Buber, 2009; Igel and Szydlik, 2011). Hank and Buber (2009) conclude that in countries like Sweden and Denmark, where public childcare services are extensive and maternal employment rates are high, many grandparents complement services by taking care of grandchildren in times of need. In southern Europe, on the other hand, mothers tend to be full-time carers for their children, and there is therefore a limited demand for grandparental help. However, the situation changes when mothers enter the labour market. Working mothers need help from the grandparent generation, and the needed support is often a 'chronic emergency' as grandparents are asked to substitute for formal care provision that is not available. Figures 2.3 and 2.4 illustrate this pattern. Higher proportions of grandparents in the Scandinavian countries, the Netherlands, Belgium and France are involved in some grandchild care, compared to grandparents in southern Europe. Being involved in (almost) daily care for grandchildren is, however, about 10 times as common among grandparents in Italy and Greece as it is among Danish and Dutch grandparents.

Grandparents as 'mother savers' or 'family savers'

Analyses of grandchild care are typically found in two different research traditions: in studies dealing with ageing and intergenerational family relations (Attias-Donfut and Segalen, 1998; Dench and Ogg, 2002; Keck and Saraceno, 2008; Hagestad and Herlofson, 2009; Hank and Buber, 2009; Attias-Donfut, 2010; Igel and Szydlik, 2011) and in literature on working mothers (Gray 2005; Leira et al, 2005; Tobío, 2007; Lewis et al, 2008). In both cases, two main pictures emerge from earlier research, as well as from the data discussed here. In the Scandinavian countries and France, where parental leaves are long and public childcare services are quite generous and affordable, many grandparents are available as supports on occasions when there is a clear and urgent need. Hagestad (2006) has discussed the back-up functions of grandparents in Norway, how they step in as babysitters for grandchildren when needed, and how important it is for parents of young children to know that their own parents can be called on in times of need. In a discussion of France, Attias-Donfut and Segalen (1998) show how essential grandparents' back-up help is, and how this type of support has increased since the 1970s. In both cases, grandparents can be described as 'family savers'.

In southern Europe, where formal childcare services are scarce, fewer grandparents are involved in care provision, but those who are often act as full-time care providers (Tobío, 2007; Hank and Buber, 2009; Svensson-Dianellou et al, 2010), allowing their daughters to remain in the labour market after having children. According to Leira and colleagues (2005), Spanish and Italian grandmothers often feel responsible for taking care of grandchildren so that their daughters can be economically active (hence the term 'mother savers'). Arpino and colleagues (2010) show how labour market participation of young Italian mothers increases substantially when they have parents or parents-in-law who help with childcare. Referring to Spain, Tobío (2007) points out that 'today's grandparents are playing a fundamental role in the rapid extension of women's economic activity' (p 192). She notes a certain paradox: Spanish grandmothers must assume the traditional female, mothering role in order for their daughters to be able to change old gender roles.

The UK is the country in Europe where grandchild care has been studied most thoroughly, and often from the perspective of working parents (mothers) (La Valle et al, 2000; Wheelock and Jones, 2002; Gray, 2005, Glaser et al, 2010). This literature seems to suggest both a 'family-saver' and a 'mother-saver' function of grandparents, the latter in particular among lone mothers. Grandparents are usually not full-time carers for their grandchildren, but complement formal part-time childcare or help out before and after school on a regular basis (weekly or more often), thus enabling mothers to be in the labour force and to work longer hours (Wheelock and Jones, 2002; Gray, 2005).

Conclusion

In our discussion, we have attempted to illustrate how demographic change, combinations of care policies and emerging work patterns of women have all contributed to a transformation of grandparenthood in Europe. The availability of parental leave and public childcare seem to be crucial in shaping how grandparent roles are defined and enacted. In societies with little public support for parents with young children, help from grandparents is often essential in enabling mothers to be active in the workforce. In such cases, grandparental responsibilities are often regular and extensive ('mother savers'). On the other hand, in societies with welfare policies aimed at reducing the work–family conflict, grandparents frequently serve a 'family-saver' function by being available when extra help and support are needed. In such 'care regime' contexts, grandparents may feel increased motivation to help offspring with young children (that is, to serve as 'family savers'), since such readiness is less 'risky' than is the case in societies with more limited formal childcare options (where grandparents are needed frequently). Here, women and men with young children are much more dependent on their parents and parents-in-law, because they often represent the only childcare solution. Without available grandparents, and in particular grandmothers, many southern European mothers would not be able to participate in the labour market.

Although the 'mother-saver' role generally includes childrearing, it differs considerably from the 'child-saver' role. 'Child savers' are described as grandparents who take on a full-time parenting role without the presence of the middle generation (the grandchildren's biological parents) (see Chapter Three). In contemporary Africa and Asia, because of the HIV/AIDS pandemic and labour migration by the middle generation from rural to urban areas, as well as in the United States, because of factors such as drug abuse, incarceration and poverty, this type of grandparent role is quite common. In European countries on the other hand, grandparents often act as 'family savers' or 'mother savers', but they rarely become 'child savers'.

One important challenge facing researchers is to further examine correlates and consequences of different care regimes. How much local variation can we observe within a national context? How do age structure and care regime interact across different local contexts? What type of regime is most strongly associated with wellbeing in old age, stress in the middle generations, help and support to young families, or children's networks of available adults? There are still many questions that should be posed in research on evolving grandparent roles.

Notes

[1] The Norwegian Life course, Ageing and Generation Study (NorLAG) was funded by the Research Council of Norway (grant number 149564), and by the Ministry of Health and Care Services, the Ministry of Labour and NOVA. The Norwegian Grandparent Study (NorGRAND) was funded by the Research Council of Norway (grant number 150223).

[2] SHARE, release 2.5.0, as of 24 May 2011. The SHARE data collection has been primarily funded by the European Commission through the fifth framework programme (project QLK6-CT-2001-00360 in the thematic programme Quality of Life), through the sixth framework programme (projects SHARE-I3, RII-CT- 2006-062193, COMPARE, CIT5-CT-2005-028857, and SHARELIFE, CIT4-CT-2006-028812) and through the seventh framework programme (SHARE-PREP, 211909 and SHARE-LEAP, 227822). Additional funding from the US National Institute on Aging (U01 AG09740-13S2, P01 AG005842, P01 AG08291, P30 AG12815, Y1-AG-4553-01 and OGHA 04-064, IAG BSR06-11, R21 AG025169) as well as from various national sources is gratefully acknowledged. For methodological details, see Börsch-Supan and Jürges (2005).

References

Aassve, A., Arpino, B. and Goisis, A. (2011) *Grandparenting and mothers' labour force participation: a comparative analysis using the Generations and Gender Survey*, Dondena Working Papers Series, no 36, Milano: Carlo F. Dondena Centre for Research on Social Dynamics, Universitá Bocconi.

Arpino, B., Pronzato, C. and Tavares, L. (2010) *All in the family: Informal childcare and mothers' labour market participation*, ISER Working Papers Series No 2010-24, Essex: Institute for Social & Economic Research.

Anttonen, A. and Sipilä, J. (1996) 'European social care services: is it possible to identify models?', *Journal of European Social Policy*, vol 6, no 2, pp 87-100.

Anttonen, A., Baldock, J. and Sipilä J. (eds) (2003) *The young, the old and the state. Social care systems in five industrial nations*, Cheltenham: Edward Elgar.

Attias-Donfut, C. (2010) 'Grandparents in Europe: new family supports', Discussion Paper No 7, Japanese Stratification Study Discussion Paper Series, www.l.u-tokyo.ac.jp/~kaiso-08/workingpaper/Discussion_Paper_07_Attias_Donfut.pdf.

Attias-Donfut, C. and Segalen, M. (1998) *Grand-parents. La famille à travers les générations*, Paris: Odile Jacobs.

Attias-Donfut, C. and Segalen, M. (2002) 'The construction of grandparenthood', *Current Sociology*, vol 50, no 2, pp 281-94.

Bengtson, V.L. (1985) 'Diversity and symbolism in grandparental roles', in V.L. Bengtson and R.F. Robertson (eds) *Grandparenthood*, Beverly Hills, CA: Sage Publications, pp 11-25.

Börsch-Supan, A. and Jürges, H. (eds) (2005) *The Survey of Health, Ageing and Retirement in Europe – methodology*, Mannheim: Mannheim Research Institute for the Economics of Aging (MEA).

Brandt, M., Haberkern, K. and Szydlik, M. (2009) 'Intergenerational help and care in Europe', *European Sociological Review*, vol 25, no 5, pp 585-601.

Burgess, E.W. (1960) 'Aging in western culture', in E.W. Burgess (ed) *Aging in western societies*, Chicago, IL: University of Chicago Press, pp 3-28.

Burton, L.M. (1992) 'Black grandparents rearing children of drug-addicted parents: stressors, outcomes, and social service needs', *The Gerontologist*, vol 32, no 6, pp 744-51.

Cherlin, A. and Furstenberg, F.F. (1985) 'Styles and strategies of grandparenting', in V.L. Bengtson and R.F. Robertson (eds) *Grandparenthood*, Beverly Hills, CA: Sage Publications, pp 97-116.

Cox, C.B. (2000) *To grandmother's house we go and stay: Perspectives on custodial grandparents*, New York, NY: Springer.

Daatland, S.O. and Herlofson, K. (2001) 'Service systems and family care – substitution or complementarity?' in S.O. Daatland and K. Herlofson (eds) *Ageing, intergenerational relations, care systems and quality of life – an introduction to the OASIS project*, Report 14/01, Oslo: NOVA, pp 53-61.

Daatland, S.O. and Herlofson, K. (2003) '"Lost solidarity" or "changed solidarity": a comparative European view of normative family solidarity', *Ageing & Society*, vol 23, no 5, pp 537-60.

Daatland, S.O, Herlofson, K. and Lima, I.A. (2011) 'Balancing generations: on the strength and character of family norms in the west and east of Europe', *Ageing & Society*, vol 31, no 7, pp 1159-79.

Dench, G. and Ogg, J. (2002) *Grandparenting in Britain: A baseline study*, London: Institute of Community Studies.

Dimova, R. and Wolff, F.-C. (2011) 'Do downward private transfers enhance maternal labor supply? Evidence from around Europe', *Journal of Population Economics*, vol 24, no 3, pp 911-33.

Dubas, J.S. (2001) 'How gender moderates the grandparent–grandchild relationship: a comparison of kin-keeper and kin-selector theories', *Journal of Family Issues*, vol 22, no 4, pp 478-92.

Eisenberg, A.R. (1988) 'Grandchildren's perspectives on relationships with grandparents: the influence of gender across generations', *Sex Roles*, vol 19, no 3/4, pp 205-17.

Elder, G.H. Jr and Conger, R.D. (2000) *Children of the land: Adversity and success in rural America*, Chicago, IL: University of Chicago Press.

Esping-Andersen, G. (1990) *The three worlds of welfare capitalism*, Princeton, NJ: Princeton University Press.

Esping-Andersen, G. (1999) *Social foundations of postindustrial economies*, Oxford: Oxford University Press.

Glaser, K., Montserrat, E., Waginger, U., Price, D., Stuchbury, R. and Tinker, A. (2010) *Grandparenting in Europe*, London: Grandparent Plus.

Goodman, C.C. and Silverstein, M. (2002) 'Grandmothers raising grandchildren: family structure and well-being in culturally diverse families', *The Gerontologist*, vol 42, no 5, pp 676-89.

Gray, A. (2005) 'The changing availability of grandparents as carers and ints implications for childcare policy in the UK', *Journal of Social Policy*, vol 34, no 4, pp 557-77.

Gutmann, D. (1987) *Reclaimed powers: Towards a new psychology of men and women in late life*, New York, NY: Basic Books.

Haberkern, K. and Szydlik, M. (2010) 'State care provision, societal opinion and children's care of older parents in 11 European countries', *Ageing & Societies*, vol 30, no 2, pp 299-323.

Hagestad, G.O. (1985) 'Continuity and connectedness', in V.L. Bengtson and R.F. Robertson (eds) *Grandparenthood*, Beverly Hills, CA: Sage Publications, pp 31-48.

Hagestad, G.O. (2006) 'Transfers between grandparents and grandchildren: the importance of taking a three-generation perspective', *Zeitschrift für Familienforschung*, vol 18, no 3, pp 315-32.

Hagestad, G.O. (2008) 'The book-ends: emerging perspectives on children and old people', in C. Saraceno (ed) *Families, ageing and social policy. Intergenerational solidarity in European welfare states*, Cheltenham: Edward Elgar, pp 20-37.

Hagestad, G.O. and Herlofson, K. (2007) 'Micro and macro perspectives on intergenerational relations and transfers in Europe', in Department of Economic and Social Affairs, United Nations Organization (UNO) *Report from United Nations Expert Group Meeting on Social and Economic Implications of Changing Population Age Structures*, New York: UNO, pp 339-57.

Hagestad, G.O. and Herlofson, K. (2009) 'Dagens besteforeldre. Småbarnsfamiliens støttespillere' ['Today's grandparents. Back-up support for families with small children',] *Samfunnsspeilet*, vol 23, no 1, pp 92-4.

Hank, K. and Buber, I. (2009) 'Grandparents caring for their grandchildren. Findings from the 2004 Survey of Health, Ageing and Retirement in Europe', *Journal of Family Issues*, vol 30, no 1, pp 53-73.

Hayslip, B. Jr and Goldberg-Glen, R. (eds) (2000) *Grandparents raising grandchildren: Theoretical, empirical, and clinical perspectives*, New York, NY: Springer.

Herlofson, K. and Hagestad, G.O. (2011) 'Challenges in moving from macro to micro: population and family structures in ageing societies', *Demographic Research*, vol 25, art 10, pp 337-70.

Hoff, A. (2007) 'Patterns of intergenerational support in grandparent–grandchild and parent–child relationships in Germany', *Ageing & Society*, vol 27, no 5, pp 643-65.

Igel, C. and Szydlik, M. (2011) 'Grandchild care and welfare state arrangements in Europe', *Journal of European Social Policy*, vol 21, no 3, pp 210-24.

Jendrek, M.P. (1994) 'Grandparents who parent their grandchildren: circumstances and decisions', *The Gerontologist*, vol 34, no 2, pp 206-16.

Kalmijn, M. and Saraceno, C. (2008) 'A comparative perspective on intergenerational support. Responsiveness to parental needs in individualistic and familialistic countries', *European Societies*, vol 10, no 3, pp 479-508.

Keck, W. and Saraceno, C. (2008) 'Grandchildhood in Germany and Italy: an exploration', in A. Leira and C. Saraceno (eds) *Childhood: Changing contexts. Comparative Social Research Vol 25*, Bingley: Emerald, pp 133-63.

Kennedy, G.E. (1990) 'College students' expectations of grandparent and grandchild role behaviours', *The Gerontologist*, vol 30, no 1, pp 43-8.

Kivnick, H.Q. (1983) 'Dimensions of grandparenthood meaning: deductive conceptualization and empirical derivation', *Journal of Personality and Social Psychology*, vol 44, no 5, pp 1056-68.

Knodel, J., Kespichayawattana, J., Saengtienchai, C. and Wiwatwanich, S. (2010) 'How left behind are rural parents of migrant children? Evidence from Thailand', *Ageing & Society*, vol 30, no 5, pp 811-41.

Koslowski, A.S. (2009) 'Grandparents and the care for their grandchildren', in J. Stillwell (ed) *Fertility, living arrangements, care and mobility*, London: Springer, pp 171-90.

Künemund, H. and Rein, M. (1999) 'There is more to receiving than needing: theoretical arguments and empirical explorations of crowding in and crowding out', *Ageing & Society*, vol 19, no 1, pp 93-121.

La Valle, I., Finch, S., Nove, A. and Lewin, C. (2000) *Parents' demand for childcare*, DfEE Research Report RR 176, Sheffield: Department for Education and Employment.

Leira, A., Tobío, C. and Trifiletti, R. (2005) 'Kinship and informal support: care resources for the first generation of working mothers in Norway, Italy and Spain', in U. Gerhard, T. Knijn and A. Weckwert (eds) *Working mothers in Europe. A comparison of policies and practices*, Cheltenham: Edward Elgar, pp 74-96.

Leitner, S. (2003) 'Varieties of familialism. The caring function of the family in comparative perspective', *European Societies*, vol 5, no 3, pp 353-75.

Lesthaeghe, R. (1983) 'A century of demographic and cultural change in Western Europe: an exploration of underlying dimensions', *Population and Development Review*, vol 9, no 33, pp 411-35.

Lewis, J., Campbell, M. and Huerta, C. (2008) 'Patterns of paid and unpaid work in Western Europe: gender, commodification, preferences and the implications for policy', *Journal of European Social Policy*, vol 18, no 1, pp 21-37.

Lingsom, S. (1997) *The substitution issue. Care policies and their consequences for family care*, Report 6/97, Oslo: NOVA.

Matthews, S.H. and Sprey, J. (1985) 'Adolescents' relationships with grandparents: an empirical contribution to conceptual clarification', *Journal of Gerontology*, vol 40, no 5, pp 621-6.

Minkler, M. and Roe, K.M. (1993) *Grandmothers as caregivers: Raising children of the crack cocaine epidemic*, Newbury Park, CA: Sage Publications.

Minkler, M. and Roe, K.M. (1996) 'Grandparents as surrogate parents', *Generations*, vol 20, no 1, pp 34-8.

Motel-Klingebiel, A., Tesch-Römer, C. and von Kondratowitz, H.-J. (2005) 'Welfare states do not crowd out the family: evidence for mixed responsibility from comparative analyses', *Ageing & Society*, vol 25, no 6, pp 863-882.

Neugarten, B.L. and Weinstein, K.K. (1964) 'The changing American grandparent', *Journal of Marriage and Family*, vol 26, no 2, pp 199-204.

Ogg, J. and Renaut, S. (2006) 'The support of parents in old age by those born during 1945-1954: a European perspective', *Ageing & Society*, vol 26, no 5, pp 723-43.

Oppong, C. (2006) 'Familial roles and social transformations. Older men and women in Sub-Saharan Africa', *Research on Aging*, vol 28, no 6, pp 654-68.

Raeymaeckers, P., Dewilde, C., Snoeckx, L. and Mortelmans, D. (2008) 'Childcare strategies of divorced mothers in Europe: a comparative analysis', *European Sociological Review*, vol 24, no 1, pp 115-31.

Robertson, J.F. (1977) 'Grandmotherhood: a study of role conceptions', *Journal of Marriage and the Family*, vol 39, no 1, pp 165-74.

Rosow, I. (1976) 'Status and role change through the life span', in R.H. Binstock and E. Shanas (eds) *Handbook of aging and the social sciences*, New York, NY: Van Nostrand Reinhold, pp 457-.

Saraceno, C. (2011) 'Childcare needs and childcare policies: a multidimensional issue', *Current Sociology*, vol 59, no 1, pp 78-96.

Saraceno, C. and Keck, W. (2008) 'The institutional framework of intergenerational family obligations in Europe: a conceptual and methodological overview', *Multilinks deliverable 1.1*, www.multilinks-project.eu.

Saraceno, C. and Keck, W. (2010) 'Can we identify intergenerational policy regimes in Europe?' *European Societies*, vol 12, no 5, pp 675-96.

Schröder-Butterfill, E. (2004) 'Inter-generational family support provided by older people in Indonesia', *Ageing & Society*, vol 24, no 4, pp 497-530.

Silverstein, M., Cong, Z. and Li, S. (2006) 'Intergenerational transfers and living arrangements of older people in rural China: consequences for psychological well-being', *Journal of Gerontology: Social Sciences*, vol 61B, no 5, pp S256-S266.

Spitze, G. and Ward, R.A. (1998) 'Gender variations', in M.E. Szinovacz (ed) *Handbook on grandparenthood*, Westport, CT: Greenwood Press, pp 113-27.

Surkyn, J. and Lesthaeghe, R. (2004) 'Value orientation and the second demographic transition (SDT) in Northern, Western and Southern Europe: an update', *Demographic Research*, Special Collection 3, art 3, pp 45-86.

Svensson-Dianellou, A, Smith, P.K. and Mestheneos, E. (2010) 'Family help by Greek grandparents', *Journal of Intergenerational Relationships*, vol 8, no 3, pp 249-63.

Szinovacz, M.E. (1998a) 'Grandparents today: a demographic profile', *The Gerontologist*, vol 38, no 1, pp 37-52.

Szinovacz, M.E. (1998b) 'Research on grandparenting: needed refinements in concepts, theories and methods', in M.E. Szinovacz (ed) *Handbook on grandparenthood*, Westport, CT: Greenwood Press, pp 257-88.

Szinovacz, M.E., DeViney, S. and Atkinson, M.P. (1999) 'Effects of surrogate parenting on grandparents' well-being', *Journal of Gerontology: Social Sciences*, vol 54B, no 6, pp S376-S388.

Tobío, C. (2007) 'Change and reciprocity in intergenerational relationships: the discourse of Spanish working mothers', in J. Véron, S. Pennec and J. Légaré (eds) *Ages, generations and the social contract: The demographic challenges facing the welfare state*, Dordrecht: Springer, pp 191-207.

Uhlenberg, P. (1996) 'Mortality decline in the twentieth century and supply of kin over the life course', *The Gerontologist*, vol 36, no 5, pp 681-5.

Uhlenberg, P. (2005) 'Historical forces shaping grandparent–grandchild relationships: demography and beyond', in M. Silverstein (ed) *Intergenerational relations across time and space. Annual Review of Gerontology and Geriatrics*, vol 38, pp 77-97.

Uhlenberg, P. and Cheuk, M. (2010) 'The significance of grandparents to grandchildren: an international perspective', in D. Dannefer and C. Phillipson (eds) *The SAGE handbook of social gerontology*, London: Sage Publications, pp 447-58.

UNICEF/UNAIDS (2004) *Children on the brink 2004. A joint report of new orphan estimates and a framework for action*, New York, NY: United Nations.

van de Kaa, D. (1987) 'Europe's second demographic transition', *Population Bulletin*, vol 42, no 1, pp 1-58.

Wheelock, J. and Jones, K. (2002) '"Grandparents are the next best thing": informal childcare for working parents in urban Britain', *Journal of Social Policy*, vol 31, no 3, pp 441-63.

THREE

The wellbeing of grandparents caring for grandchildren in China and the United States

Lindsey Baker and Merril Silverstein

Introduction

The intensity and style of care for grandchildren, as well as the precipitating conditions of grandparental involvement vary substantially across countries and regions of the world. The basic functional typology used to describe grandparents who devote substantial time to the care of their grandchildren generally classifies them into two types: 'child savers', who provide extensive childcare when parents are incapacitated or unavailable to raise their children (Minkler and Roe, 1993), and 'mother savers', who provide childcare so that parents (usually mothers) are able to work for pay outside the home or pursue educational opportunities (Gordon et al, 2004) (see Chapters One and Two). However useful this dichotomy, it does not comfortably fit patterns of grandparenting in parts of the developing world where grandparents are simultaneously child and mother savers, and may personally benefit as a result of their efforts.

Grandparent caregivers in rural China present examples of what might be called 'family maximisers', as they are embedded in an integrated multigenerational, multihousehold economic system within which resources are mutually shared. This type of caregiver is exemplified by grandparents caring full time for the children of their migrant sons in China from whom significant financial support is received in the form of remittances. Childcare provided by these grandparents enables the family to maximise its economic potential from which grandparents also materially gain (Cong and Silverstein, 2008, 2011). However, less is known about the emotional costs and benefits to grandparents associated with custodial caregiving in societies where such a role is culturally meaningful and economically rewarding, as in China.

In this chapter we examine the psychological wellbeing of grandparents in rural China who provide custodial care to their grandchildren, taking into account the unique social circumstances that have positioned them as pivotal family actors. In doing so, we investigate how the emotional wellbeing of grandparent caregivers is shaped by the positive factors that have selected them into the caregiver role and by the remittances provided by migrant sons and their wives who have left their children behind in natal villages and in the charge of grandparents. To draw attention to rural China as a distinct social context, we also compare grandparent caregivers in rural China to those in the United States, a group that experiences custodial grandparenting under starkly different societal conditions and family circumstances.

Custodial grandparenting in rural China

The role of grandparents as custodial caretakers of their grandchildren in rural China must be understood in the context of wider societal changes that have precipitated the need for grandparents to become surrogate parents. Urban economic development in China over the past three decades has created one of the largest internal migrations in human history, creating a surge of labour migrants in pursuit of better-paying service and construction jobs (Fan, 2008). Enabled by the decollectivisation of agricultural production, many rural residents took advantage of urban work opportunities, depopulating villages of their working-age populations. However, China's household registration or *hukou* system did not allow rural migrants to have permanent resident status in their new urban destinations, creating what became known as the 'floating population' – a name that denotes the temporary nature of their urban occupancy.

Because the young children of these migrants could not attend school outside of the rural area in which they were registered, many migrant parents chose to leave their children in the rural villages to be cared for by extended family members. These children along with the ageing parents of migrant workers are referred to as *liushou*, or the 'left behind' (Biao, 2007). During the 1990s, when rural-to-urban migration reached its peak, the percentage of children living in 'skipped-generation' households – households containing a grandparent and grandchild in the absence of the parent generation – nearly tripled, representing the single fastest-growing family household type in China (Yi and Wang, 2003).

Estimates of the number of 'left-behind' children are imprecise, but reports in the popular press estimate that approximately 58 million children have been left behind by migrant parents – a large majority of whom are cared for by grandparents (Stack, 2010). In rural Anhui province, the area investigated in this chapter, it is estimated that 125-250 children are 'left behind' for every 1,000 migrants and over one third of these children live apart from both parents (Biao, 2007). Given the sheer magnitude of this trend, the left-behind population is of great public concern to provincial and national policy makers, with grandparents often portrayed as too frail to handle the rigours of raising children – particularly children who have developed behavioural problems due to separation from one or both parents (Lee, 2011).

However, by agreeing to care for grandchildren, grandparents grant their adult children (most are sons in this patrilineal culture) the freedom to earn wages in excess of what they would have earned had they remained in their rural villages. There is evidence that caregiving grandparents stand to economically benefit from the financial returns enabled by these higher wages (Cong and Silverstein, 2011), and even experience improved psychological wellbeing as a result of remittances provided by migrant children (Silverstein et al, 2006). The receipt of remittances is particularly important for older adults in rural China because pensions are scarce and reliance on adult children is a virtual necessity for economic survival.

The circular flow of resources – often described as a time-for-money exchange – has a strong basis in principles of reciprocity, but reciprocity is an imperfect description in the Chinese context, as the goal is less to privately benefit from the exchange than to improve the entire family's standard of living. The Chinese model of these family dynamics has been called a 'mutual-aid' or 'corporate' system because actions taken by family members are strategically coordinated to maximise the wellbeing of the family unit (Sun, 2002). In this sense, both the efforts of grandparents and the benefits they attract are distributed where they are most needed and where they will do the most good. Caregiving for grandchildren and the provision of remittances also have deep cultural roots and are reinforced by Confucian ideals regarding the primacy of family obligation and support (Sung, 1998).

Comparing custodial grandparenting in the US and China

The Chinese model of caregiving for grandchildren does not fit comfortably within the current view of custodial grandparents – predominated by research on US African American grandparents. In this chapter, we seek to highlight an alternative model by providing a comparison of custodial grandparenting in the US and China. In the United States, grandparents who care for their grandchildren are generally typified as being either 'child savers' or 'mother savers'. 'Child savers' are those grandparents who step in when parents are incapacitated or unavailable to raise their children, often due to drug/ alcohol abuse, incarceration or death (Minkler and Roe, 1993). Initially driven by the crack-cocaine and AIDS epidemics of the 1980s, the number of 'skipped-generation' households increased substantially in the last decades of the 20th century (Bryson and Casper, 1999) and has remained common into the 21st century with approximately 2.5 million grandparents reporting primary responsibility for a grandchild in the US (Simmons and Dye, 2003). Grandparents in such households are disproportionately African American, of low socioeconomic status, and in relatively poor physical and mental health (Minkler and Fuller-Thomson, 1999; Musil and Ahmad, 2002), risk factors that were present in grandparents even before they took on the grandchild caregiver role (Minkler et al, 1997). Further, these grandparents are primarily single females (Minkler and Fuller-Thomson, 1999) with little outside support; thus, the phenomenon of grandparents raising grandchildren in the US is largely one experienced by grandmothers alone.

Grandparents who function as 'mother savers' differ from 'child savers' in that parents (usually a mother) are often still present, but call on grandparents (again, primarily grandmothers) to take over a substantial amount of childcare so the mother can work for pay outside the home or undertake educational courses (see Chapter Four). These grandparents often provide substantial financial contributions and housing to the two younger generations, in some cases acting as the sole source of income within a three-generation household (Mutchler and Baker, 2009). This type of grandparenting has expanded, driven primarily by the rise in single-parent families, increased divorce rates and the weakened ability of the working class to survive on average wages.

While 'child saver' or 'mother saver' types of grandparents are distinct, they share some common characteristics. First, in both types of grandparenting in the US, care is often triggered by an involuntary event or crisis in the parent generation and is more likely to be undertaken out of need than desire. In both cases, the grandparent often has no real choice but to intervene and little time to prepare for his/her new role. Second, grandparents of both types tend to be disadvantaged even before taking on the care of a grandchild, which further limits the social, health and financial resources they are able to draw on to handle the stressors of raising or looking after a grandchild. Finally, the flow of helping resources between generations is generally downward, as grandparents provide care for grandchildren with little or no direct reciprocity from the parent generation. Grandmothers also commonly act as 'mother savers' in southern Europe, but here the main societal driver is lack of available childcare provision (see Chapter Two).

Grandparents who raise their grandchildren in rural China can more appropriately be classified as 'family maximisers'. Rather than being a response to a crisis in the parent generation, this arrangement is often a component of a larger coordinated strategy to improve the family economy. All three generations benefit when the middle generation, enabled by the provision of childcare by grandparents, is able to take advantage of far-flung opportunities to enhance its earning power.

More so in rural China than in the United States, the formation of a 'skipped-generation' household is a decision conditioned on the ability of grandparents to adequately shelter and care for younger grandchildren. Thus, grandparents most capable of handling the stresses of raising a child full time are likely to self-select into a skipped-generation household. If grandparents are unable to properly care for grandchildren – due to functional, psychological, financial or other problems – potential migrants may choose to take their children with them despite the hardships involved, not migrate at the cost of having lower earning potential, or leave the children with an alternate set of grandparents who are more capable of handling the rigors of raising a small child. While the day-to-day care of these grandchildren traditionally falls to women as in the US, grandmothers in China generally have the advantage of being married (as divorce is relatively unheard of in rural China) with all the emotional and financial benefits this arrangement entails. Thus, Chinese grandparents in skipped-generation households are unlikely to be disadvantaged before entering the role – they are relatively advantaged, as they tend to be young, healthy and married.

In summary, we argue that rural Chinese grandparents in skipped-generation households fundamentally differ from their American counterparts in three ways: in their reasons for adopting the care role (strategy versus. crisis); in their physical, economic and psychological resources upon transitioning into the role; and in the level and type of support received from the middle generation while occupying the role. Consequently, we hypothesise that custodial grandparents in rural China will be relatively advantaged in their psychological wellbeing compared with their counterparts in the United States at the time they enter a skipped-generation household. Further, we hypothesise that the wellbeing of custodial grandparents in rural China will be better than that among non-custodial Chinese grandparents as evidenced by lower levels of depression. We propose that the higher levels of well-being of custodial versus non-custodial Chinese grandparents is explained primarily by *pre-transition resources* or the more abundant resources in their possession that originally selected them into the caregiver role (for example, better health), and *post-transition benefits* or the higher amount of money sent to these grandparents by their migrant children.

Methods and data

We address our questions using two data sources. Chinese grandparents are studied using the Longitudinal Study of Older Adults in Anhui Province, China, a multi-panel study of the older population living in rural villages surrounding Chaohu city (Silverstein et al, 2006). This region was chosen because of its high level of out-migration of working-age individuals and the resulting high concentration of older adults (Chaohui Statistical Bureau, 2001). A stratified multistage sampling frame was used to identify potential respondents age 60 and over, with an oversampling of those aged 75 and older. Out of 1,800 eligible respondents, 1,698 completed the initial survey in 2001, conducted by the Population Research Institute of Xi'an Jiaotong University in collaboration with the University of Southern California. Follow-up surveys were fielded in 2003, 2006 and 2009. This study is particularly useful for the current analysis as older respondents were asked to provide detailed information about each of their children and grandchild set(s). We use data from 1,139 grandparents who participated in at least two consecutive waves of the study.

American grandparents are studied using the Health and Retirement Survey, a nationally representative survey of the United States population aged 50 and older with over-samples of African Americans and Hispanics (Juster and Suzman, 1995). The operational sample consists of 8,468 community-dwelling respondents who reported having at least one grandchild and who responded in waves 2000 and 2002 of the study.

Measures

Depressive symptoms. In the rural Chinese sample, depressive symptoms were measured using nine questions reflecting positive affect, negative affect, feelings of marginalisation and somatic symptoms adapted from the Center for Epidemiologic Studies Depression Scale or CES-D (Radloff, 1977). Respondents were asked to indicate how often they felt the following in the previous week: happy, enjoyed life, pleasure, lonely, upset, useless, nothing to do, poor appetite, trouble sleeping. Responses were coded as: rarely or none of the time (0), some of the time (1) and most of the time (2). After scores of positively worded items were reverse coded, an additive scale was calculated ranging from 0 to 18, with a higher score indicating greater depression (α = .80). For the purpose of comparing depression levels with US grandparents, a second measure of depression was calculated as a dichotomous score with those scoring 10 or higher considered to be depressed.

Depressive symptoms of grandparents in the United States sample were measured by the shortened eight-item CES-D using a yes/no response format, a scale that has been found to be similar to the full CES-D in both internal consistency and factor structure (Turvey et al, 1999). Respondents were asked whether they felt the following for much of the time during the past week: depressed, everything was an effort, sleep was restless, happy, lonely, enjoyed life, sad, could not get going. After reversing the two positive items, an additive scale was created ranging from 0-8 (α = .78). Depression was designated by having four or more symptoms, a cut-off score found to be comparable to that using the full version of the CES-D (Wallace et al, 2000).

Household structure. We note that while only about 20% of grandparents in the Chinese study lived in a 'skipped-generation' household (SGHH) in 2001, nearly half the sample of grandparents lived in an SGHH at least once between 2001 and 2009. (Because measurements are taken at two-year intervals, it is likely that this figure underestimates the incidence of this type of living arrangement because short-term transitions would remain unobserved in our data.) Thus, SGHHs were commonly observed in our Chinese sample but were often short term or transitory. To achieve a more inclusive identification of SGHHs, we structured our data in person-period records in which each respondent has one record for each measurement period (Singer and Willet, 2003). This allows us to analyse the characteristics of grandparents both before entering an SGHH (pre-transition) and after leaving an SGHH (post-transition), and provides a more accurate identification of those respondents living in SGHHs. Each respondent may have up to three records in the analysis corresponding to the three possible periods during which a transition to or from an SGHH structure may have occurred: 2001/03, 2003/06 or 2006/09. T-1 in our analysis refers to the pre-transition wave in each interval (that is 2001, 2003 or 2006), while T-2 refers to the post-transition wave in each interval (that is 2003, 2006 or 2009).

The primary indicator of grandparent caregiving is household structure, specifically whether the respondent lived in an SGHH at Time-1 (T-1) and/or Time-2 (T-2). An SGHH is defined as a household containing a grandparent and grandchild, but no parent. Because co-resident grandchildren were defined as 16 years or younger, our assumption (borne out by inspection of a caregiving time–effort scale in the Chinese data) is that grandparents in SGHHs have custodial care responsibility for their grandchildren and are not in these living arrangements so that they can receive care from grandchildren.

Four types of respondents were identified in the analysis based on SGHH status between T-1 and T-2: those who *entered* an SGHH, those who *exited* an SGHH, and those who *stayed* in an SGHH, plus the reference category that consists of those who were *not* in an SGHH at either T-1 or T-2.

In order to contrast depressive symptoms of rural Chinese grandparents and US grandparents, we compare transitions over a single two-year period (2001–03 for Anhui and 2000–02 for the US), disaggregating grandparents by whether they entered, exited, stayed or never were in an SGHH over this interval.

Pre-transition resources. In the analysis of rural Chinese grandparents, pre-transition resources measured at T-1 include age in years, gender (0 = male; 1 = female), marital status (0 = widowed/divorced/separated; 1 = married), education (0 = no education; 1 = any formal education), total household income from earnings and pensions (logged) and functional health problems. Functional health problems were measured as the inability to perform 15 tasks in three areas of disability: personal activities of daily living (ability to bathe, put on and take off clothes, walk around the room, use the toilet, and eat a meal); instrumental activities of daily living (prepare meals, shop, take the bus or train, do housework, and manage money); and mobility and strength (ability to lift a 10-kilogram bag of rice, climb one flight of stairs, stoop, crouch or kneel, and walk 100 meters). Respondents were scored on their level of difficulty performing each task: no difficulty = 0, some difficulty = 1, cannot do it without help = 2. An additive scale was calculated ranging from 0–30 (α = .93).

Post-transition benefits. Each respondent reported on the amount of money received over the past year from each adult child at T-1 and T-2. Those who were unable or unwilling to provide an exact amount were asked to choose among eight ordered categories starting at 50 RMB (or approximately USD $7.20) – midpoints of these categories were imputed for these respondents. Change in economic support was measured as the difference in the total amount of money received from children between T-1 and T-2. The total amount of money received from children at T-1 was controlled to account for baseline differences in economic support. This variable was logged in the regression analysis to adjust for a strong positive skew in the distribution.

Control variables. We also included several control variables in our analyses including age and gender of grandparents, age of the grandparents' youngest grandchild, total number of grandchildren, dummy variables for the paired waves of data to capture any temporal effects between 2001-03, 2003-06 and 2006-09 (with 2006-09 as the reference category), and baseline (T-1) depressive symptoms.

Analytic strategy

To account for the existence of multiple transitions per respondent, we pooled all person intervals and used robust standard errors in our multivariate estimation (Singer and Willet, 2003). After selecting respondents who had at least one grandchild under the age of 16, the data structure yielded 2,638 person intervals contributed by 1,139 respondents. Table 3.1 reveals that one third of the person intervals studied involved grandparents living in an SGHH at one or both time points, about evenly divided among those who entered, exited and stayed in such a household over the two-year period.

Depression among Chinese and US custodial grandparents

We first compare depression prevalence between Chinese and American grandparents based on SGHH status. We direct our attention to differences in *the patterns of depression* across household transition types. Because the scales used to measure depression in each study lacked strict equivalence in terms of content and response categories, we warn against comparing absolute levels of depression between the two samples.

The percentage above the respective thresholds that mark moderate depression in the Chinese and US samples are shown for the four transition groups in Figure 3.1. Two aspects of this comparison are worth noting. First, the patterns of depression prevalence are different between the two samples. Where Chinese grandparents were *least* depressed before and after they entered an SGHH and *most* depressed when they had no experience of being a custodial grandparent, the reverse was true for American grandparents. Second, this cross-national difference was more exaggerated over time. There was a halving of

Table 3.1: Sample descriptives for grandparents in Anhui Province, China

	Skipped-generation household (across two-year time interval)			Non-skipped-generation household (referent)
	Entered	Exited	Stayed	
Age in years	69.0	69.9	68.1	71.5
Female (%)	49.6	51.4	41.7	51.2
Married (%)	63.7	66.6	73.7	58.6
Any formal education (%)	24.5	23.3	29.6	25.7
Income logged	4.1	4.6	5.3	3.9
Functional impairment	3.7	3.7	2.7	4.8
Age of youngest grandchild	5.2	5.9	5.3	7.3
Total number of grandchildren	7.4	7.9	7.2	7.7
Total %	10.5%	13.5%	14.1%	61.9%
n =	278	356	372	1,632

Notes: Respondents = 1,139; observations (two-year person intervals) = 2,638.

depression prevalence from T-1 to T-2 among Chinese grandparents entering an SGHH, but an increase in depression prevalence among similarly situated American grandparents over the same period. This comparison shows not only that Chinese grandparents entered the custodial role with better psychological health, but also that their psychological health improved over time in that role, which is in sharp contrast to the deterioration observed among their American counterparts. These results support our hypothesis that the process by which grandparents become custodial caregivers for grandchildren, as well as the caregiving experience itself, is dramatically different between the two societal contexts in terms of the relative advantages that this role confers.

Resources of grandparents in rural China

Next we turn to a more in-depth analysis of rural Chinese grandparents and the resources they bring to and derive from their custodial role. To illustrate differences in the resources of custodial and non-custodial grandparents, we compare Time-1 characteristics of grandparents across the four transition groups. As shown in Table 3.1, grandparents with any experience of living in an SGHH had greater health, social and financial resources at baseline compared with grandparents who had not lived in an SGHH. Skipped-generation grandparents were significantly younger and more likely to be married, and had greater household income and less functional impairment than their counterparts with no such experience. That these advantages were observed prior to the transition among those entering an SGHH suggests that the 'best qualified' grandparents were sorted into the custodial role based on the adequacy of their initial resources. Further, the resource differential was most exaggerated for grandparents who had 'stayed' in an SGHH role for at least two years, suggesting that remaining longer in the custodial role was associated with the greatest amount of resources.

Figure 3.1: Percentage of grandparents depressed in the United States (at Time-1, 2000 and Time-2, 2002) and Anhui Province, China (at Time-1, 2001 and Time-2, 2003) by household type

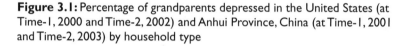
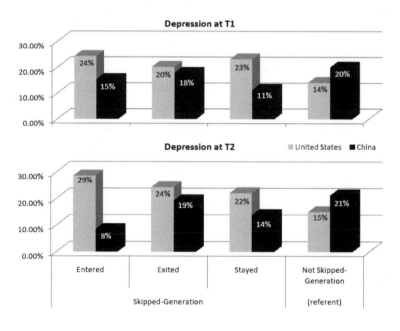

Mean levels of economic support from adult children are shown for the four transition groups in Table 3.2(a). Those grandparents who stayed in an SGHH over the two-year period received the greatest amounts of economic support from children at both Time-1 and Time-2. We suggest that grandparental custodial care for a longer duration provided time for migrant children to establish themselves in their new destinations and accumulate sufficient capital to send back to their natal villages. We also see that grandparents who entered an SGHH received the same amount from children at baseline as those with no experience in a SGHH. However, grandparents who transitioned into a SGHH received the greatest increase in remittances, nearly twice the increase received by non–SGHH grandparents.

Table 3.2: Changes among grandparents between Time-1 and Time-2 by household structure in Anhui Province, China

(a) Total financial support received from adult children (in RMB ¥ per year)

Household arrangement	Time-1	Time-2	Change
Skipped-generation			
Entered	¥1,249	¥1,974	¥723+
Exited	¥1,594	¥1,841	¥247+
Stayed	¥1,992	¥2,699	¥604+
Non-skipped-generation	¥1,175	¥1,537	¥362+

(b) Mean depressive symptoms[*]

Household arrangement	Time-1	Time-2	Change
Skipped-generation			
Entered	5.58	5.56	–.04
Exited	5.46	6.02	+.61
Stayed	4.91	5.30	+.41
Non-skipped-generation	6.25	6.61	+.36

Notes:[*] High values represent greater depressive symptoms.

Respondents = 1,158; observations (across two-year interval) = 2,638.

Depressive symptoms among grandparents in rural China

Average depressive symptoms are shown for the four transition groups in Table 3.2(b). All groups of grandparents with experience in an SGHH – particularly those living in such a household for a longer duration – reported fewer depressive symptoms at both measurement periods compared with their non–SGHH counterparts. That grandparents who transitioned into SGHHs showed a mental health advantage prior to beginning care for a grandchild is consistent with the positive selection hypothesis suggested by the distribution of resources in Table 3.1 and seen in our US–China comparative analysis in Figure 3.1. Interestingly, while the sample as a whole demonstrated a slight increase in depressive symptoms over time, grandparents who entered an SGHH showed no such increase, suggesting that wellbeing was enhanced by living in an SGHH, possibly related to the large increase in remittances among the same group shown in Table 3.2(a).

We next examined the multivariate relationship between the SGHH transition types and depressive symptoms by estimating a series of multiple regression models. Control variables representing personal resources and financial support are entered separately to better understand the selective role of pre-transition resources (namely that younger, healthier, married grandparents are predisposed to low levels of depression) and the mediating role of post-transition benefits (namely that an increase in remittances from children leads to enhanced wellbeing) in structuring depressive symptoms. The degree to which the effects of SGHH transition types on depressive symptoms are reduced with the introduction of control variables reveals how well these variables serve as explanations for the higher levels of wellbeing experienced by grandparents living in an SGHH compared with their non-SGHH counterparts. Because baseline T-1 depressive symptoms are controlled in all equations, the effects of predictor variables can be interpreted as producing relative change in depressive symptoms over the two-year intervals.

The first regression model in Table 3.3 shows that net of baseline depressive symptoms, grandparents who entered an SGHH and those who stayed in an SGHH reported significantly fewer depressive symptoms compared with those who never lived in an SGHH during the two-year period. Grandparents who exited an SGHH showed no significant difference. The pre-transition resources of grandparents were taken into account in Model 2. Grandparents who were younger and healthier, had greater education and were male all had fewer depressive symptoms. As a result of adding these variables, the beneficial effect of entering an SGHH on depressive symptoms declined in strength, but was still significant. However, the relationship between staying in an SGHH for two years and lower depressive symptoms was reduced to marginal significance.

In Model 3 we introduced control variables representing economic support from adult children. Findings revealed that grandparents who received higher initial amounts of financial support and greater increases in financial support between T-1 and T-2 tended to have fewer depressive symptoms over time. While the effect of entering an SGHH on depressive symptoms was reduced with these controls added, it remained significant. However, the association between staying in an SGHH and lower depressive symptoms was reduced to insignificance with the inclusion of these controls.

Table 3.3: OLS regression results predicting depressive symptoms in Anhui Province, China

Predictors	Model 1	Model 2	Model 3
Skipped-generation household			
Entered	−0.809 ***	−0.573 **	−0.456*
Exited	−0.282	−0.116	−0.050
Stayed	−0.806 ***	−0.379 †	−.196
Non-skipped-generation household (referent)			
Depressive symptoms T-1	0.358 ***	0.261 ***	0.241 ***
Age in years		0.076 ***	0.069 ***
Female (grandmother)		0.457 **	0.486 **
Any formal education		−0.317 †	−0.297 †
Married		0.076	0.140
Income (logged) T-1		−0.043 †	−0.066 **
Functional status T-1		0.100 ***	0.102 ***
Transition (2003-06)		0.611 ***	0.707 ***
Transition (2006-09)		0.011	0.215
Age of youngest grandchild		0.001	−0.013
Total number of grandchildren		0.006	0.032
Total financial support from children at T-1 (logged)			−0.355 ***
Change in financial support between T-1 and T-2 (logged)		-	−0.318 ***
Intercept	4.365 ***	−1.220	1.591

Notes: † $p < .10$; * $p < .05$; ** $p < .01$; *** $p < .001$.
Respondents = 1,158; observations (two-year time intervals) = 2,638.
The SURVEYREG procedure in SAS is used for analysis in order to account for the clustering of individuals within our sample due to the construction of person-period records.

To more clearly illustrate the magnitude by which the effects of SGHH type on grandparents' depressive symptoms changed with the addition of control variables, predicted levels of depressive symptoms for the four transition groups are shown in Table 3.4. Predicted values were calculated from the equations in Table 3.3 with control variables held constant at their respective means. When controlling only for baseline depression, the expected number of depressive symptoms for those who entered an SGHH and grandparents who stayed in an SGHH were identical and significantly lower than that for the reference group of grandparents who had no experience of living in SGHHs. However, net of pre-transition resources (Model 2) and post-transition economic support from children (Model 3), the predicted number of depressive symptoms for those who stayed in an SGHH climbed to be nearly as high as non-SGHH grandparents. These increases can be interpreted as the excess of depressive symptoms that would result were the transition groups equated on characteristics represented by the control variables, or in other words the expected number of depressive symptoms a grandparent would experience less the positive selective effects of pre-transition resources and post-transition economic support from adult children. While the expected number of depressive symptoms among grandparents who entered an SGHH increased as controls were added, these grandparents still experienced significantly fewer depressive symptoms in Model 3 than their non-SGHH counterparts.

Table 3.4: Predicted value of grandparents' number of depressive symptoms at Time-2 by household structure in Anhui Province, China

Household arrangement	Model I Baseline depression only	Model 2 Adds pre-transition resources	Model 3 Adds post-transition benefits
Skipped-generation			
Entered	5.66***	5.80**	5.87*
Exited	6.19***	6.26*	6.27
Stayed	5.66***	6.00†	6.13
Non-skipped-generation	6.47	6.37	6.32

Notes: † $p < .10$; * $p < .05$; ** $p < .01$; *** $p < .001$.
Respondents = 1,158; observations = 2,638.
Based on OLS regression estimates presented in Table 3.3; control variables set to sample mean.

Discussion and conclusion

In this chapter we have examined the psychological wellbeing of custodial grandparents in rural China as a function of their pre-care resources and post-transition financial support from adult children, and drawn contrasts with similarly situated grandparents in the United States. In doing so, we have shed light on the unique societal forces that govern how grandparents come to occupy the custodial role and are rewarded by it. Custodial grandparents in rural China and the United States are almost the inverse of each other in that the formation of these households in the US is reactionary and oriented towards a past event, while their formation in China is planned and oriented toward a future goal. In the United States, grandparents step in to raise their grandchildren usually under the most dire family circumstances, whereas the situation in China is quite different, with grandparent involvement representing a strategic allocation of effort intended to strengthen the economic position of the extended family.

Grandparents in rural China tend to experience relatively more favourable family circumstances and have greater access to resources on assuming the custodial grandparenting role when compared with their American counterparts, factors that appear to contribute to enhanced psychological wellbeing among Chinese grandparents in SGHHs. This finding highlights how family systems adapt to the societal demands imposed on them, with US grandparents more likely to intervene in reaction to a crisis in the middle generation such as neglect or abuse ('child savers'), and rural Chinese grandparents more likely to be involved in pursuit of a larger economic goal such as the increased economic productivity of a migrant son ('family maximisers'). The question of whether the contributions of grandparents in each nation are equally voluntary is difficult to answer, but it would seem that adverse selection into the role (as in the US) would give little choice to grandparents but to intervene, whereas positive selection into the role (as in China) would give grandparents more discretion about whether or not to become involved. Grandparents in China may choose to provide additional financial remittances to migrant children (to provide for childcare) in lieu of taking on that care themselves – a choice that is not an option for custodial grandmothers in the United States, one third of whom live in poverty (Kreider, 2008). Further, the consequences of not providing grandchild care are vastly different in the two countries – decreased economic productivity of an adult son in China versus placement within the foster care system (or with a neglectful or abusive parent) in the United States.

Our results suggest that the psychological benefit experienced by rural Chinese custodial grandparents is due largely, but not solely, to the resource advantages that select them into the role. To a more limited degree, their advantage accrues with financial transfers received from migrant adult children. In other research we showed that the psychological wellbeing of Chinese grandparents benefited in proportion to the amount of remittances received from migrant children, but benefited even more when those remittances were tied to custodial grandparenting (Cong and Silverstein, 2008). Thus, receiving remittances reduced depression most when it was part of a mutual system of exchange said to be characteristic of the multigenerational Chinese family (Cong and Silverstein, 2008).

Why do rural Chinese grandparents who recently transitioned into the custodial childcare role still exhibit less depression when resources and remittances are controlled? It is possible that cultural factors not considered in our study are responsible for this residual benefit? As traditional roles for older adults have eroded in a modernising China, caregiving for grandchildren may fill a gap by allowing grandparents to remain integral parts of their extended families and provide them with the filial authority they may have lost. Grandparents in China are traditionally accorded high status and their role within the family is unambiguous (Mjelde-Mossey, 2007). When children migrate, this role is disrupted and may contribute to decreased wellbeing. Grandparents who live in SGHHs in China may benefit from this continued integration with extended family.

Further, grandparents in rural China who engage in the culturally important activity of childcare may also derive great satisfaction from enacting such a valued family role (Raschick and Ingersoll-Dayton, 2004). Although providing intensive care is often demanding and stressful, it has also been found in the US and Europe to produce uplifts in mood due to the intrinsic reward of helping a loved one (Pinquart and Sörensen, 2003). The very activities involved in custodial grandchild care may produce practical benefits as well. The demands of managing a household with young children in 'second-time-around parenting' may impose cognitive and physical challenges that grandparents rise to meet. Roberto and Jarrott (2008) use the term 'caregiver growth' to refer to improvements in problem-solving abilities, increased self-understanding and a growing sense of competence that can derive for grandparents from the caregiving experience.

Finally, unlike their counterparts in the United States, grandparents in rural China who live in SGHHs are not disproportionately single females. Rather, the majority are married and include a large proportion of grandfathers. This gender difference may explain some of the cross-nation differential in depression, as prior research in the United States shows that grandmother caregivers tend to be more depressed than grandfather caregivers (Kolomer and McCallion, 2005). In fact, grandmothers tend to experience an increase in depressive symptoms when a grandchild moves *into* the household in the US while grandfathers tend to experience an increase when a grandchild moves *out* of the household (Szinovacz et al, 1999), probably because grandmothers are the grandparent typically responsible for the hands-on care of the grandchild.

We conclude that custodial grandparenting is an activity shaped by the familial circumstances surrounding care that are themselves shaped by social and economic forces at the societal level. In rural China, grandparents are highly adaptive as 'family-maximisers', acting strategically for the benefit of all generations within the context of an expanding economy that increasingly needs and rewards migrant labourers. In both the US and China, grandmothers are the primary caregivers for children in custodial households; however, most grandmothers in China have the advantage of being married – a status that confers many benefits including greater social and economic support. This status, combined with previously mentioned circumstances surrounding care, allows grandmothers in China to work as part of a larger family system, rather than in isolation (as is so often the case for custodial grandmothers in the US). Without rural Chinese grandmothers being full-time carers for their grandchildren, labour migration certainly would be more difficult and perhaps impossible for many parents of young children in search of better employment opportunities, leading us to the conclusion that grandparents are indeed the 'unsung heroes' of China's rapid economic expansion.

Acknowledgements

We acknowledge funding for this research from the University of Southern California (USC) US-China Institute, the USC School of Social Work, Xi'an Jiaotong University, and the National Institutes of Health Fogarty International Center. We are particularly indebted to Dr Li Shuzhou for his extraordinary efforts in coordinating the data collection in Anhui Province, China.

References

Biao, X. (2007) 'How far are the left-behind left behind? A preliminary study in rural China', *Population, Space and Place*, vol 13, no 3, pp 179-91.

Bryson, K. and Casper, L.M. (1999) *Co-resident grandparents and grandchildren*, Washington, DC: US Census Bureau.

Chaohui Statistical Bureau (2001) *Chaohu Statistical Annals*, Chaohu, China: Chaohui Statistical Bureau.

Cong, Z. and Silverstein, M. (2008) 'Intergenerational time-for-money exchanges in rural China: does reciprocity reduce depressive symptoms of older grandparents?', *Research in Human Development*, vol 5, no 1, pp 6-25.

Cong, Z. and Silverstein, M. (2011) 'Intergenerational exchange between parents and migrant and nonmigrant sons in rural China', *Journal of Marriage and Family*, vol 73, no 1, pp 93-104.

Fan, C.C. (2008) *China on the move: Migration, the state, and the household*, London and New York, NY: Routledge.

Gordon, R.A, Chase-Lansdale, P.L. and Brooks-Gunn, J. (2004) 'Extended households and the life course of young mothers: understanding the associations using a sample of mothers with premature, low birth weight babies', *Child Development*, vol 75, no 4, pp 1013-38.

Juster, F. and Suzman, R. (1995) 'An overview of the Health and Retirement Study', *The Journal of Human Resources*, vol 30, Special Issue, pp S7-S56.

Kolomer, S.R. and McCallion, P. (2005) 'Depression and caregiver mastery in grandfathers caring for their grandchildren', *International Journal of Aging and Human Development*, vol 60, no 4, pp 283-94.

Kreider, R.M. (2008) *Living arrangements of children: 2004*, Publication No. P70-114, Washington, DC: US Census Bureau.

Lee, M.H. (2011) 'Migration and children's welfare in China: the schooling and health of children left behind', *The Journal of Developing Areas*, vol 44, no 2, pp 165-82.

Minkler, M. and Fuller-Thomson, E. (1999) 'The health of grandparents raising grandchildren: results of a national study', *American Journal of Public Health*, vol 89, no 9, pp 1384-9.

Minkler, M. and Roe, K.M. (1993) *Grandmothers as caregivers: Raising children of the crack cocaine epidemic*, Newbury Park, CA: Sage Publications.

Minkler, M., Fuller-Thomson, E., Miller, D. and Driver, D. (1997) 'Depression in grandparents raising grandchildren: results of a national longitudinal study', *Archives of Family Medicine*, vol 6, no 5, pp 445-52.

Mjelde-Mossey, L.A. (2007) 'Cultural and demographic changes and their effects upon the traditional grandparent role for Chinese elders', *Journal of Human Behavior in the Social Environment*, vol 16, no 3, pp 107-20.

Musil, C. and Ahmad, M. (2002) 'Health of grandmothers: a comparison by caregiver status', *Journal of Aging and Health*, vol 14, no 1, pp 96-121.

Mutchler, J.E. and Baker, L.A. (2009) 'The implications of grandparent coresidence for economic hardship among children in mother-only families', *Journal of Family Issues*, vol 30, no 11, pp 1576-97.

Pinquart, P. and Sörensen, S. (2003) 'Associations of stressors and uplifts with caregiver burden and depressive mood: a meta-analysis', *Journals of Gerontology: Psychological Sciences*, vol 58B, no 2, pp P112-P128.

Radloff, L. (1977) 'The CES-D scale: a self-report depression scale for research in the general population', *Applied Psychological Measurement*, vol 1, no 3, pp 385-401.

Raschick, M. and Ingersoll-Dayton, B. (2004) 'The costs and rewards of caregiving among aging spouses and adult children', *Family Relations*, vol 53, no 3, pp 317-25.

Roberto, K.A. and Jarrott, S.E. (2008) 'Family caregivers of older adults: a life span perspective', *Family Relations*, vol 57, no 1, pp 100-11.

Silverstein, M., Cong, Z. and Li, S. (2006) 'Intergenerational transfers and living arrangements of older people in rural China: consequences for psychological wellbeing', *Journal of Gerontology: Social Sciences*, vol 61B, no 5, pp S256-S266.

Simmons, T. and Dye, J.L. (2003) *Grandparents living with grandchildren: 2000*, Washington, DC: US Census Bureau.

Singer, J.D. and Willet, J.B. (2003) *Applied longitudinal data analysis: Modeling change and event occurrence*, New York, NY: Oxford University Press.

Stack, M.K. (2010) 'China raising a generation of left-behind children', *Los Angeles Times*, 29 September, www.latimes.com.

Sun, R. (2002) 'Old age support in contemporary urban China from both parents' and children's perspectives', *Research on Aging*, vol 24, no 3, pp 337-59.

Sung, K.T. (1998) 'Exploration of actions of filial piety', *Journal of Aging Studies*, vol 12, no 4, pp 369-86.

Szinovacz, M.E., DeViney, S. and Atkinson, M.P. (1999) 'Effects of surrogate parenting on grandparents' wellbeing', *Journal of Gerontology: Social Sciences*, vol 54B, no 6, pp S376-S388.

Turvey, C.L., Wallace, R.B. and Herzog, R. (1999) 'A revised CES-D measure of depressive symptoms and a DSM-based measure of major depressive episodes in the elderly', *International Psychogeriatric Association*, vol 11, no 2, pp 139-48.

Wallace, R.B., Herzog, A.R., Ofstedal, M.B., Steffick, D., Fonda, S. and Langa, K. (2000) *Documentation of affective functioning measures in the Health and Retirement Study*, Report No DR-005, http://hrsonline.isr.umich.edu/sitedocs/userg/dr-005.pdf.

Yi, Z. and Wang, Z. (2003) 'Living arrangements in China: new lessons learned from the 2000 census', *The China Review*, vol 3, no 2, pp 95-119.

FOUR

Grandmothers juggling work and grandchildren in the United States

Madonna Harrington Meyer

Introduction

We tend to think of balancing work and family as something that only relatively young families contend with, yet many middle-aged grandmothers are employed and providing routine childcare for their grandchildren. Grandmothers are highly prized daycare providers because the quality is often high, the cost is often very low, and the flexibility is often maximal (Wheelock and Jones, 2002). Indeed, many young working families report that they feel that the best possible care providers for their children would be the grandmothers. Grandmothers may agree, but as the age at retirement increases with economic necessity, many grandmothers are feeling more of a pinch between paid and unpaid work (Simon-Rusinowitz et al, 1996; Wheelock and Jones, 2002; Turner, 2005; Park, 2006).

The US literature suggests that while grandfathers provide some care for grandchildren, grandmothers are a more central component of the childcare system. As many as 43% of grandmothers care for grandchildren regularly, and 20% of children with working mothers are regularly cared for by their grandmothers (Baydar and Brooks-Gunn, 1998). But these studies do not clarify whether the grandmothers are also employed and therefore juggling paid and unpaid work. There is an enormous literature on balancing work and family in the younger stages of the life course, but the literature on the impact of balancing work and family among grandparents is thin and its findings are mixed.

Caring for grandchildren while employed may affect economic security, physical and emotional health, social relationships, and the capacity to care for other family members. But the direction of the impact on grandmothers appears to be quite mixed: some fare well while others struggle (Platt Jendrek, 1994; Moen et al, 1995; Nelson,

2000; Turner, 2005). The impact may vary by race, class and marital status (Pruchno, 1999; Kataoka-Yahiro et al, 2004; Park, 2006). Caring for grandchildren may have many positive effects on grandmothers, including better physical and mental health, feelings of being needed and useful, and a very active and involved social life (Presser, 1989; Nelson, 2000; Turner, 2005). But it may have negative effects when grandmothers reduce employment hours, worry about financial implications, provide care for younger and older generations, and feel more stress and burden (Presser, 1989; Platt Jendrek, 1993; Landry-Meyer and Newman, 2004; Musil et al, 2006; Ludwig and Winston, 2007; Wang and Marcotte, 2007).

Theories of care work are becoming increasingly diverse but most do not take the life course sufficiently into account. England (2005) demonstrates that most scholarship focuses on the impact of care work on pay, neglecting the impact on other aspects of life. It also focuses on earlier and later life stages, neglecting much of middle age. Few care-work scholars fully represent the sort of everyday juggling between paid and unpaid work that women undertake not just in their younger years but across the life course (Baca and Dill, 2005; England, 2005; Lorber, 2005). An emphasis on the life course highlights the cumulative effects of various choices, opportunities, policies and programmes at different stages of life (Settersten, 2003; Moen and Spencer, 2006). For example, when women take time out from work to raise children an immediate consequence is loss of salary, but long-term consequences include reduced access to, or lower pay from, public pensions, private pensions and savings. When grandmothers reduce hours at work to care for grandchildren, they may also face reduced income, savings and pension income. The advantages and disadvantages of various life-course trajectories are not randomly distributed; they are linked to gender, race, class and marital status (Dannefer, 2003; Settersten, 2003; Baca and Dill, 2005; Lorber, 2005; Acker, 2006). While some midlife women sail through the competing demands of employment and grandparenting, others struggle as the demands outpace resources.

This chapter explores the strategies of, and impacts on, grandmothers who are juggling work and grandchildren in the United States. A life-course approach is used to explore how grandmothers juggle work and grandchildren, and how that juggling shapes their daily life, economic security, relationships and capacity to care for other family members. The chapter begins with a review of the supports available through the welfare state and employers in the US for working families in need of childcare and a discussion of the demographic shifts that may be increasing reliance on grandmothers. It then turns to data from the author's Grandmas at Work study, a convenience sample of 40 in-depth interviews with non-custodial grandmothers who balance working and minding their grandchildren in the US. It explores how grandmothers feel about minding the grandchildren and the extent to which they are readjusting work schedules, using vacation and sick leave time, emptying retirement accounts and postponing retirement. It then looks at the extent to which grandmothers care sequentially for one grandchild after the other, how intense the care work is, whether they set limits on their childcare contributions, and whether they are providing financial assistance as well. Finally the chapter explores the extent to which grandmothers are also caring for their frail older parents and the impact of these multiple care-worker roles on their retirement plans.

Decrease in support from the US welfare state and employers

Compared with most European nations, the US provides little welfare support for families as they grow. There is no federal guarantee for covering paid vacation, flexible work schedules, paid sick leave, paid maternity leave or affordable daycare. Many workers have some benefits through their employers, but these benefits are more readily available to full-time workers with higher salaries and lengthier tenure on the job and such coverage has been shrinking in recent years (IWPR, 2007; Lerner, 2010).

Paid time off is unequally distributed in the US. In contrast with 127 other countries worldwide, the US has no guaranteed vacation policy and the net effect is that one third of female workers and a quarter of male workers have no paid vacation (Lerner, 2010). Similarly, unlike many other countries, the US does not guarantee flexible work schedules and, as a result, few women are able to negotiate such arrangements. Even the best-educated and highest-paid women in the US are often unable to negotiate a flexible schedule when they have children (Stone, 2007). Lower income families are hardest hit. Only 16% of families in the bottom earnings quartile received more than two weeks of paid vacation and sick leave, compared with 59% of earners in the top earnings quartile (Heymann, 2000). Moreover, 71% of those in the bottom quartile do not receive paid leave time to care for sick children, compared with 34% in the top quartile. In 2010, 44 million US workers did not have paid sick days (Williams et al, 2010).

The lack of paid maternity leave may be what hits US families hardest. Although 98 of the 177 countries that Heymann (2000) analysed offered more than 14 weeks' maternity leave with pay, the US Family and Medical Leave Act offers only 12 weeks of unpaid leave. However, less than one half of US workers are able to make use of it either because their employer is exempted for being too small, they have not worked at that firm for a full year, or they cannot afford time off without pay. Only 39% of workers earning less than $20,000 a year are covered by this law, compared with 74% of those earning over $100,000 (Lerner, 2010). Although some women are offered paid maternity leave by their employers, this dropped from 27% of working women in 1998 to only 16% in 2008 (IWPR, 2007).

The US government provides some subsidies for daycare for poor families, but only about 15% of those entitled actually receive assistance (Mezey et al, 2002; Lerner, 2010). Waiting lists for subsidised daycare and pre-schools are often so long that some children would be high school-aged by the time they would be admitted. High-quality daycare through the private market is so expensive that increasingly families are being encouraged to pay for it through bank loans (Lerner, 2010). Although many experts have called for universal, full-day pre-school for all children aged four and older, demonstrating that it reduces reliance on welfare, teen pregnancy and criminal behaviour, only tentative progress has been made on this front (Harrington Meyer and Herd, 2007; Lerner, 2010).

The paucity of paid vacation, flexible work schedules, paid sick leave, paid maternity leave and affordable day care – either through the US welfare state or through employer benefit programmes – leaves many women turning to grandmothers, and sometimes grandfathers, for assistance with childcare. While grandmothers are not particularly likely to have many of these benefits either, grandmothers have often been in their jobs longer and may be better able than their daughters to negotiate work and family responsibilities without risk of losing their jobs.

Increase in the need for 'granny care'

Despite the paucity of welfare and employer supports, women in the US have relatively high levels of employment, particularly full-time employment, and fertility (Lerner, 2010). Many turn to grandmothers to help them juggle these competing responsibilities. Several socio-demographic trends contribute to reliance on grandmothers. Like many countries, the US has experienced a retreat from marriage and a dramatic increase in single-parent families. The US Census Bureau (2008a) reports that the percentage share of women who are married dropped from 66% in 1960 to 53% in 2008. This drop has been more pronounced among black women. In 2008, 55% of adult white compared with just 34% of black women were married.

In contrast to the many countries with falling fertility rates, in the US the fertility rate has hovered near replacement level, 2.1 births per woman, for decades (Lerner, 2010). Increasingly these births are to single women. The US Census Bureau (2008b) reports that in 2005, 39% of all births in the United States were to unmarried women. Half of these unmarried mothers may have been cohabitating, but non-marital relationships tend to be more fragile than marriages in the US (Lerner, 2010). Asians had the lowest proportion of births to single mothers, 17%, compared with whites with 28%, Latinos with 51%, and blacks with 72% of births to single mothers (US Census Bureau, 2008b). The rise in single parenting is particularly important because for many of these women, there is no partner to help them share the responsibility for juggling work and family.

Finally, US women are more likely than women in most other industrialised countries to work, and to work full time (Lerner, 2010). The US Bureau of Labor Statistics (2010) reports that among those age 16 and older, women's overall labour force participation has risen from 40% in 1975 to nearly 60% in 2009. Women with children aged 6-17 are the most likely to work, with the percentage employed rising from 55% in 1975 to 78% in 2009. But the percentage of working women with children under age three also rose, from 34% to 61% between 1975 and 2009. Relatively high fertility rates, coupled with rising rates of single motherhood and working mothers, have increased the demand for childcare, often in the form of 'grandma care'.

Grandmothers may well be the most desirable source of childcare, but increasingly women in that age group are themselves employed. Women become first-time grandmothers, on average in the US, between the ages of 48 and 52 (AARP, 2002). The US Bureau of Labor Statistics (2005) reports that in 2003, 75% of women in their early 50s and 65% of women in their late 50s are employed, suggesting that a fairly high proportion of grandmothers may be juggling work and grandchildren.

Data and methodology

The data for this chapter are drawn from the author's Grandmas at Work study in the US, which comprised in-depth interviews with 40 grandmothers who are currently employed and who often care for their grandchildren. Because there is no list or organisation of grandmothers who work and care for grandchildren from which to draw a representative sample, the sample is a non-random convenience snowball sample. The sample is diverse along race, class, marital status and geographic lines. While many of the grandmothers are white, some are African American or Native American. The women in the study range from women with PhDs who are professors to women who did not complete high school and now clean houses for a living.

The in-depth interviews provide rich descriptive data on the everyday experiences of those who are balancing work and family across the life course. To maintain confidentiality, names and areas of residence were changed. As the data were collected, the interviews were transcribed verbatim and the data then coded according to themes drawn from the review of the literature as well as along themes that emerged during the interviews. The analysis uses a life-course approach to explore how grandmothers balance work and grandchildren and how that juggling shapes their daily life, economic security, relationships and capacity to care for older relatives. While the analysis is based on the 40 interviews, this chapter highlights three women's stories, selected to illuminate important similarities and differences among working grandmothers.

Grandmothers juggling paid work and care work

All of the grandmothers in the Grandmas at Work study are happy to spend time with their grandchildren, help raise them and provide high-quality care for them. They sparkle when they talk about their grandkids. Grandchildren are a source of great joy. They love them. And they love just how much the grandkids love them. But they are also grateful when their day's duties come to a close.

Deanne loves taking care of her grandchildren but she also loves to say goodbye. Deanne is a 57-year-old, white, married, well-educated, middle-class woman with two daughters and six grandchildren. She works full time as an elected official in a small mid-western town. Like her mother before her, she also helps care for the grandchildren. But while her mother provided only occasional assistance, Deanne takes care of her three grandsons three or four days a week after work and often at weekends, in addition to caring for her mother in a nursing home three to four times a week:

> 'I love being able to help with the kids, it is so fun.... When you have your own kids you are busy with all the other things you have to do, but with your grandkids you can just sit, if the dishes get done the next day, who cares. I can take

that walk…. Being a grandma is the best job in the world:
love them, spoil them, and say goodbye.'

In addition to being happy to spend time with their grandkids, nearly all of the respondents talk about a sense of responsibility over the life course. They want to help their children and they want to help their grandchildren. They feel they will do a better job than anyone else, and they will be flexible about looking after sick kids or doing night shifts. Every one of the survey respondents provides childcare for free. In addition to feeling a great deal of joy, many see it as their responsibility.

Betty is a 59-year-old widowed black woman who lives in a city in the north-east. She completed high school and is a licensed practical nurse. When Betty's children were young she did not have help from her mother; instead she was on welfare and stayed home with her children. But she fondly remembers how much her grandmother cared for her when she was young and she is purposely providing similar care for her own grandchildren. She retired from her career job several years ago, and now is paid by the hour to work as much as 60 hours a week as a nurse at a health facility. Although she no longer receives employer benefits of healthcare, private pension, paid sick leave or paid vacation benefits, she made the switch to hourly work so that she would be able to control her paid work schedule and provide care to the grandchildren. She would like to work fewer hours, but the health facility is understaffed and she is constantly being called to work more shifts.

Betty is one of many interviewed who are sequential grandmother carers. She has four children and 14 grandchildren and has taken care of each of her children's children at various times. Currently, Betty mainly cares for her younger daughter's four children, who live nearby, while their mother works the 7 am to 7 pm, or the 3 pm to 11 pm, shift at the hospital. Although she is providing many more hours of grandchild care than she ever expected to, Betty sees this work as her responsibility. She feels it is best if she, rather than anyone else, cares for the grandchildren when they conclude their school day:

'I did not imagine I would be doing all of this. I imagined my kids would get grown and take care of their own families…. I see so many kids out, and they do not have anybody watching over them and that just bothers me. They just do not have anybody. I do not want my grandkids treated like that. I was not … I would not hire anyone to care for the kids, better if I do it myself. You have to be careful about who you leave your kids with.'

Many of the grandmothers are providing intensive grandparenting. Deanne has been working and caring for grandchildren for 10 years. Currently she is caring for her newly divorced daughter's three sons, who live just a few minutes away. In the months leading up to the interview, Deanne's daughter was working full time and attending night classes to earn a Bachelor of Arts degree. Deanne said that she and her daughter both agreed that it was best for the daughter's long-term earnings to complete her degree now. Nonetheless, that agreement means that Deanne provides many more hours of care to her grandchildren than she, or her husband, ever expected:

> 'When my daughter was in school … I left work early and picked them up from school, sometimes the boys walked here and waited in the office for me to finish…. I give them 55 cents for the candy machine, they have their treats, play on my computer, and then we head to their house, or maybe to my house to change and get toys. I would take them home and fix supper, play time, bath time, and to bed. I would be there until 9 or 11 pm … I would work 8 to 4, then take the boys from 4 to 11. I would doze on the couch waiting for my daughter to get home from her class.'

Like many of the grandmothers, Deanne feels she is constantly on call to provide even more assistance for the grandchildren. Her work day is peppered with calls and requests that she do more. She often comes to work late, leaves work early or misses the entire day to take care of the grandchildren:

> 'I have lots of phone calls at work, daily, several a day, from my daughters. "Can you pick this one up, run this over there?" – almost every day.'

Betty has also provided sequential, and intensive, grandchild care at her own home for years:

> 'Mostly I take care of the grandkids here. They come here after school and then when their Mom comes home they go home for bed at seven. If she works till 11, they will lay on the floor on a blanket at my house, and then she takes them home for bed. I feed them dinner most of the time, I cooked some beans yesterday and that is what they will have today with rice. I eat with them – we eat in the kitchen

or the living room. It is hard to find time to buy groceries sometimes.... Now that I think about it, I am working nine days in a row. And I will take care of the kids probably four of those days when I get home from work.

Betty is one of many grandmothers interviewed who has mixed feelings about juggling work and grandchildren. On the one hand, time with the grandchildren is meaningful and keeps her physically active. On the other hand, she balances so many responsibilities that she never really has time for herself. She is tired, and years away from either retiring or having independent grandchildren:

> 'Taking care of the grandkids is good for me – keeps me moving, keeps me going, when you sit and do nothing that is not good. But it gets tiring sometimes. For the most part I am used to it. This week I have been tired, I do not know why.... Only time I feel stress is when other people are begging for my time – the job, the church, my mother, my other kids. I am only one person, I can't do it all. I feel tired ... I really never have a day off.'

Estelle has a professional job that allows her to come and go largely at will, but also requires her to meet many strict deadlines. In contrast to both Deanne and Betty, Estelle rarely misses work to care for any of her grandchildren. She is a 63-year-old, well-educated white woman, who works full time. She divorced her abusive husband 30 years ago and has not remarried. She has three children and six grandchildren. Until recently, Estelle was neither a sequential nor intensive grandchild carer. Just as her own mother did not help her much when her children were young, she did not provide much care for any of her earlier grandchildren. But that changed when her youngest daughter, unmarried, had a son and they both came to live with her. Estelle works more than 40 hours a week, heads to the gym, and then goes home to make dinner and take care of her grandson. She feeds him, plays with him and puts him to bed most nights. Her daughter, who sometimes has a job and sometimes does not, either takes care of the boy all day or takes him to daycare. Then Estelle takes over in the evenings and at weekends to give her daughter a break and to spend some time with her grandson:

> 'I go exercise after work, then pick him up at the babysitter, then take him home, feed him, play with him, put him to

bed. That would get difficult at times … but I was able to stay on top of my dishes and laundry while he was playing. You just remember those lessons you had when the kids were little, you learn how to juggle all those things. He was better than having a dog, as far as my diet, I was so enthralled with him, I would just forget to eat. It was like going back to having my own babies … I am so attached to him, having him at home, I am much closer to him than I was with the other grandkids.'

Unlike Estelle, many of the grandmothers rearrange their work schedules frequently to accommodate grandchild care. Deanne changes her work schedule almost daily to care for her grandchildren. She comes in late, leaves early, takes days off, and minds the grandchildren in her office. Her divorced daughter was recently laid off, but now that she has a new job, she cannot risk missing work for the children. She has not yet built up any sick leave or vacation time, so Deanne has ramped up the amount of care she provides. Deanne says that while her daughter cannot risk missing work, she has been at her job for years and feels secure enough that she can rearrange work to accommodate the grandchildren:

'I nearly missed our interview today because I had to babysit…. My granddaughter is one, [my daughter] has a private sitter but her son was in the hospital. My daughter started a new job last spring and does not have much time built up for family time, so grandma is here…. My daughter just cannot risk missing work … I sometimes have to tell my daughter … I am too busy at work. And sometimes I will take care of them and come back to work after, if the work really has to get done.'

Like Deanne, Betty frequently rearranges her work schedule to care for her grandchildren. Betty's daughter is relatively new to her job and cannot risk missing work, while Betty has been with her company for decades and feels she can rearrange her schedule when need be. She often gets calls while at work from her children, asking her to pick up a sick grandchild. She sometimes leaves work early or brings a grandchild to work for the shift. Betty says the people at work know she has these responsibilities and they accommodate her needs to be with the grandchildren. In fact, she said that many of the nurses have similar responsibilities and they all 'pitch in' for each other to make sure the grandchildren are cared for:

> 'If I have to go from work, I just have to go. One day they were short and I had to go get my grandson [who has Down's syndrome] off the bus and then I went back to work. Sometimes I take him to work with me. We have a room that we eat in, he sits there and he likes to draw. He gets to see people – people cater to him and he likes that. If I was full time it would be bad, but because I am per diem, it is not bad. I can get off work when the kids need me. I don't have to leave that often but when I do they accept it. They have no problem with it. No, they have kids and they have to leave sometime too – I cover for them and they cover for me.'

These three women's descriptions of how they juggle paid work and grandchild care demonstrate the contrasts and similarities among the women in the sample. All are joyous about spending time with their grandchildren and happy to be providing much-needed, high-quality care. Many have provided sequential care to numerous grandchildren over the years. And many provide intensive care, multiple hours of playing, helping with homework, feeding, bathing and putting to bed. Most continually readjust their paid work schedules to accommodate care work by either coming in late, leaving early, taking days off, fielding phone calls, running errands or bringing children to the office. Unlike their daughters, few of the grandmothers are worried that caring for their grandchildren might cost them their jobs. But balancing work and grandchild care is a struggle and many of the grandmothers face long days with multiple responsibilities, lower wages or fewer benefits, and insufficient sleep. A life-course perspective reveals that for some women this labour of love is a replication of the care their grandmothers provided to them, or of the assistance their own mothers provided to them when their children were young, but for others it represents an attempt to break the existing pattern by providing a level of support for their daughters that they did not enjoy when their own children were young.

Using paid work to set boundaries

Estelle is one of the few grandmothers who feel the need to set limits. She has been careful to define what she is willing, and unwilling, to do. She rarely readjusts her work schedule and frequently tells her children "no":

> 'I said it from the beginning, and they were not young
> moms. It was always known, I am not a babysitter, do not
> come to me ... I did not want 24/7 care of the kids ... I told
> them right away that I was not their babysitter. I tell them
> I do not like kids, and I certainly do not like misbehaved
> kids. I struggle with what a grandmother's role is.'

Deanne also uses her job to set boundaries on her availability. Deanne
likes having employment in part because she loves her job and her
colleagues, and in part because the job helps to set some boundaries.
Deanne expressed concern that if she was not working she would be
asked to take care of the grandchildren even more:

> 'I could not do full-time grandkids, I need the job, the adult
> connections. I would not want to do the childcare full time,
> much as I love them. It is fun to have them come but fun
> to see them go.'

Grandmothering in the US is driven both by a joyful desire to be
with the grandchildren and a sense of responsibility to assist with the
unmet needs of the younger generation. In a society where there are
few supports for families with working parents, it often takes multiple
generations to provide sufficient care for the grandchildren. Many of
the grandmothers provide almost limitless time and resources to the
grandchildren. Others set limits, attempting to restrict just how much
care they will provide (see the discussion on boundary drawing in
Chapter Eight). But as this next section reveals, many are not limiting
their financial contributions sufficiently to protect their own old-age
'nest egg'. Some have responded to short-term economic family crises
in ways that put their own economic security across the life course
in jeopardy.

Using work to finance grandchild care

The amount of financial help that some grandmothers are providing
is astonishing. Deanne and her husband had nearly paid off their own
home in preparation for their retirement. But when their daughter
divorced, and nearly lost her home, they bought her house. Deanne's
daughter is unable to help make the monthly payments because she is
trying to complete her college degree. Moreover, Deanne's husband,
a self-employed construction worker, is disabled, and as the economy
is particularly bad in the building sector, he rarely works. In addition,

Deanne and her husband took out a second mortgage on their own home to further assist their daughter during the divorce. So Deanne is paying three mortgages: the first and second mortgage on her own home, as well as her daughter's mortgage. She is optimistic that her daughter will eventually pay back this money and that she and her husband will be financially secure when they retire. But her husband is much less certain. Deanne says he feels 'used and abused' and very worried about their finances:

> 'When my daughter divorced, they nearly lost the house to foreclosure, so I went on the loan and signed for them. But then they again nearly foreclosed, so my husband and I bought it.... And my husband has such poor health that he has had to reduce his work. The construction business has taken a downslide in the last few years, there is almost no new construction; he is mainly just a handyman now. So now I have to make the payment on my own house and most of the payment on my daughter's house, and that is hard, a bit tight. I hope she will be able to pay her share again soon. I think we will be alright when I retire, our house will be almost paid for. But we had to get a second mortgage to help our daughter with some things. I am hoping to get that money back from our daughter, to quell my husband's sense that the kids are all just taking and no one is ever giving back. He sometimes feels used and abused. He is more worried about the money than I am, he thinks he will not get this money back. But I am the optimist, I like knowing that we helped her and that our grandsons had a nice roof over their heads.'

At a time when they are supposed to be accumulating a 'nest egg', Deanne and her husband are accumulating debt. She had hoped to work for just one more four-year term in office before retiring but they will not have paid off their own, or their daughter's, mortgage by then. Because so much of Deanne's pay goes toward the mortgages, they are not saving for their retirement at this time.

Estelle has given financially until it hurts. She is now deeply in debt. Over the years, Estelle has provided a great deal of financial support to her three children and six grandchildren, but much of the money has been given to the youngest daughter and her seven-month-old son, who live in Estelle's home. Estelle's daughter does not have a job right now and is not paying for her own or her son's expenses:

'She is putting me in the poor house. I have always put a lot of money into my daughters and their kids, I will pay a phone bill or bring gifts or buy school supplies. I have always been in debt because I have chosen to support my kids and grandkids financially. But this last year with my daughter living with me has sunk me, I am now in serious financial problems … I have taken [out] most of my retirement account over the years, so it is nearly empty. I have a total of eight existing loans against my retirement account. My entire end of the month pay check pays that loan back. I have closed my credit card accounts because they were maxed out. I know where the money went – I know I was not gambling, I have been caring for my kids, and grandkids, but I still have shame, I make a decent salary, but I have used it all. I have shame over this debt.'

Estelle says she will never be able to retire. She has nothing saved for her retirement and has accumulated an enormous amount of debt. She says she will have to 'die at her desk'.

By contrast, Betty never gives her daughter money. Betty receives a private pension as well as income from her current job, generating an annual income of just under $40,000. She lives in a well-maintained home in a very run-down part of a north-eastern city. She contributes some money because she often picks up the kids and drives them around using mostly her own car and petrol. She also feeds the grandchildren dinner most week nights. But Betty's daughter, who lives with her four children in a house she owns less than a block away, holds a nursing job that pays relatively well:

'I never help her with money. She makes more than I do anyway. Sometimes she pays me, like if I go pick them up and she gives me gas [petrol] money.'

Of the grandmothers interviewed, not one is being paid to care for her grandchildren. Nearly all are helping financially in modest ways with expenditures for petrol, food and gifts. But many are also helping with major expenses such as paying monthly mortgage or daycare bills. This creates a real conflict for middle-aged women who are at a stage in the life course where they should be saving resources for their own old age. Many are not only unable to save, but are also accumulating debt. The net effect is that many are reducing their own expenditures for things such as travel and contemplating delaying their retirement plans so that they can continue to earn money.

Responsibilities for ageing parents

Several of the grandmothers I interviewed also provide regular care for their aged parents. Deanne helps to take care of her 80-year-old mother by visiting her at the nursing home in town:

> 'I also have responsibilities with my mom in the nursing home. I am the only child in town, I go to the nursing home three to four nights a week to check on her and visit with her. I have been doing this pace forever.'

Similarly, Betty helps her sister look after their mother. Most evenings, Betty drives three miles to her sister's house, while her sister is at work, and helps her mother. Some nights she takes the grandchildren with her and other nights she leaves them at her house with the 13-year-old in charge. On the nights she does not have her grandchildren, she does more for her mother, focusing more on bathing her, doing laundry and cleaning. On the nights she has the grandchildren, Betty makes a shorter trip, just getting her mother dinner and taking her to the bathroom:

> 'My mom lives with my sister and she is not doing too well, not eating. My sister works evenings, and I work days. So if I don't have the grandkids, when I get off work, around 5 or 6, I take my mom something to eat and take her to the bathroom. Last night I gave her a bath, made sure she eats, gave her Tylenol for the pain, washed the clothes and cleaned up her room. She lives about three miles from here. She walks slowly. Still getting around, but not very well. I will go tonight after I pick the kids up from school.... Tonight I just need to make sure she eats and take her to the bathroom.... In the future, I will probably be doing more for my mom, she is not doing too good.'

Unless their own parents are deceased, like Estelle's, or live quite far away, most of the grandmothers interviewed are balancing paid work, grandchild care and parent care. Their days are long and often filled with care for themselves and for others: feeding, bathing, cleaning, laundering, shopping and more. They balance paid work and care work, and they balance joy and exhaustion. Some juggle it all fairly seamlessly and others feel the pinch. Because so many are contributing their own money for the younger family's house, daycare and other payments, they expect to continue to feel that pinch for many more years.

Discussion and conclusion

Many of the grandmothers have very positive attitudes about their care work. They are joyful about the time they spend with the grandchildren and pleased to be helping to raise them. Many are sequential grandmothers, providing care for each new grandchild as it arrives. Many are also intensive grandmothers, providing long hours of hands-on care including feeding, bathing, helping with homework and tucking into bed. Some are replicating the patterns of their mothers and grandmothers before them, others are establishing new patterns to be sure their daughters have supports they never did. Finally, many are also providing care to the older generation, stopping by after work and on weekends to help their ageing parents with activities of daily living.

To balance all of these responsibilities, most of the working grandmothers interviewed are actively rearranging their own work schedules to accommodate the needs of their grandchildren. For the most part, the grandmothers have greater security and flexibility through their jobs than do their daughters. Though some set limits on the amount of care they will provide, many do not. They are at that stage of the life course where they have more time to spend with a grandchild than they did with their own children because there are fewer competing demands. But they are also at that stage of life where they should be preparing for their own retirement and old age and many are not. Though Betty does not help her daughter with major finances, Deanne, Estelle, and many of the other women interviewed are paying monthly mortgage, daycare and other bills on behalf of their children. They are not saving for their own retirement, they are eating away at their own savings, and some are even accumulating debt. Concerns about finances are forcing many to delay their retirement beyond what they had planned.

Younger and middle-aged women in the US are increasingly likely to be employed and to be single mothers, yet they receive little help from the US welfare state. In fact, the US has no federal guarantee for paid vacation, paid sick leave, flexible scheduling, paid maternity leave or affordable daycare. While many workers have some of these benefits through their employers, those benefits are more readily available for full-time workers with higher salaries and lengthier tenure in their job. Moreover, employer-based benefits are generally shrinking. Given the dearth of social support, it is not surprising that young families turn to grandma for help with the grandkids. Nor is it a surprise that ageing parents turn to their middle-aged children for help. Taking a life-course perspective reveals the extent to which middle-aged grandmothers are juggling paid work, grandchild care and parent care. Many are overflowing with joy, but some are drowning in exhaustion and debt.

References

AARP (2002) Grandparenting Survey, http://assets.aarp.org/rgcenter/general/gp_2002.pdf.

Acker, J. (2006) *Class questions: Feminist answers*, Lanham, MD: Rowman & Littlefield Publishers.

Baca Z.M. and Dill, B.T. (2005) 'What is multiracial feminism?', in J. Lorber (ed) *Gender inequality: Feminist theories and politics* (3rd edn), Los Angeles, CA: Roxbury Publishing, pp 202-7.

Baydar, N. and Brooks-Gunn, J. (1998) 'Profiles of grandmothers who help care for their grandchildren in the United States', *Family Relations*, vol 47, no 4, pp 385-93.

Dannefer, D. (2003) 'Cumulative advantage/disadvantage and the life course: cross-fertilizing age and social science theory', *Journals of Gerontology, Series B: Psychological Sciences and Social Sciences*, vol 58, no 6, pp S327-S337.

England, P. (2005) 'Emerging theories of carework', *Annual Review of Sociology*, vol 31, pp 381-99.

Harrington Meyer, M. and Herd, P. (2007) *Market friendly or family friendly? The state and gender inequality in old age*, New York, NY: Russell Sage.

Heymann, J. (2000) *The widening gap: Why America's working families are in jeopardy and what can be done about it*, New York, NY: Basic Books.

IWPR (Institute for Women's Policy and Research) (2007) *Maternity leave in the United States*, A131, August, Washington DC: IWPR.

Kataoka-Yahiro, M., Ceria, C. and Caulfield, R. (2004) 'Grandparent caregiving role in ethnically diverse families', *Journal of Pediatric Nursing*, vol 19, no 5, pp 315-28.

Landry-Meyer, L. and Newman, B.M. (2004) 'An exploration of the grandparent caregiver role', *Journal of Family Issues*, vol 25, no 8, pp 1005-25.

Lerner, S. (2010) *The war on moms: On life in a family-unfriendly nation*, Hoboken, NJ: John Wiley and Sons.

Lorber, J. (2005) *Gender inequality: Feminist theories and politics* (3rd edn), Los Angeles, CA: Roxbury Publishing.

Ludwig, F.M. and Winston, K. (2007) 'How caregiving for grandchildren affects grandmothers' meaningful occupations', *Journal of Occupational Science*, vol 14, no 1, pp 40-51.

Mezey, J., Greenberg, M. and Schumacher, R. (2002) *The vast majority of federally-eligible children did not receive child care assistance in FY 2000*, Washington, DC: Center for Law and Social Policy.

Moen, P. and Spencer, D. (2006) 'Converging divergences in age, gender, health, and well-being: strategic selection in the third age', in R.H. Binstock and L.K. George (eds) *Handbook of aging and the social sciences* (6th edn), New York, NY: Academic Press.

Moen, P., Robison, J. and Dempster-McClain, D. (1995) 'Caregiving and women's well-being: a life course approach', *Journal of Health and Social Behavior*, vol 36, no 3, pp 259-73.

Musil, C.M, Warner, C.B, Zausniewski, J.A, Jeanblac, A.B. and Kercher, K. (2006) 'Grandmothers, caregiving, and family functioning', *Journals of Gerontology Series B: Psychological Sciences and Social Sciences,* vol 61, no 2, pp S89-S98.

Nelson, J.L. (2000) 'Contemplating grandmotherhood', *Ageing International*, vol 26, no 1-2, pp 3-9.

Park, H.H. (2006) 'The economic well-being of houses headed by a grandmother as caregiver', *Social Service Review*, vol 80, no 2, pp 264-96.

Platt Jendrek, M.P. (1993) 'Grandparents who parent their grandchildren: effects on lifestyle', *Journal of Marriage and the Family*, vol 55, no 3, pp 609-21.

Platt Jendrek, M.P. (1994) 'Grandparents who parent their grandchildren: circumstances and decisions,' *The Gerontologist*, vol 34, no 2, pp 206-16.

Presser, H.B. (1989) 'Some economic complexities of child care provided by grandmothers', *Journal of Marriage and the Family*, vol 51, no 3, pp 581-91.

Pruchno, R. (1999) 'Raising grandchildren: the experiences of black and white grandmothers', *The Gerontologist*, vol 39, no 2, pp 209-21.

Settersten, R.A. (2003) 'Introduction', in R.A. Settersten (ed) *Invitation to the life course: Toward new understandings of later life*, Amityville, NY: Baywood Publishing.

Simon-Rusinowitz, L., Krach, C.A., Marks, L.N., Piktialis, D. and Wilson, L.B. (1996) 'Grandparents in the workplace: the effects of economic and labor trends', *Generations*, vol 20, no 1, pp 41-4.

Stone, P. (2007) *Opting out: Why women really quit careers and head home*, Berkeley and Los Angeles, CA: University of California Press.

Turner, F.J. (2005) *Social work diagnosis in contemporary practice*, New York, NY: Oxford University Press.

US Bureau of Labor Statistics (2010) *Women in the labor force: A databook*, Washington, DC: US Department of Labor, www.bls.gov/cps/wlf-databook2010.htm.

US Census Bureau (2008a) 'Table MS-1. Marital status of the population 15 years old and over by sex and race, 1950 to present', www.census.gov/population/www/socdemo/hh-fam.html#ht.

US Census Bureau (2008b) 'Table FM-1. Families by presence of own children under 18, 1950 to present', www.census.gov/population/www/socdemo/hh-fam.html#ht.

Wang, Y. and Marcotte, D.E. (2007) 'Golden years? The labor market effects of caring for grandchildren', *Journal of Marriage and Family*, vol 69, no 5, pp 1283-96.

Wheelock, J. and Jones, K. (2002) '"Grandparents are the next best thing": informal childcare for working parents in urban Britain', *Journal of Social Policy*, vol 31, no 3, pp 441-63.

Williams, C., Drago, R. and Miller, K. (2010) '44 million US workers lacked paid sick days in 2010', IWPR B293, Washington, DC: Institute for Women's Policy Research, www.iwpr.org/pdf/B293PSD.pdf.

FIVE

Solidarity, ambivalence and multigenerational co-residence in Hong Kong

Lisanne S.F. Ko

Introduction

In most western societies, three-generational co-residence is not the norm. However, the US Census, for instance, has noted a sharp increase of co-residence with grandparent(s) since the economic downturn in 2007. At present, one child in 10 lives with a grandparent in the US (Livingston and Parker, 2010). Living with grandparents is more prevalent in a number of Asian societies. For instance, in Thailand, 59% of older adults aged 60 and above lived with at least one child and/ or grandchild in 2007 (United Nations, 2010a). The corresponding proportion is 43% in Japan (United Nations, 2010a) and 53% in Hong Kong (Census and Statistics Department, 2008). Multigenerational households are not only widely accepted in Asian societies as the most common household type for older adults, but are also regarded by many as the ideal living arrangement.

Existing studies on intergenerational relationships have largely focused on factors that influence the frequency of contact and quality of relationship between grandparents and grandchildren (Yi and Farrell, 2006); the extent and content of intergenerational transfers (Hoff, 2007); and impacts of grandparental caregiving on both grandchildren (Moyi et al, 2004) and grandparents themselves (Baker and Silverstein, 2008). In this literature, the intergenerational solidarity model proposed by Bengtson (1975) has received much attention. On the one hand, the proposed six dimensions of intergenerational solidarity have provided researchers with a framework for empirical studies (Katz et al, 2005). On the other hand, the model has given rise to many debates and further theorising on intergenerational relationships, most notably the concepts of intergenerational solidarity–conflict (Silverstein et al, 1996) and intergenerational ambivalence (Luescher and Pillemer, 1998;

Connidis and McMullin, 2002). Most of these debates and findings on intergenerational solidarity, conflict and ambivalence were based on the experiences of societies in which multigenerational co-residence is unusual and on the assumption that geographic proximity is conducive to cohesion across generations. Whether these findings and arguments hold in societies where multigenerational co-residence has remained a widespread and normative practice is not fully understood.

This chapter presents the findings of an exploratory study on grandparents' experiences and views about living in multigenerational households in Hong Kong. Hong Kong is selected because it shares a similar high level of development with other rich countries (Hong Kong ranks 21st on the human development index according to the United Nations, 2010b), but contrasts with most of them due to the sustained high prevalence of intergenerational co-residence. Because of its colonial history, Hong Kong is the most westernised among all the cities in China (Chen et al, 2007). Hong Kong is also a typical society in which the Confucian ideal of cohesiveness of the family is still widely observed but with diminishing importance (Chen et al, 2007). Investigating perceptions of multigenerational co-residence within a developed westernised economy, but with traditional cultural values, may shed new light on studies of intergenerational relationships (see also Izuhara, 2010).

This chapter is divided into five major parts. Theoretical approaches to intergenerational relationships are first discussed, followed by an overview of the social context of Hong Kong. The methodology and findings of the exploratory study are then discussed before the concluding remarks.

Theoretical approaches to intergenerational relationships

Bengtson's (2001) intergenerational solidarity model has been widely adopted as a key reference in studies of intergenerational relationships since its inception in the mid-1970s. The model incorporates six multifaceted and multidimensional constructs to explain the parent–adult child relationship, but it has also been widely applied in studies on grandparent–grandchild relationships (Silverstein and Bengtson, 1997; Lin and Harwood, 2003; Hoff, 2007). In Bengtson's words (2001, p 8), the six dimensions are:

> Affectual solidarity: the sentiments and evaluations family members express about their relationship with other

> members....Associational solidarity: the type and frequency
> of contact between intergenerational family members....
> Consensual solidarity: agreement in opinions, values, and
> orientations between generations.... Functional solidarity
> (assistance): the giving and receiving of support across
> generations....Normative solidarity: expectations regarding
> filial obligations and parental obligations, as well as norms
> about the importance of familistic values.... Structural
> solidarity: the 'opportunity structure' for cross-generational
> interaction reflecting geographic proximity between family
> members.

Bengtson's (1975) typology has given rise to many debates among
researchers of intergenerational relationships including discussion on
intergenerational conflict (Silverstein et al, 1996). Parott and Bengtson
(1999) argued that conflict is inevitable in family relationships.
Bengtson et al (2002, p 571) therefore incorporated conflict in their
revised intergenerational solidarity–conflict model by highlighting
both positive and negative valences along each of the six dimensions:

> [E]ach of the multiple dimensions of solidarity is distinct
> (orthogonal) and each represents a dialectic: intimacy
> and distance (affectual solidarity), agreement and dissent
> (consensual solidarity), dependence and autonomy
> (functional solidarity), integration and isolation (associational
> solidarity), opportunities and barriers (structural solidarity),
> familism and individualism (normative solidarity).

As further elaborated by Lowenstein (2007, p 107), these valences of
'solidarity and conflict do not represent a single continuum from high
solidarity to high conflict'. Instead, they coexist in different directions
and magnitudes, depending on family dynamics.

Another key concept in the literature is intergenerational ambivalence.
The concept of ambivalence was first developed by Luescher and
Pillemer (1998) in a study on parent–adult child relationships. It refers to
irreconcilable contradictions or ambiguities within family relationships.
The concept was further developed by Connidis and McMullin (2002).
They described ambivalence found in family relationships as a feature
of structured sets of social relationships as well as a vehicle for social
action. That is, personal experiences of family relationships resemble
what people experience in other social relationships. Social structures
such as age, gender, ethnicity and socioeconomic class usually favour

certain groups of people over others (for example, the young over the old, and men over women). Less privileged groups may therefore encounter ambivalence caused by the paradoxes or conflicts embedded in these structured variables when they attempt to exercise control in the context of their family relationships.

Bengtson and colleagues (2002) affirmed the contributions made by Connidis and McMullin (2002), including the importance of conflict theory in understanding intergenerational relationships. By normalising conflict as something inevitable in intergenerational relationships, related studies focus not only on cohesiveness but also on conflicts and ambiguities. Empirical research adopting these concepts seeks to capture the dialectics between solidarity and conflict within each of the six dimensions of the intergenerational solidarity–conflict model (Bengtson, 2001). In addition, as implicated in the concept of intergenerational ambivalence, structural constraints can be identified. Appropriate policy change may then be formulated to reduce or remove these structural constraints.

Living in Hong Kong

Over the past 150 years, Hong Kong has been transformed from a small fishing village into a global financial centre with a population of over seven million. In 2010, the gross domestic product (GDP) per capita was US$31,799, ranking 24th in the world and third in Asia (International Monetary Fund, 2010). Despite the handover of sovereignty from Britain back to China in 1997, the capitalist, market-oriented economic system remains unchanged, and the laissez-faire economic policy adopted by the colonial government is upheld by the new administration. This laissez-faire model led to an overemphasis on economic development. There were only fragmented policies and initiatives on social development, which were formulated mostly in response to crises that were perceived as threatening the legitimacy of the colonial rule. As the prime objective of the government has been to provide an environment conducive to economic growth, any social policy interventions including old-age policies have been minimal.

There was no official retirement protection scheme until the launch of the Mandatory Provident Fund in 2000. However, due to its short history and poor or negative investment return rate since inception, the fund cannot provide the required retirement protection for current and future retirees. In fact, the low contribution rate, 5% of income payable by both the employer and the employee, with a maximum contribution level capped at HK$1,000 (US$128) per month, relegates the fund to merely a source of 'minimum safety net income' for retirees, according to actuarial projections (Chan, 2001). Besides, it does not cover all the people but only the working population. The fight for a statutory minimum wage has also taken more than a decade to succeed. Though the Hong Kong Government used to argue that a statuatory minimum wage would drive up costs and scare away international and local investors, the first statutory minimum wage came into effect in May 2011, with the wage set at HK$28 (US$3.60) per hour, but it is not certain whether this first statutory minimum wage will protect low-wage earners. For those in difficult financial situations, the Hong Kong Government provides a social security scheme. However, the principle behind this safety net is the long-standing residual model of welfare. Coupled with the Chinese traditional value of self-reliance, public assistance carries a stigma. In fact, public discourses on poverty have focused on individual laziness rather than structural issues. This argument might have been reasonable in the 1960s and 1970s when Hong Kong was undergoing rapid industrialisation and abundant job opportunities were available. However, because of the change from a secondary economy to a tertiary economy, large numbers of the Hong Kongese could not match up their skills with this economic change and find appropriate jobs. The latest income inequality denoted by the Gini-coefficient of 0.43, ranking the highest among all the developed economies, further reflects the seriousness of poverty in Hong Kong (United Nations, 2009).

With regard to health status, Hong Kong ranks among the best in the world, with long life expectancy (79.8 for men and 86.1 for women), a low infant mortality rate (1.7 per 1,000 live births) and a low maternal mortality rate (2.4 per 100,000 live births) in 2009 (Centre for Health Protection, 2011). The public health facilities and management in Hong Kong are also world-renowned. However, the extent to which good population health is attributable to the public health services is questionable, because comprehensive primary health services are still lacking. Public expenditure on health is very low at 2.5% of GDP in 2006/07 (compared with 7% or above in the US, Canada, Belgium, Austria and the Netherlands) (Food and Health Bureau, 2011).

The Hong Kong Government housing policies were successful in accommodating the population in the 1970s and 1980s. As a consequence of a 10-year housing project in the 1970s, around 30% of the current older population lives in public rental housing and 20% lives in subsidised sale flats (Census and Statistics Department, 2007). Concomitantly, to combat problems associated with high population density in the core urban areas, the government has also been developing new towns in rural areas by building transportation infrastructures and launching massive public rental housing projects. Many younger adults, driven by the government's encouragement of home ownership, were attracted to establish their own households in these new towns and therefore moved away from their ageing parents. Redevelopment of old public rental housing estates and urban gentrification projects since the 1970s have further encouraged the splitting of extended households.

Very often, older people chose to stay in the old neighbourhoods where they feel secure and can maintain long-standing social ties while their adult children moved away from the city centre (Census and Statistics Department, 2007). Consequently, Hong Kong has experienced nuclearisation of household structures. The proportion of nuclear households has steadily increased from 59.2% in 1986 to 63.6% in 1996, and 67% in 2006 (Census and Statistics Department, 2007). In contrast, the proportion of three-generational extended family households has decreased from 9.9% in 1996 to 7.4% in 2006. Further, although the majority of Hong Kong senior citizens aged 60 and above still share a household with their adult children, the percentage has been continuously decreasing, from 60.3% in 1996 to 53.5% in 2006 (Census and Statistics Department, 2007). However, such changes in household types do not necessarily lead to the demise of traditional extended families. Instead of living together and rendering immediate support to family members (within the same household), families nowadays are more flexible in their living arrangements and resource exchange patterns.

The domestic arrangements of families in Hong Kong have also undergone significant changes. Women's participation in the labour market has risen since the 1960s. In the 1990s, almost half of working-age women were in the labour force and the proportion increased to 52% in 2011 (Census and Statistics Department, 2011). Although this percentage is not especially high when compared with many European countries or the US, the increase has brought drastic changes to the gender roles and functions in Chinese families. It has led to an increasing number of dual-career families in which wives and mothers have to redistribute the domestic work and caregiving responsibilities that were traditionally prescribed to them. The nuclearisation trend of households may further exacerbate the situation because of the absence of an older member in the household to act as a substitute domestic or childcare helper. To ease women's household burden, since the 1980s, domestic housekeepers have been hired from other East Asian countries, including the Philippines, Indonesia and Thailand. In 2001, about one in 10 households in Hong Kong employed a migrant domestic housekeeper (Census and Statistics Department, 2001). Strong gender norms still designate domestic tasks as women's work, which poses a big challenge to working women.

Methods

This chapter aims to explore grandparents' experiences and perceptions of intergenerational relationships and co-residence in three-generational families in Hong Kong. It is based on a study that focused on the grandparents' relationships with co-residing grandchildren or grandchildren they were in regular contact with. Purposive sampling was employed to select grandparents who were aged 60 or above, had at least one adolescent grandchild of high-school age and were able to communicate in Cantonese (local dialect). Grandparents with adolescent grandchild(ren) were selected because they were likely to have a longer experience of multigenerational co-residence (compared with those who have recently become grandparents) and hence were in a better position to offer reflections on multigenerational relationships.

The 16 participants included seven grandparents who were living with their grandchild(ren) at the time of the interview (for at least one year prior to the interview); four grandparents who had previously lived with their grandchild(ren) for at least one year but currently did not live with any of them; and five grandparents who had no multigenerational co-residence experience but had frequent face-to-face contact with their grandchild(ren) (at least three days a week). Fourteen grandmothers and two grandfathers were interviewed; participants were aged between 60 and 96, with an average age of 76. In-depth interviews were conducted in early 2010 and the interview time ranged between 90 minutes and two hours. The open-ended questions focused on the reasons for multigenerational co-residence/non-co-residence, respondents' desire for this co-residence pattern, relationships between the interviewees and the designated grandchild, factors affecting intergenerational relationships in the family, and roles of grandparents in these families. For this chapter, analysis of interview data was oriented by the intergenerational solidarity–conflict and ambivalence frameworks as described above.

Multigenerational co-residence as an act of filial piety

Living with the older generation under the same roof has always been regarded as an act of filial piety and a virtue in the traditional Chinese culture. In the past, this referred to the situation where the eldest son remained in his parents' household even after he had married. Such patrilocal residence, in which a married couple lives with the husband's parent(s), is rooted in traditional Chinese culture where the family was regarded as an important system for inheritance of property through the male line and as an important socialisation agent. In contrast to 'the role-less role', a term that Johnson and Troll (1994) used to refer to the lack of consensus on norms associated with the grandparent role in western cultures, roles of grandparents are clearly defined in traditional Chinese culture. Chinese grandparents, according to Mjelde-Mossey (2007), know that they should maintain and enhance positive relationships with their grandchildren through teaching, coaching and caring. These are the manifestations of *Renqing*, a central concept in Chinese culture. *Renqing* refers to social exchanges, with a connotation that giving is more important than receiving (Cheung et al, 1996). It is also a guiding principle for maintaining the highest value in traditional Chinese culture, namely, harmony in relationships. *Renqing,* coupled with filial piety (the virtue of respect for parents and ancestors), is a normative guide to intergenerational relationships. The solidarity implied in these intergenerational relationships is similar to Durkheim's mechanical solidarity, which is found in societies that are homogeneous in work, education and lifestyles, and adhere to strong normative ethics based on a person's age, gender and social position.

Cowgill and Holmes (1972) argued that the degree of modernisation of a society is inversely related to the status of older people. Accompanying this phenomenon is the changing relationship between elders and others resulting from individualism associated with urbanisation and industrialisation, which plays a key role in weakening traditional norms of filial obligation (Kemp, 2004). For instance, nowadays ageing parents in Hong Kong have no preference for living with the eldest son or the youngest one, and whether the involved son remains in the parental home after marriage or the ageing parents move into the son's home is immaterial, so long as they live with a married son. This is because the resources (mainly the practical wisdom gained by experience and land ownership) and power (mainly the traditional power based on normative ethics) that an elder used to enjoy in the past have been eroded.

In Hong Kong, the social conditions have not been favourable for maintaining traditional relationships and virtues since the 1960s. There are several reasons for this. First, Hong Kong is basically a migrant society. The parents or grandparents of most people in Hong Kong as well as the current oldest cohorts originally came from mainland China. They were geographically separated from their original extended

—

families. In the struggle for survival under a foreign regime (the British colonial government) that was focused on economic prosperity, self-reliance rather than mutual dependency on family members became an important strategy. Second, the massive social assistance schemes introduced by European missionaries after the Second World War changed the cultural values and practices of filial piety (Ho, 1996). Development of public facilities (such as new town projects) and basic social provisions (such as the 10-year housing project and free primary education) launched in the 1970s directly shook the foundation of traditional Chinese culture, *Renqing*. Grandparents were no longer required to provide teaching and accommodation for the younger generations. Such institutionalised individualism was further accelerated by the concomitant industrialisation and urbanisation in the 1960s and 1970s. Nonetheless, familial (including intergenerational) relationships remain important to individuals. The family is still a significant source of support for members in a society where the government spends little on welfare services (Chung, 2001). A familial ideology, utilitarianistic familism, is defined by Lau (1981, p 201) as:

> [A] normative and behavioral tendency of an individual to place his familial interests above the interests of society or any of its component individuals and groups, and to structure his relationships with other individuals and groups in such a fashion that the furtherance of these familial interests is the primary consideration. Moreover, among the familial interests materialistic interests take priority over all other interests.

However, the emphasis on materialism has sown the seeds for cultural change. In parallel to the completion of the massive projects of public rental housing and new town development in the 1980s, the nuclear family, which is composed of parents and unmarried children, became the most prevalent family form in this industrialised urban society.

These developments are reflected in the findings of this study. All seven co-residing informants mentioned that three-generational co-residence was traditional and it would be natural for ageing parents to live with one of their sons even after the sons got married and had children of their own. Two lived with their daughter's family, and three chose to live with their only son's family even though they had daughter(s). They believed that living with the son was their only choice, and they had never thought about moving in with their daughter's family. The living arrangements of the remaining two co-residing informants were dependent on the decisions made by their adult children after negotiation among themselves. For instance, the youngest son of Ms Chui, a widow, had promised his two elder brothers that he would take care of his mother until her death. All the above mentioned practices followed the norm of Confucian filial piety with a preference for patrilocal residence. As pointed out by Ms Chui, there are also principles guiding which son she should live with:

> 'If there is only one son, the elder usually lives with this only son. But if there is more than one son, s/he will live with either the youngest or the eldest.' (Ms Chui, aged 96, co-residing with her youngest son's family)

Besides these norms, conflicting norms were noted in the research findings. Three of the seven co-residing informants felt ashamed when their son did not move out of the parental household after getting married. For them, a son being able to set up a household of his own is seen as a success in contemporary society. The traditional ideal of patrilocal multigenerational households therefore runs counter to the modern-day ideal of having a successful son with his own home. These conflicting ideals are not uncommon among adult children with low-status jobs (Martin, 1990) or where there are housing shortages and the cost of housing is high (Harwood, 2004). The view of Mr Lam, who chose to invite his only son to remain living in his own household but not his daughter, is illustrative of these ambivalences:

> 'How can he [the son] have the [financial] ability to move out? He's very disappointing! If it wouldn't be me, his life would have been more difficult.... We're a family. Where could I live [if I do not live with them]? Besides, my importance to the family is more than that of a Filipino maid [a migrant domestic helper]. How can they live without me? I'm here just for the two granddaughters ... I have nobody, except the granddaughters, the son, and the daughter-in-law. Where can I go? I'd only be with them.' (Mr Lam, aged 77, widowed, co-residing with his son's family)

Irrespective of Mr Lam's high regard for multigenerational co-residence, he gained no feelings of affectual solidarity through living with his son's family. Instead, he encountered at least two different types of ambivalence. The first one came from the constraints of realities. Mr Lam had been expecting a happy life in a three-generational patrilocal residence. However, the change from being an adviser and symbolic head of the family to being 'an unpaid maid' did not bring Mr Lam the traditionally expected trust and respect associated with the term 'grandparent'. In addition, he chose to continue the current living arrangement and repeatedly told himself that this was the only choice available to him, even though he had another daughter and some personal savings. Further ambivalence was caused by two conflicting norms, namely, the ideals of multigenerational co-residence and having a successful son. What made his situation even worse was his son's family's dependency on him (functional solidarity). Mr Lam provided the family with substantial instrumental support such as doing housework. Similar observations were noted among all the co-residing informants. Their co-residence with their children and grandchildren was motivated by the ideal of familism (normative solidarity), and yet five of the seven co-residing interviewees did not experience affectual solidarity with their co-residing grandchild.

Distant relationships (lack of affectual solidarity) were also observed among three of the four grandparents who had previously lived with their child's family and the grandchild. Yet all these informants agreed that living in a multigenerational family was a blessing for an elder. They had provided childcare support to their grandchild (from infancy to childhood) during the time of co-residence. The reasons for moving out from the multigenerational households were varied, including poor health of the informant (Mrs Leung), conflicts due to different lifestyles and parenting (Mrs Chan and Ms Ho) and cessation of childcare needs when the grandchild reached adolescence (Ms Chung and Ms Ho). An interesting point was noted. The multigenerational co-residence experience referred to by all these previously co-residing grandmothers came from the experience of living with their daughter. As there were no grandfathers in this category, whether or not the dissent (lack of consensual solidarity) is an outcome related to gender of the co-residing dyads of grandmothers and daughters is not known. Ms Ho, who had two years of co-residence experience with her daughter's family, described the problems as follows:

> 'I've no problem with my grandson. But it may not be good to live with his mum, my eldest daughter. Saying this doesn't mean that she is not good. The problem is that she's too serious about her child. She's really too serious ... I haven't lived with other grandchildren before.... Well, I guess there could be something good and something bad [about multigenerational co-residence]. In case we need to

have direct contact daily, we may have conflict quite easily.' (Ms Ho, aged 70, currently living alone but with earlier co-residence experience)

Centrality of functional solidarity?

Functional solidarity, denoted as the giving and receiving of support across generations within a family, has been widely discussed in existing literature. Studies also show that functional solidarity is not necessarily unidirectional from adult children to their ageing parents (Phua and Loh, 2008). This study also yielded similar findings. Older adults provided both material and non-material help to their adult children and grandchildren. Four out of the seven co-residing informants, for example, reported that doing housework for their children's families was part of their daily routine. Four gave financial support to their children periodically. Similar types of support had been provided by all four previously co-residing informants during their period of multigenerational co-residence. The centrality of functional support was also evident among the five informants who had never lived with their children's families. For instance, two (Mr Choy and Ms Wu) regularly went to the markets to get food and performed housekeeping duties for their children who lived very close to them (within walking distance). Similarly, Ms Chung, previously co-residing with her daughter, helped take care of her two adolescent grandchildren who lived at quite a distance from her (30-minute commuting time). Her two grandchildren came to her home by bus after school almost every day, did their home work and ate supper at her home before going back to their parents. As argued by family researchers (Martin, 1990), basic family functions, such as meal sharing and care giving, can be performed by members not living under the same roof. This is a prominent feature of family relationships in Hong Kong. The well-developed mass transportation system and the relatively small geographical area of Hong Kong make this family arrangement possible even when the households live in different areas.

Carrying out household chores and taking care of family members were frequently mentioned as the main roles of our informants. Some even described these as their 'duties' that they had to fulfil daily. The description by Ms Lai, a co-residing widow, was the most detailed:

'I'm responsible for all the household chores. When they [my daughter and her husband] come back [from work], they'll get a rest for a while and they'll then have dinner.

After the dinner, they need a rest as well. All the household chores are done by me ... I'm usually responsible for going to the market, cooking meals, doing housework and so on ... all these nitty-gritty.... For instance, they [my daughter and her husband] take a bath every morning before going to work. I'll then do laundry ... I've to do many things and I'm not free most of the time.... But it's okay. That's what we call "we're a family".... Yes, my role in the family is very important. They [my daughter and her husband] also think that I'm important to the family.... They've never worried about their home.... As long as I've been living here, I'd help them, shouldn't I? I'd make them [my daughter and her husband] go to work without worry, without worry about the family. I'll take care of it.... We're so close to one another. I've to take care of the whole family, of course.' (Ms Lai, aged 73, living with her daughter's family)

Grandparents doing household chores for their adult children who live in the same or a separate household is a common practice among dual-career families in Hong Kong. In many cases, couples with young children ask their parents to help supervise the migrant domestic helpers they have hired to take care of their children (see also Chapter Six). Couples without a domestic helper usually resort to grandparents' help with meal preparation and household chores. The work done by Ms Lai was equivalent to the work of a full-time housekeeper. Despite her seemingly very onerous daily duties (functional solidarity), Ms Lai's account evinces strong normative and affectual solidarities. As noted by Koyano (1996), multigenerational co-residence (structural solidarity) and emotional closeness (affectual solidarity) are not necessarily related. A similar account was given by Mr Lam, who was a widower taking care of his three-generational family since the birth of his eldest granddaughter 14 years ago:

'I've done all the housework ... buying food and preparing meals ... I even lay the table and place the rice in bowls for them [all the other family members].... The daughter-in-law doesn't care about these things. She does nothing.... Frankly, even when you employ a Filipino maid, she won't do the things like what I've been doing.... If it was not me, how could the family sustain itself? But if I don't do these, nobody will take care of my two granddaughters. They'll be miserable. She [the daughter-in-law] really doesn't care [about] anything.' (Mr Lam, aged 77, co-residing with his son's family)

Although the case of Mr Lam exhibited the normative and functional solidarities evident in the case of Ms Lai, no affectual solidarity is present. Mr Lam even described his role in this multigenerational family as unpaid housekeeper. Such a mentality was frequently mentioned among all four co-residing informants who were providing functional support to their extended family, alongside accounts of tense relationships with their children. As concluded by Chow (1999), the status of the elders (including ageing grandparents) in Hong Kong is now determined more by their actual contribution to the family (such as helping with household chores and taking care of grandchildren) than by normative expectations and values held by them. However, when these functions can be easily replaced by recruiting a domestic housekeeper, the contributions made by these ageing grandparents may no longer be treasured and their status in the family may not be as high as that in the past.

Health status and physical functioning were emphasised by some co-residing informants (including Ms Chu, Mr Lam, Ms Lai and Ms Wong). It seems that a functional body is central for maintaining their status and remaining on good terms with their adult children in multigenerational co-residence, as described by Mr Lam:

'I'm still in good shape.... This is a blessing to me. If I'm not fit enough, how could I do all these [household care support services]? It'd be hopeless in case I'm in poor health and need them to take care of me.' (Mr Lam, aged 77, co-residing with his son's family)

Failure to demonstrate this 'utility function' may lead to frustration and low self-esteem, as in the case of Ms Wong:

'An older person is useless unless s/he can do the housework.... I'm not important in the family now. She [the daughter] has already got a Filipino maid. I've been made redundant like "scrap wood".... I'm still quite healthy. I'm already 88, but I still walk quite fast.' (Ms Wong, aged 88, co-residing with her daughter's family)

Moreover, the traditional Chinese family structure is often characterised as patriarchal with the power distribution in a family based on age, generation and gender. Traditionally an old grandfather enjoys the greatest power and most respect. However, this was not the case for Mr Lam. He did not receive respect from his son and daughter-in-law. He even had to 'set the table for dinner and fill the bowls with rice for them'. This is quite a common scenario in Hong Kong where dual-career couples are prevalent and live in multigenerational households. In the traditional Chinese culture, it is usually the younger generation who invite their seniors (such as parents and grandparents) to the table to have meals with them. Reversing this practice generates further ambivalence for the grandparents.

Functional solidarity as described in Bengtson's (2001) model emphasises reciprocity in care and material support across generations. However, some participants in this study (including co-residing Ms Lee, previously co-residing Mrs Chan, and Ms Fong and Ms Chan who had no experience in multigenerational co-residence) had often provided functional support to their children's families yet their children and grandchildren had not reciprocated in any form. Ms Fong stated that she would consider seeking support from her children only as a last resort:

> 'I don't want to bring people [my children] trouble. I won't tell people [my children] unless my problem is so big that I won't be able to solve it…. No, I don't call them [my children] if nothing special [is happening]. I really don't want to give them [my children] any pressure.' (Ms Fong, aged 72, no experience of co-residence)

Normative solidarity in connection with ambivalence

Preference for patrilocal residence in a multigenerational family still prevailed even among those participants for whom the co-residence experience had not brought intimacy, respect or feelings of integration, but rather resulted in conflicts. The provision of functional support for their children's families, ranging from financial support to housework, childcare and accommodation, was based on strong normative obligations. Ms Lee, a co-residing informant who had two unmarried daughters and a married son with a 19-year old son, said:

> 'It's okay. I only have a son and a daughter-in-law … I'll give them everything I've got…. Anyway, I can't bring it [property] all into my coffin.' (Ms Lee, aged 75, co-residing with her husband and her son's family)

A similar view is shared by Mr Lam, who co-resided with his son and also had a married daughter. Following a request from his only son he gave his son all his personal savings to save his son's business. Yet he still mentioned:

> 'Yes, I did it [give all the money to the son]. I'd help him [the son].... But it didn't mean that I love him. Frankly, I love my daughter more than the son. Why? In Hong Kong, it's nothing about son or daughter. It's only the cultural tradition saying that we spoil sons.' (Mr Lam, aged 77, co-residing with his son's family)

Irrespective of the quality of experience with intergenerational co-residence, the majority of informants considered themselves as having 'no choice' when they accounted for the support they gave. The fatalistic attitude towards multigenerational co-residence is evident in this statement by Ms Wu, a non-co-residing informant:

> 'You've no choice. Who makes you the grandmother of these grandchildren and the mother of this daughter? You've got no choice. You'd help whenever you can. You couldn't care too much.' (Ms Wu, aged 60, no experience of multigenerational co-residence but living close to her daughter's family)

Multigenerational co-residence, as an act of filial piety, may therefore be detrimental to both grandparents and their families since many family tensions develop. Conflict and ambivalences can arise within the 'ideal' family living arrangement of multigenerational co-residence but remain unacknowledged (Phua and Loh, 2008). Apart from the conflicting norms between the ideal of patrilocal multigenerational co-residence and the ideal of a successful son (who is supposed to afford his own apartment after marriage) and conflicts between realities and norms (the cultural ideal prescribed for a respected and beloved grandparent) as discussed above, the relationship between grandparents and their children-in-law was found to be a source of ambivalence among some of our informants. For example, when asked if living with a married child's family was a preferable arrangement, Ms Wu, who was providing regular help in taking care of her grand-daughter but did not live with her grand-daughter's family, chose 'keeping a distance' with her son-in-law as preferable to maintaining a closer relationship with him:

'If you're talking about co-residence with grandchildren only, I've no special preference. But if you're talking about living with my daughter and her husband, I don't want it. It's much better to keep a distance between us.... Living together may too easily lead to conflict.' (Ms Wu, aged 60, no experience of multigenerational co-residence)

Discussion and conclusion

Chinese people have a long tradition of multigenerational co-residence. Hong Kong has been influenced by both the Chinese and western cultures due to its historical development. On the one hand, living in a three-generational family is still seen as an act of filial piety and a virtue. On the other hand, our findings show that actualising this cultural norm seems to be difficult among the current grandparent cohorts. Multigenerational co-residence, in itself, may not lead to the fulfillment or enactment of all types of solidarity. The assumption that increased opportunities for interaction brought about by multigenerational co-residence make relations between generations cohesive has to be re-examined. As suggested by our findings, this argument overlooks the possible negative consequences of the normative bases and practical drivers of multigenerational co-residence. Tension may replace affection and integration to become a dominant experience in situations where a grandparent does not derive the traditionally expected trust and respect from multigenerational co-residence (which is highly valued as a manifestation of filial piety). Besides, with the well-developed mass transportation system and wide use of communication technology, geographic distance may no longer be an obstacle to intergenerational solidarity in Hong Kong.

Functional solidarity manifested in the housework and childcare provided by grandparents is in some cases the only form of solidarity that is present in Hong Kong Chinese families. Although living together enhances functional support from grandparents to the middle and third generations, the support may not primarily be based on reciprocal support exchange across generations. Because of strong normative altruism, grandparents are willing to give more and receive less. In some cases, grandparents even move out from multigenerational households simply because they are unable to help the family due to their poor health or because their help is no longer needed when the grandchildren reach adolescence. Grandparents also clearly indicate that providing help with household chores and care for grandchildren is important to them. As such, the role of grandparents in multigenerational co-residence needs further investigation. The relationships between structural solidarity, functional solidarity and normative solidarity have to be revisited, too.

Further, the findings show that when striving to fulfill the normative familial obligations in intergenerational relationships, grandparents inevitably encounter ambivalences generated by conflicts between norms, as well as conflicts between norms and realities. This is most evident when the prestige and respect normatively bestowed on grandparents cannot be found in multigenerational co-residing families or when grandparents' preference for multigenerational co-residence clashes with their ideal of having a successful son (who can financially afford a separate household). The ambivalence faced by grandfathers deserves closer attention because they once enjoyed the most status and power in the family, even more so than grandmothers, and thus changes in intergenerational relations may exert a greater impact on them. Lastly, future studies of multigenerational co-residence should also focus on the relationships of grandparents with their children-in-law, as they are an important mediator of the grandparent–grandchild relationships.

References

Baker, L.A. and Silverstein, M. (2008) 'Depressive symptoms among grandparents raising grandchildren: the impact of participation in multiple roles', *Journal of Intergenerational Relationships*, vol 6, no 3, pp 285-304.

Bengtson, V.L. (1975) 'Generations and family effects in value socialization', *American Sociological Review*, vol 40, no 3, pp 358-71.

Bengtson, V.L. (2001) 'Beyond the nuclear family: the increasing importance of multigenerational bonds', *Journal of Marriage and Family*, vol 63, no 1, pp 1-16.

Bengtson, V.L, Giarrusso, R., Mabry, J.B. and Silverstein, M. (2002) 'Solidarity, conflict and ambivalence: complementary or competing perspectives on intergenerational relationships?', *Journal of Marriage and Family*, vol 64, no3, pp 568-76.

Census and Statistics Department of Hong Kong Special Administrative Region Government (2001) *Thematic household survey report no. 5'*, http://www.statistics.gov.hk/publication/stat_report/social_data/B11302052001XXXXB0100.pdf.

Census and Statistics Department of Hong Kong Special Administrative Region Government (2007) *Hong Kong annual digest of statistics*, Hong Kong: Hong Kong Special Administrative Region Government.

Census and Statistics Department of Hong Kong Special Administrative Region Government (2008) '2006 Population by-census – thematic report: older persons', www.censtatd.gov. hk/freedownload.jsp?file=publication/stat_report/population/ B11200532006XXXXB0100.pdf.

Census and Statistics Department of Hong Kong Special Administrative Region Government (2011) 'Labor force and labor force participation rates (LFPRs) by sex', http://censtatd.gov.hk/hong_kong_statistics/ statistical_tables/index.jsp?tableID=007&ID=&subjectID=2.

Centre for Health Protection of Hong Kong Special Administrative Region Government (2011) 'Major health indicators in 2009 and 2010', www.chp.gov.hk/en/data/4/10/27/110.html.

Chan, W.S. (2001) 'The first mandated social security pension scheme in Hong Kong', *Benefits: A Journal of Social Security Research, Policy & Practice*, vol 32, pp 15-21.

Chen, S.X., Bond, M.H. and Tang, D. (2007) 'Decomposing filial piety into filial attitudes and filial enactments', *Asian Journal of Social Psychology*, vol 10, no 4, pp 213-23.

Cheung, F.M.C., Leung, K., Fan, R., Song, W.Z., Zhang, J.X. and Zhang, J.P. (1996) 'Development of the Chinese personality assessment inventory', *Journal of Cross-Cultural Psychology*, vol 27, no 2, pp 182-99.

Chow, N.W.S. (1999) 'Diminishing filial piety and the changing role and status of the elders in Hong Kong', *Hallym International Journal of Aging*, vol 1, no 1, pp 67-77.

Chung, G.W. (2001) 'Elders in the family and the strain of the discourse of filial piety', *Korea Journal*, vol 41, no 4, pp 144-58.

Connidis, I. and McMullin, J.A. (2002) 'Sociological ambivalence and family ties: a critical perspective', *Journal of Marriage and Family*, vol 64, no 3, pp 558-67.

Cowgill, D.O. and Holmes, L.D. (eds) (1972) *Aging and modernization*, New York, NY: Appleton-Century-Crofts.

Food and Health Bureau (2011) 'Hong Kong's domestic health accounts – estimates of health expenditure, 1989/90-2006/07', www.fhb.gov. hk/statistics/download/dha/en/tf5_0607.pdf.

Harwood, J. (2004) 'Relational, role, and social identity as expressed in grandparents' personal web sites', *Communication Studies*, vol 55, no 2, pp 300-18.

Ho, D.Y.F. (1996) 'Filial piety and its psychological consequences', in M.H. Bond (eds) *The handbook of Chinese psychology*, Hong Kong: Oxford University Press, pp 155-65.

Hoff, A. (2007) 'Patterns of intergenerational support in grandparent–grandchild and parent–child relationships in Germany', *Ageing & Society*, vol 27, no 5, pp 643-65.

International Monetary Fund (2010) 'World economic outlook database', www.imf.org/external/pubs/ft/weo/2010/02/weodata/index.aspx.

Izuhara, M. (ed) (2010) *Ageing and intergenerational relations: Family reciprocity from a global perspective*, Bristol: The Policy Press.

Johnson, C.L. and Troll, L.E. (1994) 'Constraints and facilitators to friendships in late, late life', *Gerontologist*, vol 34, no 1, pp 79-87.

Katz, R., Lowenstein, A., Phillips, J. and Daatland, S.O. (2005) 'Theorizing intergenerational family relations. Solidarity, conflict, and ambivalence in cross-national contexts', in V.L. Bengtson, A.C. Acock, K.R. Allen, P. Dilworth-Anderson and D.M. Klein (eds) *Sourcebook of family theory and research*, Thousand Oaks, CA: Sage, pp 393-407.

Kemp, C.L. (2004) '"Grand" expectations: the experiences of grandparents and adult grandchildren', *Canadian Journal of Sociology*, vol 29, no 4, pp 499-525.

Koyano, W. (1996) 'Filial piety and intergenerational solidarity in Japan', *Australasian Journal on Ageing*, vol 15, no 2, pp 51-6.

Lau, S.K. (1981) 'Chinese familism in an urban-industrial setting: the case of Hong Kong', *Journal of Marriage and the Family*, vol 43, no 4, pp 977-92.

Lin, M.C. and Harwood, J. (2003) 'Accommodation predictors of grandparent–grandchild relational solidarity in Taiwan', *Journal of Social and Personal Relationships*, vol 20, no 4, pp 537-63.

Livingston, G.. and Parker, K. (2010) 'Since the start of the Great Recession, more children raised by grandparents', http://pewresearch.org/pubs/1724/sharp-increase-children-with-grandparent-caregivers.

Lowenstein, A. (2007) 'Solidarity–conflict and ambivalence: testing two conceptual frameworks and their impact on quality of life for older family members', *Journal of Gerontology: Social Sciences*, vol 62B, no 2, pp S100-7.

Luescher, K. and Pillemer, K. (1998) 'Intergenerational ambivalence: a new approach to the study of parent–child relations in later life', *Journal of Marriage and Family*, vol 60, no 2, pp 413-45.

Martin, L.G.. (1990) 'Changing intergenerational family relations in East Asia', Annals of the American Academy of Political and Social Science, vol 510, July, pp 102-14.

Mjelde-Mossey, L.A. (2007) 'Cultural and demographic changes and their effects upon the traditional grandparent role for Chinese elders', *Journal of Human Behavior in the Social Environment*, vol 16, no 3, pp 107-20.

Moyi, P., Pong, S.L. and Frick, W. (2004) *Co-resident grandparents and grandchildren's academic performance*, Philadelphia, PA: Population Research Institute, Pennsylvania State University.

Parrot, T.M. and Bengtson, V.L. (1999) 'The effects of earlier intergenerational affection, normative expectations, and family conflict on contemporary exchanges of help and support', *Research on Aging*, vol 21, no 1, pp 73-105.

Phua, V.C. and Loh, J. (2008) 'Filial piety and intergenerational co-residence: the case of Chinese Singaporeans', *Asian Journal of Social Science*, vol 36, no 3-4, pp 659-79.

Silverstein, M. and Bengtson, V.L. (1997) 'Intergenerational solidarity and the structure of adult child–parent relationships in American families', *American Journal of Sociology*, vol 103, no 2, pp 429-60.

Silverstein, M., Chen, X. and Heller, K. (1996) 'Too much of a good thing? Intergenerational social support and the psychological well-being of aging parents', *Journal of Marriage and Family*, vol 58, no 4, pp 970-82.

United Nations (2009) 'United Nations development programme: human development report 2009', http://hdr.undp.org/en/media/HDR_2009_Tables_rev.xls.

United Nations (2010a) 'Current status of the social situation, well-being, participation in development and rights of older persons worldwide', www.un.org/ageing/whatsnew%20PDF/Ageing%20Comprehensive%20report%202010%202%20September.pdf.

United Nations (2010b) 'International human development indicators', http://hdrstats.undp.org/en/countries/profiles/HKG.html.

Yi, C.C. and Farrell, M. (2006) 'Globalization and the intergenerational relation: cross-cultural perspectives on support and interaction patterns', *Journal of Family Issues*, vol 27, no 8, pp 1035-41.

SIX

Grandparenting in the context of care for grandchildren by foreign domestic workers

Shirley Hsiao-Li Sun

Introduction

Historically, childcare needs in Asia have been met within the family. Moreover, participation of grandparents in providing care for their grandchildren has been the norm. In the context of declining fertility and an ageing population, as in some contemporary South East Asian societies, it is pertinent to consider how the nature and character of intergenerational relations is changing with respect to childcare. For example, to what extent does the norm of obligation for grandparents to provide childcare assistance still hold? What happens to intergenerational interactions when co-residence of three generations of family members declines? In the midst of global migration, what is the relationship between parents, grandparents and foreign domestic workers (FDWs) in a host country? This chapter addresses these questions by drawing on qualitative data obtained in the fast-changing globalised city-state of Singapore.

Intergenerational solidarity, conflict and ambivalence

Intergenerational relations can be analysed primarily through three lenses – intergenerational solidarity, conflict and ambivalence (see Chapter One). Bengtson and colleagues (1976) developed the intergenerational solidarity model to describe sentiments, behaviours and attitudes associated with intergenerational relationships in families. According to Bengtson and Oyama (2007, p 2), intergenerational solidarity can be succinctly defined as 'social cohesion between generations'. Bengtson and Schrader (1982) suggested that there are six dimensions of parent–adult child solidarity: associational, affectual, consensual, functional, normative and structural. Bengtson and Oyama (2007, p 8) reiterated the six dimensions as follows:

- affectual solidarity: sentiments and evaluations that family members express concerning their relationships with one another;
- associational solidarity: type and frequency of contact between family members;
- consensual solidarity: agreement in opinions, values, and orientations between generations;
- functional solidarity: giving and receiving of support across generations;
- normative solidarity: expectations regarding filial obligations and parental obligations, as well as norms concerning the importance of familial values;
- structural solidarity: the 'opportunity structure' for cross-generational interaction, for example reflecting geographic proximity between family members.

This model has been adopted in studying parent–child relationships in cross-national comparisons (Lowenstein and Ogg, 2003) and in multicultural societies (Katz, 2009). However, conflict is also a prominent aspect of intergenerational relations. Indeed, Clarke and colleagues (1999) found that about one in five relationships between older parents and adult children in the US were characterised by either significant conflict or detachment. Thus, the intergenerational solidarity paradigm was later modified into the 'family solidarity–conflict' model, which incorporates the existence of conflict (Silverstein et al, 1996).

Luescher and Pillemer (1998) proposed the intergenerational ambivalence paradigm as a framework for studying intergenerational relationships. They defined intergenerational ambivalence as 'contradictions in relationships between parents and adult offspring that cannot be reconciled' (p 416). Connidis and McMullen (2002, p 565) further conceptualised ambivalence as 'socially structured contradictions made manifest in interaction'. Moreover, as Connidis and McMullen pointed out:

> Assuming ambivalence in intergenerational relationships and in structural arrangements forces us to consider how ambivalence is resolved. In daily life, it is resolved not merely by choosing between roles but also by redefining them. Emphasizing ambivalence forces an examination of how the taken-for-grantedness of roles is negotiated. (2002, p 565)

For example, regarding parental support to divorced and separated adult children in Ireland, Timonen and colleagues (2011, p 21) demonstrated that 'the contexts where feelings of ambivalence were particularly acute were childcare support that proved more extensive or of longer duration than anticipated; and co-residence that lasted longer than expected'.

Bengtson and colleagues (2002) concluded that the solidarity–conflict and ambivalence models are 'not competing, antagonistic approaches to family relationships', but 'each of these concepts can be useful in understanding and explaining intergenerational ties' (p 575). Moreover, a given set of intergenerational relationships can be characterised differently depending on a subject's position within the family structure. Hagestad (2006, p S321) wrote perceptively, 'in designing and executing studies of modern grandparents, researchers need to be aware of asymmetry as a potential problem and be very clear on where in vertical connections the research is anchored'. Thus, this chapter explores the nature and character of intergenerational relations seen through both the parental generation and the grandparental generation in Singapore during the first decade of the 21st century, where it is estimated that one in six families hired live-in FDWs in 2008 (Wong, 2008). With the notable exception of Lan (2002), whose work reveals intergenerational conflicts in Taiwan, there has been little research on the dynamics among parents (usually mothers), grandparents (usually grandmothers) and FDWs in caring for (grand)children in Asia. Although Lan's (2002) empirical evidence and analysis shed light on these intergenerational conflicts, the division of childcare among the grandmother, the mother and the FDWs was not discussed. This chapter seeks to fill this gap, drawing on empirical evidence collected through in-depth personal and focus-group interviews to give texture and nuances to the theoretical notions of intergenerational solidarity and intergenerational ambivalence.

Childcare by foreign domestic workers and grandparents

Most of the literature on the topic of childcare provided by FDWs focuses on the relationship between the female employer (the mother) and the domestic worker. The domestic workers' position in the household is often viewed as under a 'total institution' (Arat-Koc, 1989; Bakan and Stasiulis, 1997; Tronto, 2002; Lin and Sun, 2010). Nonetheless, it has also been shown that domestic workers develop coping strategies to mitigate against their total subordination (Cohen, 1991; Lin and Sun, 2010). The female employer–domestic worker relationship is characterised by a shared subordination to men and the notion that it is women's responsibility to clean the house. However, this shared subordination 'does not lead to solidarity between the two' (Arat-Koc, 1989, p 44). In the US, Hochschild (1993) suggested that the relationship between the female employer and the domestic worker is maternal. Moreover, regarding childcare, female employers tend to reinforce the distinction that domestic workers are only helpers, and that employers are the primary caregivers, although a greater proportion of care work is usually performed by the domestic workers (Colen, 1995).

Wheelock and Jones (2002) examined a family's choice between paid childcare (through formal services) and complementary childcare (by friends, neighbours or primarily grandparents) in urban Britain, and suggested that employed parents made decisions based on economic factors (such as the price of formal childcare), but that financial considerations were not the primary factor. They suggested that 'a clear understanding of why working parents use complementary childcare (particularly from grandparents) is essential for any childcare policy that hopes to be attuned to what families actually want' (p 441). They concluded that:

> Many parents, as we have seen, do indeed access market-based childcare, but they may still wish to draw on family support too. The type of care that grandparents are seen to provide is often critical to what families perceived as high quality; it is the 'best' childcare: best for children, best for parents, and from the grandparents' point of view, best for them, too: complementary childcare is based on values about childrearing that are shared between the generations ... what is valued by parents when it comes to grandparenting is that it comes from love. This was in contrast to the way that 'outsiders' or 'strangers' who work in the formal childcare sector were sometimes seen. (Wheelock and Jones, 2002, p 441)

Timonen and Doyle (2010, p 38), however, found that migrant care workers in both institutional and home settings described themselves as 'altruistic, compassionate and trusting' and suggested that researchers and policy makers need to gain a better understanding of the affective components of formal care work. Sarti (2010) demonstrated that unpaid grandparents and paid domestic workers were not mutually exclusive actors within childcare. Indeed, a proportion of families in Italy rely on both grandparents and paid domestic workers:

> In some cases, the domestic worker carries out both domestic chores and childcare and the grandparents step in only in exceptional circumstances or if they want to spend some time with their grandchildren. In other cases childcare seems to be considered a task that requires more trust and is thus normally entrusted to grandparents, whereas cleaning is entrusted to paid workers who do not belong to the family. (Sarti, 2010, p 802)

As noted, there has been very little research on the triad of parents, domestic workers and grandparents, with the exception of Lan's (2002) work. Lan's analysis focused more on power dynamics and tensions than on the division of labour in caring for a child among the triad. Lan pointed out various power dynamics between the daughter-in-law, foreign domestic worker and mother-in-law in the Taiwanese family. She suggested that 'modern daughters-in-law often prefer to hire migrant workers rather than accept the kin labour offered by their mothers-in-law, because they fear excessive intervention in their families' domestic lives' (p188). Lan interpreted the choice of these daughters-in-law to hire domestic workers as a move to safeguard the nuclear family and resist three-generational cohabitation, and observed that 'the daughter-in-law and the domestic worker may develop a sisterly camaraderie when they face the mother-in-law's authority together' (p 175). On the other hand, mothers-in-law tended to be angry with the presence of domestic workers, as that denied the link they might have enjoyed with their sons' families and grandchildren. Moreover, as the authority and old-age support for mothers-in-law was perceived to depend on their provision of grandparental childcare, mothers-in law felt insecure when they were not caring for their grandchildren. Lan noted that 'a daughter-in-law who hires a migrant worker may have lightened her physical workload, but she has often taken on the additional emotional labour of soothing her mother-in-law's tensions and anxieties' (p 183).

Singapore also relies on migrant domestic workers for caregiving tasks. The first survey to describe FDW caregivers for older people in Singapore was the 1995 National Survey of Senior Citizens in Singapore (MCYS, 1995). This survey reported that the majority of these FDWs were employed for dual purposes, such as housework and looking after elderly relatives (61%) or looking after grandchildren and elderly relatives (31%). Yeoh and colleagues (1999) investigated the perceived influence of the foreign domestic worker in the family setting, highlighting a concern of female employers that 'the availability of foreign maids will lead to a generation of kids that are really pampered and spoiled' (p 126). Many women interviewed were also worried about domestic workers' influence on their children's value system. At the same time, they acknowledged that having a FDW helped relieve them from basic household tasks, thereby freeing them for more time and activities within the family, such as spending quality time with their children.

Study context: contemporary Singapore (since 2000)

Singapore is a multi-ethnic city-state located in Southeast Asia with a population size of 5.08 million in 2010, consisting of 3.77 million residents and 1.31 million non-residents on employment passes, work permits, student passes and long-term social visit passes (Singapore Department of Statistics, 2010a). The resident population consisted of 74.1% Chinese, 13.4% Malays, 9.2% Indians and 3.3% Others (Singapore Department of Statistics 2010a, p v). Economic development in Singapore has been dramatic since independence from Britain in 1965. For example, per capita gross domestic product has increased 37 fold, from approximately S$1,600 (approximately US$512) in 1965 to S$59,813 (approximately US$47,252) in 2010 (Singapore Department of Statistics, 2010b).

The labour force participation of women age 15 years and older increased from 24.2% in 1965 to 56.5% in 2010 (Ministry of Trade and Industry, 2010). Dual-income families comprised 40% of married couples in 2000 (Teo, 2000). The government introduced the Foreign Domestic Maid Scheme in 1978 to help Singaporean women enter and stay in the workforce. The number of FDWs in Singapore grew from 5,000 in 1978 to 180,000 in 2008 (Reisman, 2009, p 186). Most FDWs in Singapore are live-in maids from Indonesia, the Philippines, Sri Lanka and India. There is no guaranteed minimum wage, and FDWs are excluded from Singapore's Employment Act, which stipulates minimum days off and maximum weekly working hours. As Ochiai (2010, pp 16-17) pointed out, 'in some societies like Singapore and Taiwan, families purchase care services from the market'.

Despite the normative acceptance of FDWs in Singapore, and the relatively cheap cost of FDWs as providers of childcare, Singapore has experienced rapidly declining fertility rates. Fertility fell below replacement level in 1977, and has remained there; it was reported to be 1.16 children per resident female in 2010 (Li, 2011). Detailed descriptions and discussions of various aspects of Singapore's population policies that encourage its citizens to get married and have more children can be found in Sun (2009, 2010, 2012). Two policy provisions – maid-levy subsidies and grandparent caregiver tax relief – are particularly relevant to the state's mobilisation of grandparents and foreign domestic helpers for the purpose of childcare:

- Maid-levy subsidies: maid-levy tax relief was introduced for working mothers in 1987; the amount of the levy was reduced in 2004 from S$345 to S$250 (or US$259 to US$188) per month and this reduced amount remained in force at the time of writing in 2011.
- Grandparent caregiver tax relief: since 2004, working mothers have been able to claim annual tax relief of S$3,000 (approximately US$2,250) if their parents or parents-in-law look after their children under 12 years old. This remained in force at the time of writing in 2011.

Finally, persistent below-replacement fertility is associated with a rapidly ageing society. According to a United Nations (2002, p 14) report:

> By the year 2030, the two oldest Asian countries will be Singapore and Japan. Japan can expect 28% of its population to be aged 65 and above in the year 2030, whereas Singapore will have at least 19% of its population above the age of 65 by the year 2030.

Methods and data collection

This chapter focuses on attitudes towards the ideal caregiver for children under three years old, using data derived from a research project funded by the Singaporean Ministry of Education titled Multi-level Analysis of the Impact of State Population Policies on Birth Rates in Singapore since 1987. Snowball sampling facilitated access to respondents through existing networks with built-in trust. It was considered an appropriate sampling strategy, since previous research has found that Singaporeans treat childbearing as a 'private' and 'personal' decision (Graham, 1995; Teo and Yeoh, 1999). Eleven senior university students (seven Singaporean-Chinese, two Singaporean-Indians and two Singaporean-Malays) were trained in interviewing techniques. Each research assistant then contacted 15 interviewees who were women of childbearing age, the target group for Singaporean population policies.

During the first stage, these research assistants conducted semi-structured interviews with 165 women. Among the interviewees,

51 were married and 114 were unmarried (most in the 19-24 age group), as the larger project also explored the younger generation's knowledge and attitudes toward state pronatalist policies. Interviews were conducted in English, Malay or Tamil, based on respondents' preference. The length of interviews was usually 30–45 minutes. Each interview was recorded on tape and transcribed (and translated where necessary) verbatim.

The second stage involved focus groups with participants nominated by women in the first stage as individuals who had had or who would have a significant influence on their own childbearing decision making. These focus groups were conducted with individual women, their significant others and their parents or parents-in-law. A total of 39 focus groups were conducted either in respondents' homes or an interview room at the author's university workplace. Length of discussions was usually 60–90 minutes.

Within the 'snowball sampling' strategy, the approach included 'quota sampling' according to two criteria. First, to ensure ethnic minority groups' representation, the minimum number of respondents from the Singaporean-Indian and Singaporean-Malay communities was set at 30. Numbers of respondents from these two communities eventually exceeded the minimum requirement. Second, the sample reflected the national profile according to monthly household income level. Between 20 and 30% of employed households had monthly incomes below S$3,000 (low income), and 20 to 30% had monthly household incomes above S$8,000 (high income) in 2006 and 2007 (Singapore Department of Statistics, 2009). All interviewee names are pseudonyms. Married interviewees are referred to as 'Mr' or 'Mrs' and unmarried interviewees are referred to by first names.

'Assumed' consensual solidarity and normative solidarity between the (prospective) parental generation and grandparent generation

As highlighted above, consensual solidarity refers to 'agreement in opinions, values, and orientations between generations', while normative solidarity refers to 'expectations regarding filial obligations and parental obligations' (Bengston and Oyama, 2007, p 8). This section discusses 'assumed' consensual solidarity concerning opinions and values about seeking grandparental childcare as women's labour force participation becomes the norm in Singapore, by drawing on data primarily from the younger generation (age 19-24). Consistent with previous research (Wheelock and Jones, 2002; Sun, 2008; Sarti,

2010), the recurrent theme is that the younger generation believed that grandparents in Singapore should be called on to provide nurturing and caretaking functions because, first, childcare is collectively understood as a task that requires trust, and is given to grandparents who are seen as the most trustworthy caregivers, and second, because grandparents are seen as transmitters of family values. For instance, when the interviewer asked, 'For children up to three years old, who do you think is best to look after them? Would it be yourself? Your husband or partner? Your parents? Your parents-in-law? Other relatives? A maid, nanny, babysitter, or other paid help? A daycare centre? Or any others?', Agnes (age 21, Chinese, S$3,000–3,999 monthly household income) replied:

> 'My ambition is that even when I have kids I want to continue working. So, my parents, I trust their expertise because they [brought] me up to who I am today, I believe they have the skills.…And moreover I wouldn't be thinking [worrying about] my maid running away with my child or my babysitter feeding him the wrong stuff. [As for] my parents, why wouldn't I trust them?'

Hui Lin (age 21, Chinese, female, S$10,000 and over) said:

> 'It depends on different needs of the child, for example, maybe educational wise, I may not know what a two-year-old child should learn, but if you're talking about the normal moral things, I think teaching them myself or with my parents will be very good already.'

Similarly, in a focus-group discussion among young male unmarried participants, when asked why there would be childcare difficulties, despite the common practice of employing foreign domestic workers, one group member replied:

> 'Domestic helpers can be there to help out, but somebody that I trust [would have to be there], mainly because I don't trust a domestic helper.' (Chee Keong, age 24, Chinese, male, S$10,000 and over)

In terms of 'normative solidarity,' grandparents are expected to support their adult children's paid employment by providing them with childcare assistance. In a group discussion, Wee Leong (age 25, Chinese, S$6,000–6,999) thought his parents 'should' help:

Moderator: 'Who are you going to turn to for support?'

Wee Leong: 'Relatives. Parents.'

Moderator: 'Why should they help you?'

Wee Leong: 'They should, right? Because I am their child, right?'

Indeed, the pattern of assuming grandparental childcare could be seen in most of the focus-group discussions. Siew Cheng (age 22, Chinese, S$5,000-5,999) had 'not really talked to' her parents, but noted in her exchange with Albert (age 24, Chinese, S$2,000-2,999) that her parents would not mind providing support:

Siew Cheng: 'I mean, there's always our parents …'

Albert: 'Then it will become a burden for them instead of a burden for you.'

Siew Cheng: 'No, they might like to take care of grandkids.'

Moderator: 'You talked to them already?'

Siew Cheng: 'I have not really talked to them about it. But they did mention that they don't mind taking care of my kids, but I think it's just in the day, of course at night, I have to take them home.'

Similarly, Mei Ling (age 23, Chinese, female, S$9,000-9,999) and Kenneth (age 23, Chinese, S$9,000-9,999) had not had any discussions with their parents about needing help with childcare; however, both seemed confident that they would receive such help when they needed it:

Mei Ling: 'The best case would be if I've a relative to take care of the child.'

Moderator: 'Do you have someone in mind?'

Mei Ling: 'My mum.'

Moderator: 'Have you talked about this?'

Mei Ling: 'That's what I feel, but I also feel that it's important to have both parents working because I would want to provide the best for my child, at least materially.'

Kenneth: 'Yes, I think that, in today's society, you need some kind of help, from our parents. I would prefer our parents, their grandparents taking care of them.'

Moderator: 'Have you talked to them [parents] about this?'

Kenneth: 'No, but I think they're ready.'

It is not uncommon for young unmarried interviewees to presume that their parents will help in the event that they have children. For example, when asked how they planned to balance their paid employment and future childcare responsibilities, a typical answer was to rely on their own parents. Furthermore, such 'assumed' solidarity became manifest in the process of deciding *when* to have children. The following draws on married participants talking retrospectively about taking into account whether they would receive childcare help from their parents when making their own childbearing decisions. For example, Mrs Lee (age 36, Chinese, S$10,000 and over) pointed out that her mother's childcare help was a key factor in deciding when to have children:

'So, to start the family, you have to save up. You have to think through, plan and think; what is good is at least, for me, [is] that sometimes my mom can help look after the child, the baby.'

Similarly, in a conversation with Mrs Majid and some of her family members (age 28, Malay, S$5,000–5,999), she explained that she would 'ask permission' first to see if her mother was ready to take care of a second child before she proceeded to have that child:

'Right now, my mother will tell me, "You shouldn't have a second one yet". My mother is not ready to take care of a second one. Even among friends … they'll ask their parents whether they're willing to take care of another one [before] then they'll have the second one. Maybe because among my friends we don't use a maid. We use our parents.'

In summary, young interviewees and participants from different socioeconomic classes and ethnic backgrounds believed that childcare provided by their parents (primarily mothers and mothers-in-law) remained preferable to childcare by FDWs because of issues of trust and the normative expectation of parental obligations. Moreover, the younger generation presumes that such requests for help will be honoured if they do have children. Finally, married respondents indicated that their own normative expectations about how much help their parents would provide actually influenced their childbearing decisions.

Negotiating solidarity: grandparents as moral guardians

As Connidis and McMullin (2002, p 562) pointed out, 'in daily life, [ambivalence] is resolved not merely by choosing between roles but also by redefining them'. This section suggests that some families employ FDWs to resolve contradictions between the grandmother's desire to care for their grandchildren and the restrictions they face with their own paid employment and/or limited physical abilities. For married respondents who were already receiving childcare help from parents or parents-in-law, the most prominent finding was that grandparents tend to care for grandchildren *together with* foreign domestic helpers, as the following examples illustrate. First, for example, during a focus-group discussion, Mr and Mrs Ramasamy (both in their late 40s, Indian, S$10,000 and over, taking care of their grandchildren in a three-generation household) stated:

> Mrs Ramasamy: 'They [their children] are working couples, and we would like them [grandchildren] to be here; we have a maid, so we are happy with her helping us [the daughter pays the maid levy] as well as looking after the three [children].... Now for three kids here, with us, and we are both working still. With a maid, it's manageable. Of course if it is only me, I couldn't manage the three children.'

> Mr Ramasamy: 'The family member to be there together with a maid, and I think the child would be much happier

and grown up [better behaved]. At least the morals will be much there, you know?'

Mrs Ramasamy: 'Our case is a little bit different, because the [grand]children are always with us. Let's say like for most cases, the [grand]children are here on weekdays, and weekends they're brought back by their parents, back home, it will definitely be easier. But we're different, because they are always with us, seven days, 24 hours.'

This exchange contains several important elements also prominent in other interviews and discussions. First, one of the primary reasons for the grandparents to offer grandchild care was to support the younger couples' paid employment and strengthen intergenerational solidarity. Second, the availability of foreign domestic helpers offered significant support to the older generation's desire to help with grandchild care and the younger generation's need for help. Third, it was suggested that the mother (the grandparents' daughter) pay part of the fees for the grandparents to employ a foreign domestic helper. Finally, the grandparents themselves understood their grandchild care to be qualitatively different from childcare provided by domestic helpers – as the grandfather said, 'at least the morals will be much there'.

Indeed, the idea that grandparents can function as moral guardians or supervisors in the nexus of 'market-based yet family-centered' childcare is also evident in focus group discussions with unmarried participants and their parents, in which parents expressed their expectations to offer their daughters childcare help together with a foreign domestic helper:

Mrs Nair: 'The moral support, as parents we have to give. Once she is married, then we can help her to raise the kids right…. She will definitely have a maid. And then we can take care of the child while she is working … why should she stay at home?' (Age 51, Indian, S$5,000-5,999)

Mrs Tan: 'Oh, we will support, in the sense that if she [daughter] can afford it, she will have a maid. Then yes, we'll support in the sense that yes, as grandparents, I'll be there. But not in the physical part of taking care of the grandchild. If in my capacity, I can teach the child, yes.' (Age 51, Chinese, S$3,000-3,999)

These examples illustrate how grandparents would help guide their grandchildren through teaching them moral values (Mrs Nair) or perhaps educate the grandchildren (Mrs Tan).

Like Mr and Mrs Ramasamy's family, discussed earlier, the Khaw family (Mr Khaw, age 30 and Mrs Khaw, age 28, Chinese, S$7,000-7,999) provide an example of the upper-middle-income family's reliance on grandparents and foreign domestic helpers to provide childcare. Indeed, Mrs Khaw eventually left her paid job to fully devote herself to childrearing. In other words, the baby, Nicholas, is cared for by five people – the father (financial provision), the mother (developmental labour), the paternal grandparents (moral labour) and the foreign domestic helper (housework). The following excerpt is from the group discussion with the parental (middle) generation:

> Mr Khaw: 'We don't believe in letting a maid look after the child, or only the grandparent looking after the child. Perhaps [they can] look after the child when the parents are away. But more in the development process, it must be the parent. That's why she [the wife] takes no-pay leave, extended.'

> Moderator: 'You have grandparents right now taking care of Nicholas [grandson]?'

> Mrs Khaw: 'Our parents.'

> Mr Khaw: 'They're actually working. They're here on weekends or at night after they finish work, they come here for dinner. Then they take over the caring for a while, while she [the wife] gets a chance to wash up and bathe.'

In contrast to the maternal grandparental childcare assistance in the Ramasamy family, the Khaw's family practices paternal grandparenting. Moreover, Mr Khaw's mother (the grandmother) wanted to stay in paid employment and helped the younger generation to pay the foreign domestic workers' fees.

> Mr Khaw: 'Actually, we didn't plan to engage a maid. What happened was that I asked whether my mum wants to resign from her work and look after [Nicholas]. She said, given her current income, which can amount to about $3,000 a month, for her age, no one will give her this kind of money

per month. There's no way at 62 anyone will employ her. Rather than she gives up her job, why not we engage a maid? And she will help us with the maid levy.... But the maid is more to cover the household chores than the child caretaking responsibilities.'

Similarly, Mrs Owyong (age 50, Chinese, S$10,000 and over) described how her mother took care of the grandchildren:

'The grandchildren come to her house with the maids and everything.... So, her timetable goes according to the grandchildren's timetable so that her children [Mrs Owyong and her brothers/sisters] are free to carry on with their careers.'

The desire and expectation on the part of grandparents to engage foreign domestic workers is overt and also echoed in the personal interviews with unmarried young women:

Kamariah: 'Just recently, my mum talked to me ... she said ... "Oh ... if you want ... you get a maid, send the child and the maid to my house. I look after. I make sure the maid takes care of the kid, but under my supervision." I don't mind that but, then again, it might be expensive.' (Age 23, Malay, S$2,000-2,999)

Grace: 'My mom said, "I'm not looking after your children ... I mean, I want to be a cool, hip grandma that goes out. It's not like I won't look after them [the grandchildren], I will supervise the maid." So I thought, fine!' (Age 21, Chinese, S$10,000 and over)

In short, unlike Lan's (2002) finding that Taiwanese grandparents are hostile towards engaging FDWs, this study shows that grandparents in Singapore actively expressed the desirability of employing them, sometimes even helping the younger generation to pay for them. This might reflect the different composition of our samples in terms of household income level, as Lan (2002) focused on middle-income households, while the majority of focus-group participants in this sample come from middle, upper-middle and upper-income households. The role of the grandparents and the foreign domestic helper found in this research can be characterised as complementary rather than substitutive.

Existence of functional solidarity and patterns of associational solidarity

Another recurrent theme concerning intergenerational solidarity is that grandchild care is not discouraged by non-co-residence, partly because of good transportation and ease of travel within Singapore. Thus, Siti Isah talked about the prospect of being an evening and weekend ('off-work') parent while relying on the older generation's help while she is in paid employment:

> 'I would rather have my own mother take care of my kids while I work. So I'll probably send my kids to my mother or mother-in-law, then go to work and then fetch them again.' (Age 22, Malay, S$4,000-4,999)

Another feature of relying on non-co-resident grandparents is that parents sometimes undertake their parenting roles only at the weekend. Recall that Mrs Ramasamy remarked: "For most cases, the children are here on weekdays, and weekends they're brought back by their parents, back home". Similarly, Mr Wong (age 27, unmarried, Chinese, S$6,000-6,999) firmly stated: "From Monday to Friday, you surely send the kid back to the mother-in-law". In short, grandparenting may take different forms – co-residence, or caring for grandchildren on a daily, weekend or hourly basis.

Intergenerational (consensual) solidarity may also take the form of an agreement between the parental and the grandparental generation to send the grandchildren to childcare centres, as the following conversation with Mr and Mrs Chong (age 49 and 45 respectively, S$2,000-2,999) and their childless daughter Gim Mei (age 23) illustrates:

> Gim Mei: 'Actually, both of my parents cannot do it. They are too outdated.'

> Mr Chong: 'I accept [agree].'

> Gim Mei: 'The children are educated once they are put into nursery. What can they learn with my parents? They would only learn dialects. I do not mean it is useless, but just that [that] era is over.'

> Mr Chong: 'I agree. If you have lost at the starting point, you will lose.'
>
> Moderator: 'So, who do you want to leave them with?'
>
> Gim Mei: 'The childcare centre.'

In summary, the functional solidarity between the two generations takes different forms. It seems that couples in higher-income households, who have long work hours, tend to leave their children in grandparents' care (in most cases assisted by foreign domestic workers) and only pick them up on the weekends; couples in the middle-income households who hold 9-to-5 jobs tend to pick their children up on a daily basis; and couples in the lower-income households might send their children to a childcare centre because they deem education for their children as particularly important and less educated grandparents were not seen as capable of meeting this requirement.

Ambivalence

While the majority of study participants successfully negotitate intergenerational solidarity, there were also signs of intergenerational ambivalence emerging, for reasons including, but not limited to, cost and availability of appropriate foreign domestic workers, complex co-residence family dynamics, and ageing of the older generation. The focus group with Mr and Mrs Balasingam (both age 34, Indian, S$4,000-4,999) and their friends Mr and Mrs Velayuthan (age 30 and 27 respectively, Indian, S$3,000-3,999) illustrates this ambivalence:

> Moderator: 'You have two kids and they are being taken care of, right? So how do you manage as working parents?'
>
> Mrs Balasingam: 'Get a maid. But like what she [Mrs Velayuthan] said, half my salary went to the maid. She is comfortable in my home. And I was slogging.... So, it came to a point of thinking, who's the maid? But my children were very well taken care of. We had a good maid and she really took care of my kids. Then she left ... we were stranded. So we turned to the next source we had ... the only source we have, parents.'

Mr Balasingam: 'When you get your parents, you get the real Singaporean deal, cheap and good.'

Mrs Balasingam: 'And hope nothing would happen, the child won't fall sick; I go to work, come back and the child is still happy. Grandparents maybe will shower more love and genuine [affection].... But at the back of your mind, you keep thinking, what is best for your kid? Still, who's the best caregiver? You want your grandparents; I mean they are getting old as well.... Do they have the time? Are they able to do it physically?'

Mr Velayuthan: 'Is it fair to them?'

In the discussion above, we see that both the normative assumption and the low financial cost contribute to reliance on grandparental childcare. However, a sense of ambivalence is also apparent. On the one hand, the belief that grandparental childcare comes from love is upheld; on the other hand, there is considerable hesitation due to other factors, such as fairness to the grandparents, what constitutes the best interests of the child, and physical ability of the grandparents. Last but not least, in order to acquire grandparental childcare assistance, Mr and Mrs Balasingam had to move to co-reside with Mr Balasingam's parents, which exacerbated tensions and anxieties between the generations.

In the following focus group extract with unmarried Chinese participants, the younger generation also noticed a change in the degree of willingness of grandparents to treat their childcare assistance as taken for granted. Moreover, one of the participants noted the need to provide financial support for the grandparents themselves. It is also evident that the younger generation do not believe grandparents can meet the intellectual/developmental needs of the grandchild (Hwee Ann, age 21, female, S$2,000-2,999; Hui Lin, age 21, female, S$10,000 and over; Chee Keong, age 24, female, S$10,000 and over):

Hwee Ann: 'I think, in the past, the grandparents would be more than willing, but right now, I think the trend is changing.'

Hui Lin: 'I think mine [her parents] would want to play with the kid only, that's it.'

Moderator: 'But you want them to also take some responsibility when you are working?'

Hwee Ann: 'I feel that it's quite unfair for them also. They should enjoy. It's no longer their responsibility to take care of a kid anymore.'

Chee Keong: 'I think now families have fewer kids, so it's very difficult for the kid to support the parents [the grandparents]. So you cannot expect the grandparents to just sit there and just take care of the kids, they may have their work.'

Hui Lin: 'You have to understand that some grandparents may not be as educated. They may be able to take care of kids, but they may not be able to teach your kids new things or teach your kids to prepare for education in the future.'

In summary, there is an emerging sense of intergenerational ambivalence and some new patterns: the (middle) parental generation (for example, Mr and Mrs Balasingam) and prospective parental generation (for example, Hwee Ann, Chee Keong and Hui Lin), while needing their parents' help with the 'love'-based childcare to enable them to engage in paid employment, are deeply concerned about whether it would be fair for their parents and whether their parents could appropriately handle their grandchildren's developmental and educational needs.

Discussion and conclusion

In this chapter, interview data collected on the topic of best caregiver for children up to three years of age in Singapore lends substantial support to the intergenerational solidarity perspective on intergenerational relations – particularly in the form of 'assumed' consensual solidarity, normative solidarity and functional solidarity. More specifically, the younger generations from various socioeconomic and ethnic backgrounds still idealise and expect childcare assistance from their own parents. Grandparents in Singapore are perceived by the younger generation as a 'regular army' during normal times (characterised as 'mother savers' in Chapter Two), instead of a 'reserve army' to be mobilised under exceptional circumstances. Moreover, grandparents try to offer help, despite their own paid employment and non-co-residence with their adult children.

At the same time, there are signs of intergenerational ambivalence. As Connidis and McMullin (2002, p 567) noted, 'ambivalence is a particularly useful concept when embedded in a theoretical framework that views social structure as structured social relations, and individuals as actors who exercise agency as they negotiate relationships within the constraints of social structure'. In this chapter, intergenerational ambivalence can be seen where, on the one hand, the younger generation prefers a kind of 'trustworthy' childcare assistance from their parents to enable their worry-free paid labour force participation. On the other hand, the younger generation is also concerned with issues of fairness to their parents, the ability of their parents to teach the grandchildren both educationally and morally, and the tensions and anxieties of three-generational co-residence.

Regarding the perspective of the grandparents(-to-be), the chapter shows that the grandparental generation in Singapore is renegotiating the norm of obligation to care for their grandchildren by contracting out part of the grandchildcare to FDWs. This is illustrated by the prospective grandparents' explicit references to employing FDWs to carry out certain caring tasks (for instance, physical care and housework) and to redefine and restrict their own role to 'moral guardians' of the grandchildren or 'supervisors' of the FDWs. Such desires and practices are particularly prominent among higher-income Singaporean families. Moreover, the middle generation tended to ask for childcare assistance from grandmothers, and it was also the grandmothers who appeared to be more ready to offer such help, even though some grandfathers acted alongside the grandmothers. In other words, the gendered patterns of intergenerational support remain more or less traditional in this fast-changing society.

The data presented in this chapter suggest the need to consider to what extent intergenerational solidarity, ambivalence and conflict characterise the relationship between older parents and their adult children in caring for (grand)children, and whether this is primarily a function of the socioeconomic class positions of the families. This chapter has shown that, when family members have resources to travel between their own and family members' homes, and/or to employ a foreign domestic helper, cross-generational cohesion and exchanges of informal support seem sustainable. However, given the very limited data on low-income households in this study, future research is needed to explore what happens when financial resources to employ FDWs are not available, or when grandparental help is only feasible with co-residence. Among lower-income Singaporeans the emerging ideals and practices of grandparenting may differ from those documented in this chapter.

References

Arat-Koc, S. (1989) 'In the privacy of our own home: foreign domestic workers as solution to the crisis in the domestic sphere in Canada', *Studies in Political Economy*, vol 28, no 1, pp 33-58.

Bakan, A.B. and Stasiulis, D. (1997) 'Foreign domestic worker policy in Canada and the social boundaries of modern citizenship', in A. Bakan and D. Stasiulis (eds) *Not one of the family: Foreign domestic workers in Canada*, Toronto: University of Toronto Press, pp 29-52.

Bengtson, V.L. and Oyama, P.S. (2007) 'Intergenerational solidarity: strengthening economic and social ties', Paper presented at the Expert Group Meeting, United Nations Headquarters, New York, 23-25 October, www.un.org/esa/socdev/unyin/documents/egm_unhq_oct07_recommendations.pdf (accessed 4 June 2011).

Bengtson, V.L. and Schrader, S. (1982) 'Parent–child relations', in D. Mangen and W.A. Peterson (eds) *Research instruments in social gerontology*, Minneapolis, MN: University of Minnesota Press, pp 115-86.

Bengtson, V.L, Giarrusso, R., Mabry, J.B. and Silverstein, M. (2002) 'Solidarity, conflict and ambivalence: complementary or competing perspectives on intergenerational relationships?', *Journal of Marriage and Family*, vol 64, no 3, pp 568-76.

Bengtson, V.L, Olander, E.B. and Haddad, A.A. (1976) 'The generation gap and aging family members: toward a conceptual model', in J.E. Gubrium (ed) *Time, roles and self in old age*, New York, NY: Human Sciences Press, pp 237-63.

Clarke, E., Preston, M., Raksin, J. and Bengtson, V.L. (1999) 'Types of conflicts and tensions between older parents and adult children', *The Gerontologist*, vol 39, no 3, pp 261-70.

Cohen, R. (1991) 'Women of color in the white households: coping strategies of live-in domestic workers', *Qualitative Sociology*, vol 14, no 2, pp 197-215.

Colen, S. (1995) '"Like a mother to them": stratified reproduction and West Indian childcare workers and employers in New York', in F.D. Ginsburg and R. Rapp (eds) *Conceiving the new world order: The global politics of reproduction*, Los Angeles, CA: University of California Press, pp 78-102.

Connidis, I.A. and McMullin, J.A. (2002) 'Sociological ambivalence and family ties: a critical perspective', *Journal of Marriage and Family*, vol 64, no 3, pp 558-67.

Graham, E. (1995) 'Singapore in the 1990s: can population policies reverse the demographic transition?', *Applied Geography*, vol 15, no 3, pp 219-32.

Hagestad, G.. (2006) 'Transfers between grandparents and grandchildren: the importance of taking a three-generation perspective', *Zeitschrift fur Familienforschung*, vol 18, no 3, pp S315-332.

Hochschild, A.R. (1993) 'The managed heart', in A.M. Jaggar and P.S. Rothenberg (eds) *Feminist frameworks: Alternative theoretical accounts of the relations between women and men* (2nd edn), New York, NY: McGraw-Hill Companies, pp 328-245.

Katz, R. (2009) 'Intergenerational family relations and life satisfaction among three elderly population groups in transition in the Israeli multi-cultural society', *Journal of Cross-Cultural Gerontology*, vol 24, no 1, pp 77-91.

Lan, P.C. (2002) 'Among women: Filipina domestics and their Taiwanese employers across generations', in B. Ehrenreich and A. Hochschild (eds) *Global woman: Nannies, maids, and sex workers in the new economy*, New York, NY: Metropolitan.

Li, X. (2011) 'Singapore's fertility rate hits record low of 1.16', *The Straits Times*, 18 January, www.straitstimes.com/BreakingNews/Singapore/ Story/STIStory_625319.html (accessed 26 March 2011).

Lin, T.C.T. and Sun, S.H.L. (2010) 'Connection as a form of resisting control: foreign domestic workers' mobile phone use in Singapore', *Media Asia: An Asian Communication Quarterly*, vol 37, no 4, pp 183-92.

Lowenstein, A. and Ogg, J. (2003) *OASIS – old age and autonomy: The role of service systems and intergenerational family solidarity*, Final Report, Haifa, Israel: Center For Research and Study of Aging, University of Haifa.

Luescher, K. and Pillemer, K. (1998) 'Intergenerational ambivalence: a new approach to the study of parent–child relations in later life', *Journal of Marriage and the Family*, vol 60, pp 413-25.

MCYS (Ministry of Community, Youth, and Sports) (1995) 'National survey of senior citizens 1995', www.mcys.gov.sg/MCDSFiles/ Resource/Materials/SC_NationalSurvey1995.pdf (accessed 26 March 2011).

Ministry of Trade and Industry (2010) 'Age-sex specific resident: Labour force participation rates', www.singstat.gov.sg/stats/themes/ economy/ess/aesa26.pdf (accessed 26 March 2011).

Ochiai, E. (2010) 'Reconstruction of intimate and public spheres in Asian modernity: familialism and beyond', *Journal of Intimate and Public Spheres*, vol 1, no 1, pp 2-22.

Reisman, D.A. (2009) *Social policy in an aging society: Age and health in Singapore*, Cheltenham: Edward Elgar Publishing.

Sarti, R. (2010) 'Who cares for me? Grandparents, nannies and babysitters caring for children in contemporary Italy', *Paedagogica Historica*, vol 46, no 6, pp 789-802.

Silverstein, M, Chen, X. and Heller, K. (1996) 'Too much of a good thing? Intergenerational social support and the psychological well-being of older parents', *Journal of Marriage and Family*, vol 58, no 4, pp 970-82.

Singapore Department of Statistics (2009) 'Key household income trends, 2008', www.straitstimes.com/STI/STIMEDIA/pdf/20090120/op-s15.pdf (accessed 26 March 2011).

Singapore Department of Statistics (2010a) 'Census of population 2010. Advance release', www.singstat.gov.sg/pubn/popn/c2010acr.pdf (accessed 26 March 2011).

Singapore Department of Statistics (2010b) 'Key annual indicators', www.singstat.gov.sg/stats/keyind.html (accessed 11 November 2011).

Sun, S.H.L. (2008) 'Not just a business transaction: the logic and limits of grandparental childcare assistance in Taiwan', *Childhood: New Themes in the Sociology of Childhood*, vol 15, no 2, pp 203-24.

Sun, S.H.L. (2009) 'Re-producing citizens: gender, employment, and work–family-balance policies in Singapore', *Journal of Workplace Rights*, vol 14, no 3, pp 351-74.

Sun, S.H.L. (2010) 'From citizen-duty to state-responsibility: globalization and nationhood in Singapore', *New Global Studies*, vol 4, no 3, pp 1-26.

Sun, S.H.L. (2012) *Population policy and reproduction in Singapore: Making future citizens*, London and New York, NY: Routledge.

Teo, E. (2000) 'Singapore 21', www.singapore21.org.sg/speeches_110600.html (accessed 26 March 2011).

Teo, P. and Yeoh, B. (1999) 'Interweaving the public and the private: women's responses to population policy shifts in Singapore', *International Journal of Population Geography*, vol 5, no 2, pp 79-96.

Timonen, V. and Doyle, M. (2010) 'Caring and collaborating across cultures? Migrant care workers' relationships with care recipients, colleagues and employers', *European Journal of Women's Studies*, vol 17, no 1, pp 25-41.

Timonen, V., Doyle, M. and O'Dwyer, C. (2011) '"He really leant on me a lot": parents' perspectives on the provision of support to divorced and separated adult children in Ireland', *Journal of Family Issues*, vol 32, no 12, pp 1-25.

Tronto, J.C. (2002) 'The "nanny" question in feminism', *Hypatia*, vol 17, no 2, pp 34-51.

United Nations (2002) 'Aging in Asia and the Pacific: emerging issues and successful practices', www.unescap.org/esid/psis/publications/spps/10/SPP10.pdf (accessed 26 March 2011).

Wheelock, J. and Jones, K. (2002) 'Grandparents are the next best thing: informal childcare for working parents in urban Britain', *International Journal of Social Policy*, vol 31, no 3, pp 441-63.

Wong, G. (2008) 'Singapore advocacy groups campaign' *The Irrawaddy*, 2 May 2008, www.irrawaddy.org/article.php?art_id=11709 (accessed 3 June 2011).

Yeoh, B., Huang, S. and Gonzalez, J. III. (1999) 'Migrant female domestic workers: debating the economic, social and political impacts in Singapore', *International Migration Review*, vol 33, no 1, pp 114-36.

Part Two
Grandparent identities and agency

SEVEN

Being there yet not interfering: the paradoxes of grandparenting

Vanessa May, Jennifer Mason and Lynda Clarke

Introduction

> 'You can send them [grandchildren] home when you've had enough, but sometimes you don't want to.' (Mrs Wilkinson, grandmother, 74)

Grandparenting is an increasingly common experience (Mann, 2007), and it is also an ambivalent one for many grandparents, as Mrs Wilkinson (pseudonym) indicates. She hints at the pleasures of grandparenting, including a relative freedom from the kinds of responsibilities that parents have for children, but she betrays a sense of regret that she lacks control over the relationship – sometimes 'you don't want to' send them home, but, she implies, *you must*. She also speaks of grandparenting using a form of 'normative talk' that she expects will be familiar to the listener.

This chapter[1] focuses on 'normative talk' about grandparenting. It is based on analysis of 46 interviews conducted with grandparents in the UK, from which we have identified two main cultural norms of grandparenting. There were very high levels of consensus in the study over what grandparents 'should' do, namely 'not interfere' and 'be there'. We explore how these two cultural norms concerning grandparenting resonate in contemporary accounts of what grandparenting is and how it 'should be done'.

We also argue that these 'grandparenting norms' conflict with others that are significant for contemporary grandparents, specifically norms about good parenting, and about the moral value of independence and self-determination. The grandparents interviewed for this study had a keen sense that being a 'good parent' (to their own adult children) should mean allowing them to be independent and thereby 'not interfering', but this could sometimes conflict with their sense of responsibility to their grandchildren. In addition, the character and quantity of 'being there' that was required of grandparents was often determined not by themselves but by their children. This was in clear contradiction with the grandparents' sense that they should be allowed to be independent as well.

Norms like these are moral abstractions that are not straightforwardly translatable into everyday practice, and the conflict that can exist between norms and practices is likely to produce inherent paradoxes in the meaning and experience of contemporary grandparenting. We propose that a focus on ambivalence is a useful way of revealing these paradoxes. The chapter concludes with a discussion of some of the limitations of the data and the analysis, and with suggestions for the development of further work in this area.

Norms, paradoxes and ambivalence

Our analytical approach is to view our interview data as cases of 'normative talk'. This is because one of the ways in which individuals work out the 'fit' between cultural norms and their own everyday experiences is through the narratives they tell of their lives. Family 'roles' in particular are associated with normative assumptions about how people in families 'should' behave, and it is therefore not surprising that people tend to talk about their family life in normative terms (Smart and Neale, 1999; Ribbens McCarthy et al, 2003; May, 2008). We consider such accounts as 'presentations of self' that are often concerned with presenting a *moral* self by telling normative(ly acceptable) narratives of oneself as a grandparent (Goffman, 1959; Green et al, 2006). This is accomplished through appealing to shared cultural understandings by using a well-known language about grandparenting.

However, because people's rather complex lives rarely fit within simple normative prescriptions (expressed as dictums such as 'never interfere' or 'be there'), this telling of normative tales often involves a degree of negotiation between different social norms (May, 2008). In addition, such norms are often vague and abstract to begin with, or '*qualified* guides for action' (Sykes and Matza, 1957, p 666, emphasis in original) rather than categorical imperatives. This means that people have to figure out what a norm means for them in practice given their family circumstances (Finch and Mason, 1993). In doing so, they are marking a moral boundary and identifying themselves as people who are not only fully aware of where the boundary is, but also securely located on the 'right' side of it – that is, presenting themselves as moral actors (May, 2008). However, in the interviews in this study, the grandparents were often ambivalent about the 'fit' between different norms and their own experiences.

Ambivalence as a sociological concept is used to argue that individuals are confronted by conflicting pressures and ideas (Luescher and Pillemer, 1998). It has been used particularly in relation to intergenerational relations between parents and children, as a way of examining how structured sets of social relations are reproduced in interpersonal relationships and how taken-for-granted expectations within families are negotiated (Luescher and Pillemer, 1998; Goldscheider et al, 2001; Connidis and McMullin, 2002). For example, individuals may experience ambivalence when they feel that their ability to exercise agency in how they conduct their relationships is constrained by social structural arrangements (such as socially prescribed roles of 'mother' or 'son').

We employ the concept of ambivalence throughout the chapter because of its capacity to encompass simultaneously occurring negative and positive feelings (for example, resentment and affection, care and control) as well as practices and norms in family relationships. We suggest that such ambivalences abound in the lives of grandparents (see also Smart, 2005), and more generally that ambivalence usefully complicates normative views of family as expressing *either* solidarity *or* conflict, and/or positive *or* negative emotions, because it establishes that these sentiments and practices are frequently concurrent.

The study

This chapter is based on analysis of data from a follow-up interview study conducted in 2000 as part of a larger project on grandparenting funded by the UK Economic and Social Research Council (ESRC) Growing Older Programme (Clarke and Roberts, 2004).[2] Overall, the project involved a survey of 850 grandparents in the Office for National Statistics Omnibus Survey (National Statistics Omnibus Survey, 1999) and 46 more detailed structured interviews with a sub-sample of the national study. Although the follow-up study was successful in gaining a mix of gender, marital status and experience of family breakdown in grandchildren's families, it did not manage to recruit any minority ethnic grandparents. Partly this was because only seven ethnic minority grandparents had participated in the national survey – low ethnic minority response rates are a general problem in surveys. Some interviews were conducted with couples and others with individuals; in total, 23 grandfathers and 38 grandmothers were interviewed. The youngest grandparent was aged 44 and the oldest was

86 years of age – the median age was 65 years. The majority (70%) were retired, 13% were working full-time, 10% part-time, and 7% of the grandparents were unemployed.

The national survey revealed great diversity in the characteristics of grandparents and their families (Clarke and Roberts, 2004). One third of grandparents were below the age of 60, one third were in their sixties and one third were 70 or older. Three quarters (73%) were married or partnered, 30% were working (63% of those under age 60), over one third (38%) had some grandchildren whose parents had separated and a quarter (24%) had step-grandchildren. Six out of 10 (61%) grandparents saw a grandchild at least once a week, but 20% saw them only in the school holidays or less frequently, and 2% never saw their grandchildren.

The follow-up interview study asked a standard set of survey-style questions using a mix of open-ended and pre-coded formats.[3] The focus was primarily on grandparents' views of grandparenting in general, together with gaining more information about their own grandparenting experiences than was possible in the quantitative study. The data set does not include detailed qualitative case study material.

This chapter focuses on *publicly expressed norms about grandparenting* and the ambivalence surrounding these. We begin by examining the tensions expressed by the participants between the norm of 'not interfering' *as a grandparent* on the one hand, and the norms and practices involved in *parenting their own grown-up children* on the other. We have called this the paradox of parenting. We then turn to examine the contradiction between 'being there' and 'having time to oneself', which we have called the paradox of self-determination. Finally, we explore the role that the parents, that is, the adult children of the grandparents interviewed, played in this configuration.

'Not interfering' and the paradox of parenting

The edict that grandparents should 'not interfere' was the most prominent normative theme running through the interview data. In fact, 88% of answers to the direct open-ended question 'What do you think grandparents should and should not do?' mentioned 'not interfering' explicitly, using those very words.[4]

Other studies conducted in Anglo-American societies have also identified this strong social norm of non-interference. For example, Bates notes the existence of an implicit rule that 'grandparents are not to interfere in the lives of grandchildren without an invitation from parents' (2009, p 338). Mann argues that the 'norm of non-interference' is the result of the priority that is given to parent–child relations, and that it entails that 'grandparents must not interfere in the upbringing or the discipline of the child', while 'the involvement of grandparents is largely sanctioned by parents', who 'disfavour a heavily involved and influential role' (2007, p 283). Not surprisingly therefore, the 'involvement' of grandparents is in some families a major source of conflict between parents and grandparents (Hilton and Koperafrye, 2007).

Thus our finding of a very high level of normative (and linguistic) consensus that a good grandparent should 'not interfere' is perhaps in itself not unforeseen. What is, however, particularly noteworthy is that in our study, this finding applied to all grandparents, regardless of socioeconomic and demographic characteristics, including gender and age. While gender and age were found to be characteristics on which grandparents varied in terms of contact with and practical support of grandchildren in the analysis of the quantitative survey (Clarke and Cairns, 2001), these characteristics were not important discriminators in the findings from the follow-up interviews.

Overall, people in the follow-up study were keen to point out that interfering was wrong, and to distance themselves from this practice. Mrs Young's response was typical: "[Grandparents should] not interfere for a start, don't interfere. But always be there" (Grandmother, 70).

Defining what 'interfering' means in practice is a more difficult task. We know that it does not mean that grandparents should not be involved in the lives of their grandchildren because all of those who identified 'not interfering' as important had regular and frequent contact with their grandchildren, with most having some contact every week or daily, and most were involved in providing some kind of practical support.

We also found in the quantitative data that grandparents offered substantial amounts of a variety of supports. For example, 61% of grandparents reported that they had looked after a grandchild under the age of 15 in the daytime, and 55% babysit in the evenings (National Statistics Omnibus Survey, 1999). Over half (52%) of grandparents take grandchildren to activities outside the home and 53% have grandchildren under 15 to stay overnight, while 13% have taken grandchildren under 15 on holidays. Two thirds (65%) of grandparents have given money to grandchildren under 15. Similar findings have emerged from European surveys, which indicate that a large proportion of grandparents provide care for their grandchildren (Lewis et al, 2008; Hank and Buber, 2009). Lewis and colleagues maintain that '[g]randparents (often grandmothers) are a highly significant source of child-care' in most European countries (2008, p 33).

Although there was almost universal agreement that grandparents should not interfere, grandparents in the follow-up study suggested that in practice there were certain circumstances that might make this acceptable. At times of crisis – divorce and separation being the most commonly cited example – some grandparents had stepped in and taken over *major* childcare responsibilities (see also Arthur et al, 2003; Douglas and Ferguson, 2003; Smart, 2005; Tan et al, 2010; see also Chapter Eight in this book). The level of involvement that these grandparents had in their grandchildren's lives would in 'normal' situations perhaps have been seen as 'interfering'.

However, in practice the boundary between being involved and interfering is not self-evident, and it is one that the grandparents in the interview study sometimes had considerable difficulty in negotiating. We suggest that in order to understand why 'not interfering' is simultaneously so important and so difficult, it is important to acknowledge that grandparents are trying to *parent* and grandparent simultaneously. The norms attached to each are not always synonymous, which can result in considerable ambivalence.

A clear norm about the parenting of adult children is that you should allow them to be, indeed facilitate their becoming, both independent and autonomous. Parenting adult children is said to be about a process of 'letting go', while providing the right kind of support to allow them to become independent (Finch and Mason, 1993, 2000; Holdsworth, 2004). As Mrs Smith (76) put it: "They're adults, they've got their lives to lead". For the grandparents in the follow-up study, allowing children to lead their own lives also involved allowing them to bring up their own children in their own way, and recognising the legitimacy of their parental authority. The following interview excerpt illustrates these points:

> Mrs Graham: '[Grandparents should] support their children, maybe give them a little respite, not interfere, because different generations bring up their children differently and it doesn't necessarily mean that whatever's been right for one generation is [right for another].... Kids are brought up differently with each generation and I don't really see that it's really the grandparents' business to interfere. If they've brought up their children in terms of what they think is right and proper, the parents would I think automatically hand on these values to their own children.' (Grandmother, 69)

The interview participants indicated that to 'interfere' is *not the way to parent* one's own children. Mrs Graham elaborates this point by suggesting that grandparents who have brought their children up well would have no need to interfere because good parenting values are passed on through good parenting itself. By 'interfering', grandparents potentially damage their own reputations as good parents, either because good parents should not interfere, or because if they had brought their own children up well they would not need to. There was general consensus about this among the grandparents interviewed.

At times, however, this norm of good parenting (of adult children) can come into conflict with grandparents' sense *as grandparents* of some responsibility for descendant generations, which might push them towards 'interfering' in the upbringing of their grandchildren. Given their long-term experience of (successfully) parenting their own children, grandparents generally have a first-hand sense of what works in parenting, as well as what does damage, and what makes no difference. We therefore suggest that in order to understand both the strength and the ambivalence in grandparenting norms we have to keep parenting firmly in the frame.

We now discuss the other key grandparenting norm, that of 'being there', and its uneasy relationship with general contemporary norms of independence and self-determination both for older people and their adult children.

'Being there' and the paradox of self-determination

In the last section, we quoted Mrs Young on the importance of 'not interfering'. She finished the sentence with the words 'but always be there'. 'Being there' is the normative companion – we might even say the 'caring face' – of 'not interfering', and was the other central norm of grandparenting to emerge from the follow-up study; it was evoked in 86% of the interviews. The 'being there' response also applied regardless of socioeconomic and demographic characteristics including gender and age, although there were some differences in terms of what it meant in practice.

Being there evokes the image of a grandparent waiting in the wings, at the ready to be called on for practical, emotional or financial support when the time is right for the parents and grandchildren, and in that sense it is an 'other-orientated' concept. Normatively, it establishes that 'not interfering' is nothing to do with a lack of love or interest but rather than the grandparent who 'is there' is someone who is constant and supportive, but does not make 'unreasonable' demands or initiate contact 'out of turn'. 'Being there', along with 'not interfering', is thus a highly passive norm. Yet at the same time, grandparents in this study evoked the ideal of each individual (themselves and their offspring) as self-determining and 'independent'.

There is much debate around the idea of individual life projects and specifically about how that can be reconciled with the connectivity and relatedness of people's lives (Jamieson, 1999; Mason, 2004; Brannen and Nilsen, 2005). However, most theorists would agree that a capacity for self-determination, including both a sense of personal agency and a willingness to take responsibility for one's own actions, has come to be seen as a morally desirable component of personhood (Ribbens McCarthy et al, 2003; McNay, 2004; Brannen and Nilsen, 2005). In her overview of research in the US, Lye (1996) found that the conflicting norms of obligation and independence must be delicately balanced in intergenerational relationships. In our study, we found that the ambivalence some grandparents were expressing was the result of a conflict between normative expectations of what a grandparent 'should' do and their own wish to determine their lives in an autonomous fashion. For example, Mrs Hampson talks about having other interests beyond her grandchildren that she would like to be able pursue *at a time of her choosing*:

> 'I think my son took, not took advantage, but I think he thinks I'm the nanny so I'll have him [grandson], but I do, now I do say "no" at times because I do get really tired and I think I'm not just here, although I love them, I feel as though I'm not here for them all the time. Although I don't go out, I mean I'm not one for partying or anything like that, but I've got other interests, I like reading and, but it is very tiring, it does tire me out.' (Grandmother, 51)

Indeed, the grandparents in the follow-up study tended to portray their lives in terms of choosing how to conduct family relationships, being responsible for their own lives and not expecting their adult children to take on too many responsibilities for caring for them as they aged. At the same time, they viewed their children as independent adults who should only expect a certain level of support from the grandparents. Banks (2009) suggests that perhaps the dictum 'I do not want to interfere' could also be interpreted as 'a veiled statement that they [grandparents] prefer their offspring to be less enmeshed in the grandparents' personal day-to-day lives' (Banks, 2009, p 186). Indeed, the grandparents in Banks' study seemed concerned that they would be asked to take 'too much' responsibility for the lives of their children and grandchildren.

In emphasising the significance of a norm of self-determination, we are not suggesting that grandparents wanted little or no involvement in their grandchildren's lives. As pointed out earlier, the majority of grandparents saw at least some of their grandchildren weekly, and most were involved in providing practical support. Furthermore, in the Omnibus survey, 94% of respondents agreed with the statement 'my grandchildren are a very rewarding part of my life' (National Statistics Omnibus Survey, 1999). But the norm of 'being there' is at odds with current notions of identity as self-determining and autonomous and the passivity required of a grandparent who 'is there' and does not 'interfere' does not sit comfortably with the agentic individual who shapes her or his own relationships (see also Chapter Eight in this volume). Reconciling these opposing norms requires a negotiation between relationality and independence, as well as balancing one's own needs and wishes with those of different family members. These various pushes and pulls can often compete with each other, sometimes requiring grandparents to make a choice between, for example, offering regular childcare support or developing their own interests and activities.

Unsurprisingly therefore, although the ideal of 'being there' sounds laudable and positive, it did pose a problem to the grandparents in this study and they were ambivalent about it (compare Douglas and Ferguson, 2003). Some felt that they were not expected to 'be there' according to their own wishes, but as a reserve and a childcare repository, to be called on when required by the parents. Thus, although the grandparents almost unanimously gave support to the sentiment that a 'good' grandparent should 'be there' for their children and grandchildren, they did express some resentment over the expectation that they relinquish their self-determination and there was no small degree of ambivalence when talking of specific relationships and situations. For example, the Murphys were circumspect when discussing the impact that their grandchildren's frequent, practically daily, visits had on how they experienced their own home:

> Interviewer: 'Do you think that being a grandparent has changed your life in any way, good or bad?'
>
> Mrs Murphy: 'It's difficult to say. Well it's only changed in that the house isn't our own, it isn't, let's be honest, it isn't, because one or the other of them is always in or out.'

Mr Murphy: 'There's more work for you [wife] isn't there? Because you know, if they're here, she's got to get some food.'

Mrs Murphy: 'Sometimes Tom [grandson] will bring in two boys with him and they all want food and drink' (laughs).

Mr Murphy: 'Oh yes.'

Mrs Murphy: 'Yes that is nothing unusual, oh yes, and he [grandson] knows that's alright, so, you know.' (Grandmother and grandfather, 65 and 67)

The ambivalence the Murphys experienced was the result of their lack of control over their own space and time. This affected each of them differently, with Mrs Murphy shouldering more of the domestic responsibilities, as most of the women in the follow-up study tended to do. The gendered relations of domestic space in later life, taken together with grandmothers' greater involvement in practical and childcare support for their grandchildren, means that the practices involved in 'being there', as well as ambivalence arising from contradictory norms, are themselves likely to be gendered (see also Mason, 1990).

In seven of the interviews (involving three men and six women), grandparents talked of the importance of 'having time to oneself' or of not always being 'on call', which in some ways conflicted with the norm of 'being there', and this was the source of some ambivalence. The strong theme in these interviews was that grandparents felt they had already brought up one generation of children and had fulfilled their duty. They were willing to offer occasional support but did not want to be relied on in a routine fashion or to 'be there' unequivocally. Some grandparents who were in employment felt they deserved free time to themselves without extra responsibilities (see also Chapter Four). Others, who were retired, felt they wanted to enjoy their retirement, something they felt they had earned by bringing up their own children and working all their adult lives. However, the follow-up interview data and other research indicate that this ideal is not easily reached, particularly for women who continue to carry the main responsibility for domestic work (Arber and Ginn, 1991).

Parents as gatekeepers

Overall, the grandparents tended to present their involvement with their grandchildren as dependent on what the parents wanted and needed, and their accounts suggested that they did not exhibit a high degree of self-determination in this respect, even where they had very frequent contact. Tan and colleagues (2010, p 996) found similarly in a study of grandparenting in the US that parents act as gatekeepers, largely determining the nature and frequency of contact with grandchildren. In addition, the better the relationship between the parents and the grandparents, the more the parents encouraged their children to be involved with their grandparents – with the result that in these families, contact between grandparents and grandchildren was more frequent and the emotional relationship was stronger (Tan et al, 2010).

The grandparents in our study who played a significant role in the lives of their grandchildren by looking after them regularly expressed an awareness that because this involved making decisions about their grandchildren's lives, such as what they should eat, this could in the future be interpreted as 'interfering'. This in turn might risk jeopardising the quality of their relationships with their own children as well as their grandchildren and other relatives. The ultimate sanction for interfering too much, which several grandparents told us they were keenly aware of, would be that their children would break off contact with them, or between them and the grandchildren. For example, Mrs Elliott looked after her granddaughter on a regular basis but still did not feel she had a guaranteed right of access to her:

> Mrs Elliott: 'I mean, I've had to grovel to [daughter] before when I know I've been right. But I've had to do because I've always had the fear that …'

> Interviewer: 'You've had to grovel to see [granddaughter]?'

> Mrs Elliott: 'Well, not to see [granddaughter] but I've had the fear that if I hadn't grovelled that day then she might have done that, because I think [daughter] would sometimes, when she's really, really piggy [obstinate] she would stop me…'

> Interviewer: 'But you have to keep on her good side.'

> Mrs Elliott: 'Yes.'

Interviewer: 'That's terrible; it's like a power relationship.'

Mrs Elliott: 'Yes, it's awful, I can't believe it. I mean, being a grandparent is a privilege, but it's not something you should have to grovel for.' (Grandmother, 56)

The fact that Mrs Elliott talks about '*grovelling*' to sustain a relationship with her granddaughter that her daughter could potentially put a stop to at any moment is particularly significant when it is revealed that she looks after her granddaughter six days a week (see Chapter Eight for a case study of paternal grandparents who were heavily involved in childcare and felt they needed to do this in order to secure contact with their grandchild). She describes a situation that she feels is dependent on the mother's approval, apparently almost on a daily basis, despite the fact that she offers regular childcare. This is why Mrs Elliott feels she needs to keep on her daughter's good side, which she clearly resents. The situation was particularly sensitive because Mrs Elliott explained that although she is not close to her daughter, she feels (sometimes uncomfortably) almost a parent to her granddaughter.

That the quality of the relationship grandparents had with their grandchildren was largely dependent on how good their relationship was with the parents was particularly evident in cases where the parents had separated and the grandchildren lived with the interviewees' ex-daughter-in-law, and we see some differences between maternal and paternal grandparents here. The quantitative results showed that, overall, grandparents had less contact with a son's children than with a daughter's children. Also other studies in both the UK and the US have found that maternal grandparents (particularly grandmothers) have more frequent contact with their grandchildren (Mills et al, 2001; Tan et al, 2010) and are more likely to provide care and less likely to experience disruptions of contact than paternal grandparents are (Drew and Silverstein, 2007; Banks, 2009; Hank and Buber, 2009; see also Chapter Eleven).

These differences between maternal and paternal grandparents were even more pronounced in our study if the parents were separated or divorced (compare Douglas and Ferguson, 2003; Smart, 2004). Hilton and Koperafrye (2007) suggest that this is because mothers are more likely to be the residential parent and are also more likely to have contact with their own parents than with their former in-laws after a divorce. Consequently, grandchildren whose parents are divorced are likely to see more of their maternal than their paternal grandparents. The interviews in the present study shed some more light on this matter. Where the grandparents and the residential parent had no relationship, the grandparents also tended to have no relationship with the grandchildren. At the other extreme, some paternal grandparents continued to have a close relationship with their grandchildren, almost stepping in to take the role of the non-residential parent, as in the case of the Murphys (see also Finch and Mason, 1990). The following excerpt indicates that the Murphys to some extent saw their initial decision to provide support to the grandchildren and their ex-daughter-in-law as atoning for the 'sins' of their son (compare the compensatory behaviour of grandparents discussed in Chapter Eight). However, this set in train a relationship involving regular and routine support, about which they now felt ambivalent:

> Mr Murphy: 'I mean, I suppose we've had so much [to do] with the grandchildren because of what [our son] did.'

> Mrs Murphy: 'Yes, when he left his wife and she had two young, a baby and a little boy, so we were there all those years really for them.'

> Mr Murphy: 'Yes, I mean, really she didn't have, well, she was left with nothing and we were fortunate that we were able to do it, and we did it. I think sometimes she thinks we're here to do everything, that's what I think.'

> Interviewer: 'Oh, you mean she thinks that you should be responsible because your son left her?'

> Mrs Murphy: 'Well, it was for a very long time, yes.'

> Mr Murphy: 'For a very long time.'

> Mrs Murphy: 'And it's even a little that way now, I mean, we don't mind the children coming anytime, they always ring up and say, "Can I come and sleep tonight Nanna?" and I'll say, "Yes alright, well mum's going out is it?" But she takes it for granted that we're going to have them and we will, no problem, but she does take it for granted.'

> Mr Murphy: 'If she would ask sometimes, we would never say "no", but I would feel much better, but she doesn't

ask, and she doesn't tell us a thing, so.' (Grandmother and grandfather, 65 and 67)

Continuing to be close to and offer considerable support to a former daughter-in-law, which could perhaps be regarded as 'out of the ordinary', was not straightforward. On the one hand, the grandparents were pleased to continue to play an important role in the lives of their grandchildren, but on the other, they could complain that the 'ex-in-law' parent expected too much of them (Ribbens McCarthy et al, 2003).

Discussion and conclusion

The interview data that form the basis of this chapter provide us essentially with tales about being a 'good' grandparent, which involves telling normative(ly acceptable) narratives of one's own grandparenting. Two social norms of grandparenting – 'not interfering' and 'being there' – emerged from the interviews with grandparents. While our observations are based on a diverse rather than a statistically representative sample, the ubiquity of these norms in the follow-up interview data, together with the uniform colloquial language in which they were articulated, indicates that they were being referred to as, and assumed to be, culturally familiar norms of considerable authority and applicability.

Although previous studies have already identified 'not interfering' and 'being there' as prevalent norms of grandparenting, we argue that the degree of consensus among grandparents in this study over them is worth remarking on for two reasons. First, as we and others before us have noted, grandparenting is not a uniform experience (Kemp, 2007). There is considerable diversity among grandparents, for example in terms of their age, gender, marital and employment status, and in the generational combinations of their children, grandchildren and great-grandchildren, and this diversity was reflected in the sample for the follow-up interview study. There is thus no such thing as a 'typical' grandparent, yet in this study there were at least two agreed norms about what a grandparent should be and do that applied across the different socioeconomic and demographic characteristics. Second, we know that family obligations and responsibilities are not in general governed by such a consensus (Finch and Mason, 1991).

Despite the unanimity with which the grandparents voiced that they should 'be there' yet 'not interfere', these two norms do not always sit comfortably with each other, or with other social norms. We have used the concept of ambivalence to help understand both coexistence and conflict between these norms and others that apply to grandparents, namely norms of good parenting and self-determination. We have suggested that grandparenthood is at the fulcrum of a contradiction between two influential contemporary frameworks of understanding about responsibility for 'the self' – namely one's own 'self', and other people's 'selves'. Crudely put, the first involves the idea that adult individuals are or should be solely responsible for themselves (or their 'selves') and for their actions. The second involves an argument that parents are partially responsible for the 'selves' of their children whose upbringing they influence. Each of these frameworks of understanding has its own history and body of influential expert knowledge as well as popular cultural interpretations and manifestations (Rose, 1996).

The idea of ambivalence has also helped to reveal the relationship between abstract norms and what the grandparents said about the lived reality of family relationships. Given the findings of other research on the negotiated character of family and normative or moral practices, we should perhaps not be surprised that abstract norms are not simply 'applied to' grandparents' relationships with their children and grandchildren (Finch and Mason, 1993; Smart et al, 2001; Ribbens McCarthy et al, 2003; Brannen, 2006). Parents and children clearly have to negotiate their positions over time in relation to these familiar forms of understanding, but, arguably, grandparents (who are simultaneously parents) are in a much more troubling position because of the presence of second- and third-generation descendants, which complicates the picture of who, ultimately, is responsible for whose 'self'. Grandparents in our study expressed a wish to find a balance between allowing their adult children to live their own lives while at the same time caring deeply about how they did so. They talked of the difficulties of feeling some sense of responsibility for, or investment in, how the grandchildren are brought up, while also allowing their adult children to be independent and self-determining.

The issue of the informal childcare provided by grandparents is one that fairly regularly surfaces in public debate in the UK. Representatives of both main political parties have in the past decade suggested they would like to offer grandparents some form of childcare grant, while some local councils encourage grandparents to register as childminders. What policy makers seem to be suggesting is that grandparents could step up to fill the emerging childcare gap as increasing numbers of mothers seek employment outside the home, yet this seems not to take into consideration the reality of grandparents' lives. The grandparents in our study expressed their right to an autonomous and independent existence, rather than being called on when parents need them (see also Chapter Eight).

Although our analysis has begun to tell us about relationships between norms of grandparenting and parenting, and ambivalence about them, we propose that this is only part of the picture. There are two particular ways in which our analysis is limited, which we suggest indicates productive directions for future work. First, our analysis is highly likely to be culturally specific; we cannot say anything about normative understandings among minority ethnic people because none were included in the follow-up study. Yet we know that there are differences in relation to norms of parenting between women of different ethnic origin (see Duncan and Edwards, 1999). It is highly likely that norms of grandparenting, and their conflict or otherwise with norms of parenting, take distinctive shapes and forms for people from different ethnic backgrounds, and in different cultural contexts, and this requires further exploration. The findings of our study also relate specifically to the UK context. It is likely that in, for example, Southern European countries, where family policies as well as normative ideologies about the role of the family (in particular mothers) differ considerably from the UK, grandparents would raise quite different issues and paradoxes in relation to grandparenting (see Chapter Two).

Second, our study could be complemented by analyses of nuances and differences in the experiences and contexts of grandparenting. This would further our understanding of how people relate normative understandings to the realities of their everyday lives, and would enable an exploration of the significance of the salience of different experiences of, for example, social class, ethnicity, age, gender, partnering and so on. It would also allow an exploration of the development over time of specific grandparental relationships, which could contribute to the theorising of relationalities and personal histories in grandparenting. In our view, there is considerable benefit to be gained from a mixed-methods approach to these kinds of questions, to harness the different capabilities of national large-scale surveys, and more qualitative approaches in addressing the complexities and ambivalences of contemporary grandparenting. The study with which we have been involved has taken a small step in this direction, but there is a good deal further to go.

The findings of our study have nevertheless contributed a nuanced understanding of the paradoxes that grandparents experience as they try to find the right balance of 'being there' yet 'not interfering'. We found that this balancing act may lead to a sense of ambivalence, which in turn may be further heightened when these rather passive grandparenting norms conflict with norms around self-determination. First, as 'good' parents who are expected to facilitate the independence of their own adult children, the grandparents in our study questioned how much they should really 'be there'. Second, the grandparents also felt a sense of ambivalence around the fact that they themselves lacked a degree of self-determination in their relationship with their grandchildren, which was largely mediated by the parents. In addition, they experienced a paradox between the norm expecting them to 'be there' (as much as the parents needed) and their wish to lead independent lives.

We have also suggested that, in order to understand the apparent strength and ubiquity of these grandparenting norms, we need to keep parent–adult child relationships and cultural understandings of what is important in these relationships firmly in the frame. Although we have identified an uneasy fit between different sets of norms, as well as between norms and everyday practices, we have also suggested that this is a situation that grandparents can readily speak about and that they live with routinely. Ambivalence is a productive concept in the analysis of such relationships because it allows us to conceptualise this kind of routine discordance as part of ordinary family lives.

Notes

[1] The authors are grateful for permission to publish this chapter, which is a revised and updated version of the following article published in *Sociological Review*: Mason, J., May, V. and Clarke, L. (2007) 'Ambivalence and the paradoxes of grandparenting', *Sociological Review*, vol 55, no 4, pp 687-706.

[2] 'Grandparenthood: its meaning and its contribution to older people's lives', ESRC L480254040, 1999–2002, Lynda Clarke, Ceridwen Roberts, Francis McGlone, Helen Cairns. Jennifer Mason and Vanessa May were not part of the original project team, but conducted a secondary analysis of the data from the follow-up interview study in collaboration with Lynda Clarke.

[3] The interviews were audio-recorded and answers to open-ended questions were transcribed. Cross-sectional thematic and discursive analysis was carried out on a question-by-question basis, and using QSR NVivo. This was supported by more holistic analysis of key cases where sufficient personal data were available.

[4] The small number of alternative answers were not at odds with the sentiment of 'not interfering', but tended to emphasise the idea of 'being there'.

References

Arber, S. and Ginn, J. (1991) *Gender and later life: A sociological analysis of resources and constraints*, London: Sage Publications.

Arthur, S., Snape, D. and Dench, G. (2003) *The moral economy of grandparenting*, London: National Centre for Social Research.

Banks, S.P. (2009) 'Intergenerational ties across borders: grandparenting narratives by expatriate retirees in Mexico', *Journal of Aging Studies*, vol 23, no 3, pp 178-87.

Bates, J.S. (2009) 'Generative grandfathering: a conceptual framework for nurturing grandchildren', *Marriage & Family Review*, vol 45, no 4, pp 331-52.

Brannen, J. (2006) 'Cultures of intergenerational transmission in four-generation families', *Sociological Review*, vol 54, no 1, pp 133-54.

Brannen, J. and Nilsen, A. (2005) 'Individualisation, choice and structure: a discussion of current trends in sociological analysis', *Sociological Review*, vol 53, no 3, pp 412-28.

Clarke, L. and Cairns, H. (2001) 'Grandparents and childcare: the research evidence', in B. Broad (ed) *Kinship care: The placement choice for children and young people*, Lyme Regis: Russell House Publishing.

Clarke, L. and Roberts, C. (2004) 'The meaning of grandparenthood and its contribution to the quality of life of older people', in A. Walker and C. Hagan Hennessy (eds) *Growing older: Quality of life in old age*, Milton Keynes: Open University Press, pp 188-208.

Connidis, I.A. and McMullin, J.A. (2002) 'Sociological ambivalence and family ties: a critical perspective', *Journal of Marriage and Family*, vol 64, no 3, pp 558-67.

Douglas, G. and Ferguson, N. (2003) 'The role of grandparents in divorced families', *International Journal of Law, Policy and the Family*, vol 17, no 1, pp 41-67.

Drew, L.M. and Silverstein, M. (2007) 'Grandparents' psychological well-being after loss of contact with their grandchildren', *Journal of Family Psychology*, vol 21, no 3, pp 372-9.

Duncan, S. and Edwards, R. (1999) *Lone mothers, paid work and gendered moral rationalities*, Basingstoke: Macmillan.

Finch, J. and Mason, J. (1990) 'Divorce, remarriage and family obligations', *Sociological Review*, vol 38, no 2, pp 219-75.

Finch, J. and Mason, J. (1991) 'Obligations of kinship in contemporary Britain: is there normative agreement?', *British Journal of Sociology*, vol 42, no 3, pp 345-67.

Finch, J. and Mason, J. (1993) *Negotiating family responsibilities*, London: Routledge.

Finch, J. and Mason, J. (2000) *Passing on: Kinship and inheritance in England*, London: Routledge.

Goffman, E. (1959) *The presentation of self in everyday life*, New York, NY: Doubleday.

Goldscheider, F.K, Thornton, A. and Yang, L.S. (2001) 'Helping out the kids: expectations about parental support in young adulthood', *Journal of Marriage and Family*, vol 63, no 3, pp 727-40.

Green, G., South, N. and Smith, R. (2006) '"They say that you are a danger but you are not": representations and construction of the moral self in narratives of "dangerous individuals"', *Deviant Behavior*, vol 27, no 3, pp 299-328.

Hank, K. and Buber, I. (2009) 'Grandparents caring for their grandchildren: findings from the 2004 Survey of Health, Ageing and Retirement in Europe', *Journal of Family Issues*, vol 30, no 1, pp 53-73.

Hilton, J.M. and Koperafrye, K. (2007) 'Differences in resources provided by grandparents in single and married parent families', *Journal of Divorce & Remarriage*, vol 47, no 1, pp 33-54.

Holdsworth, C. (2004) 'Family support during the transition out of the parental home in Britain, Spain and Norway', *Sociology*, vol 38, no 5, pp 909-26.

Jamieson, L. (1999) 'Intimacy transformed?: A critical look at the "pure relationship"', *Sociology*, vol 33, no 3, pp 477-94.

Kemp, C.L. (2007) 'Grandparent–grandchild ties: reflections on continuity and change across three generations', *Journal of Family Issues*, vol 28, no 7, pp 855-81.

Lewis, J., Campbell, M. and Huerta, C. (2008) 'Patterns of paid and unpaid work in Western Europe: gender, commodification, preferences and the implications for policy', *Journal of European Social Policy*, vol 18, no 1, pp 21-37.

Luescher, K. and Pillemer, K. (1998) 'Intergenerational ambivalence: a new approach to the study of parent–child relations in later life', *Journal of Marriage and Family*, vol 60, no 2, pp 413-25.

Lye, D.L. (1996) 'Adult child–parent relationships', *Annual Review of Sociology*, vol 22, pp 79-102.

Mann, R. (2007) 'Out of the shadows? Grandfatherhood, age and masculinities', *Journal of Aging Studies*, vol 21, no 4, 281-91.

Mason, J. (1990) 'Reconstructing the public and the private: the home and marriage in later life', in G. Allan and G. Crow (eds) *Home and family*, London: Macmillan, pp 101-21.

Mason, J. (2004) 'Personal narratives, relational selves: residential histories in the living and telling', *Sociological Review*, vol 52, no 2, pp 162-79.

May, V. (2008) 'On being a 'good' mother: the moral presentation of self in written life stories', *Sociology*, vol 42, no 3, pp 470-86.

McNay, L. (2004) 'Agency and experience: gender as a lived relation', in L. Adkins and B. Skeggs (eds) *Feminism after Bourdieu*, Oxford: Blackwell/Sociological Review, pp 175-90.

Mills, T.L, Wakeman, M.A. and Fea, C.B. (2001) 'Adult grandchildren's perceptions of emotional closeness and consensus with their maternal and paternal grandparents', *Journal of Family Issues*, vol 22, no 4, pp 427-55.

National Statistics Omnibus Survey (1999) *Module – Grandparents*, Produced for London School of Hygiene and Tropical Medicine, London: Office for National Statistics.

Ribbens McCarthy, J, Edwards, R. and Gillies, V. (2003) *Making families: Moral tales of parenting and step-parenting*, Durham: sociologypress.

Rose, N. (1996) *Inventing our selves: Psychology, power and personhood*, Cambridge: Cambridge University Press.

Smart, C. (2004) 'Changing landscapes of family life: rethinking divorce', *Social Policy and Society*, vol 3, no 4, pp 401-08.

Smart, C. (2005) 'Textures of family life: further thoughts on change and commitment', *Journal of Social Policy*, vol 34, no 4, pp 541-56.

Smart, C. and Neale, B. (1999) *Family fragments?*, Cambridge: Polity.

Smart, C., Neale, B. and Wade, A. (2001). *The changing experience of childhood: Families and divorce*, Cambridge: Polity.

Sykes, G.M. and Matza, D. (1957) 'Techniques of neutralization: a theory of delinquency', *American Sociological Review*, vol 22, no 6, pp 664-70.

Tan, J.-P., Buchanan, A., Flouri, E., Attar-Schwartz, S. and Griggs, J. (2010) 'Filling the parenting gap? Grandparent involvement with UK adolescents', *Journal of Family Issues*, vol 31, no 7, pp 992-1015.

EIGHT

Grandparental agency after adult children's divorce

Virpi Timonen and Martha Doyle

Introduction

One of the major social changes that have shaped grandparenting in the modern world is the increased incidence of divorce and separation, both among grandparents themselves and among their adult children. In this chapter, we focus on grandparenting in families where members of the middle (or 'intermediate') generation have divorced or separated. Having divorced children is a common experience for older adults in many countries. In the United States, for instance, over half of all parents aged 60 or older with at least one ever-married adult child are estimated to have experienced a child's divorce (Spitze et al, 1994). Grandparents' roles in divorced and separated families range from intensive co-parenting alongside their divorced son or daughter to situations where they experience a drastic reduction or complete withdrawal of contact with grandchildren. Despite this variation, at the aggregate societal level adult children's divorce is associated with growing downward intergenerational transfers from parents to their divorced or separated adult children (Bengtson, 2001).

Johnson (1985, p 91) posits that grandparents are 'constrained by the mandate on the autonomy and privacy of the nuclear family in each generation' and that grandparents' relationships with their grandchildren 'ultimately rest on the wishes of their children and children-in-law'. It follows that the quality of the middle generation's relationship with their own parents and parents-in-law is a powerful determinant of the quality of grandparent– grandchild relationships (Johnson and Barer, 1987; Hodgson, 1992). The grandparent–grandchild relationship is therefore 'mediated' (Gladstone, 1989) or 'derived' (Johnson, 1998, p 188). The power of the middle generation can be accentuated in families following divorce, for instance if the resident parent denies access or makes access to children difficult for the non-resident parent and grandparents. However, Ferguson (2004, p 13) in a study on grandparenting in divorced families in the UK comments that '[t]he view that grandparenting is a mediated or derived role needs to be qualified and refined'.

Existing research literature contains some strong arguments about the position of grandparents following divorce or separation in the intermediate generation. Dench and Ogg (2003, p 107) argue that paternal grandparents' position is 'routinely delicate' and that, with divorce in the middle generation, 'their say' virtually disappears. Paternal grandparents are more likely than maternal grandparents to experience reduction in or loss of contact with grandchildren following divorce or separation in the middle generation (Cherlin and Furstenberg, 1992). This is due to the strengthening of 'the matrifocal bias' (Chan and Elder, 2000) and 'the female tilt in the kinship structure' (Aldous, 1995, p 108) following divorce or separation, brought about by the socialisation of women as kin keepers and the widespread norm of children remaining with their mothers (Johnson, 1998; Ferguson, 2004). Furthermore, Rossi and Rossi (1990) have argued that separated and divorced mothers have a greater developmental stake than fathers in preserving and strengthening their ties with their own parents. Ferguson (2004, p 1) states that '[F]ollowing a divorce, the mother normally becomes the resident parent ... and the paternal grandparent connection is likely to break should *fathers* fail to maintain contact and keep the connection alive' (emphasis added). Gender and lineage (maternal versus paternal) are therefore highlighted in the literature as key variables that influence contact and support provision between (grand)parents and (grand)children following marriage breakdown in the middle generation (Amato and Cheadle, 2005). Grandparents' gender is also important, as grandmothers tend to be more active than grandfathers in the provision of assistance to divorced children, especially daughters (Johnson, 1998).

Ferguson (2004, p 31) argues that 'the nature of the grandparent–grandchild relationship before the break-up of the family is ... an important predictor of the post-divorce relationship' and that 'the evidence of changes in pre- and post-divorce grandparenting is less compelling than the evidence of continuities'. Their study therefore paints a rather static picture where established roles and patterns are carried on through and beyond the relationship breakdown in the middle generation. Johnson (1998, p 196) states that grandparents achieve 'close, rewarding relationships with their grandchildren through their own efforts' but 'do not generally see themselves as operating as free agents'.

Existing research literature has largely overlooked the possibility that (paternal) grandparents may be determined and successful agents in maintaining the connection with their grandchildren following an adult child's divorce. In contrast, the picture that emerges from our research is considerably more dynamic and indicative of considerable grandparental agency. We argue that grandparents can not only proactively sustain and regenerate the connection between themselves and their grandchildren but also keep alive the link between the middle and grandchild generations of their family (Doyle et al, 2010). Phrasing this argument in more general terms, we posit that grandparents can be influential and strategic agents who actively shape their relationship with grandchildren and with both former and remaining kin.

Some of the existing literature on grandparents does flag their actual and potential agency. It has been argued that grandparents can 'serve as a catalyst for wider family cohesion' (Hagestad, 1985); that they may mediate disagreements between their children and grandchildren (Ross et al, 2003); that 'paternal grandparents sometimes devise complex strategies to ensure continued contact with noncustodial grandchildren' (Szinovacz, 1998, p 16); and that paternal grandparents may be 'invisible' facilitators who help sons to maintain relationships with their children (Bradshaw et al, 1999). However, we argue that grandparental agency has remained an under-appreciated and under-theorised aspect of grandparenting, and that deeper understanding of agency is central to advancing our understanding of contemporary grandparenting.

The intergenerational solidarity (Bengtson et al, 2002) and ambivalence theories (Luescher and Pillemer, 1998) are widely applied in the literature on intergenerational relations, and are useful in seeking to understand grandparents' experiences in the context of their adult children's separation or divorce (Timonen et al, 2011). The concept of *structural* ambivalence is also useful when seeking to understand the ways in which grandparents respond and feel when their son or daughter undergoes relationship breakdown: 'individuals experience ambivalence when social structural arrangements collide with their attempts to exercise *agency* when negotiating relationships' (Connidis and McMullin, 2002, p 565, emphasis added). The framework developed by Connidis and McMullin is particularly useful as it highlights, to a greater extent than others, the centrality of agency. However, current understanding of how agency manifests itself is very inadequate. This chapter seeks to develop a fuller understanding of grandparental agency by analysing data from a project carried out in Ireland that focused on grandparents' experiences and perceptions at the time of a major status transition (divorce or separation) in their adult children's and grandchildren's lives (see also Timonen et al, 2009, 2011; Doyle et al, 2010).

Highlighting and understanding grandparental agency is important because the existing theoretical frameworks tend to situate grandparents within powerful structural constraints (see Chapter One in this volume). It can therefore be difficult to understand how grandparents make choices and sometimes act in ways that the framework would not 'allow' or predict. The existing theoretical frameworks have a tendency to portray situations as largely static, and grandparents as operating under pressures and forces that push them in the direction of certain behaviours and eliminate the possibility of alternative courses of action or outcomes. Existing theories emphasise lineage and gender on the one hand and the norms and constraints that surround grandparents on the other; thus, existing theories are not well adapted to elucidating choices. This is perhaps a more general problem with the ways in which researchers study older adults: many social gerontological theoretical frameworks construe older people as confined and limited by social and economic structures such as families and their demands and expectations, as well as by social policies and the incentives and disincentives that are imposed on older people by, for instance, pension and benefit systems (Pierce and Timonen, 2010).

There is considerable empirical evidence that maternal grandparents are less likely than paternal grandparents to experience negative changes in their relationship with grandchildren following an adult child's divorce or separation (Ahrons, 2007; Bridges et al, 2007). In seeking to gain a deeper understanding of grandparental agency, this chapter focuses primarily on paternal grandparents within our sample (which contains both maternal and paternal grandparents) because paternal grandparents are generally at a greater disadvantage in families where adult children divorce. Paternal grandparents can be expected to engage in behaviours that are intended to combat that disadvantage, hence yielding greater scope to understand how grandparental agency is enacted. However, we also draw on some examples of maternal grandparents' agency in this chapter. We do *not* wish to argue that paternal grandparents are invariably more strategic or exercise their agency to a greater extent than maternal grandparents do – further research is required to explore the possible differences in the amount and types of agency exercised by maternal and paternal grandparents.

Societal context of the study

Divorce has been possible in Ireland only since 1997. Divorce legislation was passed after a second referendum on divorce that only resulted in a very narrow majority for the pro-divorce campaign. Divorce is a long and highly controlled process in Ireland. Spouses must be able to prove that they have lived apart for at least four years before initiating divorce proceedings. The number of people who have experienced marriage breakdown in Ireland (including separated, divorced and remarried after divorce) increased five-fold between 1986 and 2006 (Lunn et al, 2009). However, in comparison with most Western countries, the divorce rate in Ireland remains low.

Divorced fathers, separated fathers, and members of the extended paternal kin network in Ireland have to live within a policy framework that is arguably very unaccommodating towards them. Fathers who were not married to the mother of their child before the relationship ended are at a particular disadvantage as they have no automatic right to shared custody or even rights to see their children (visiting rights), but rather have to enter protracted and expensive legal proceedings to secure access. Family law and policy in Ireland have not evolved in tandem with the rapidly changing patterns of partnership formation and dissolution, in particular the increased number of children born to parents who are not married, and the increased rate of dissolution of both marital and non-marital unions. Under Irish legislation, grandparents can apply to the courts for access to a grandchild; they have no right to this access, but it can be granted where it is shown to be 'in the best interests of the child' (Timonen et al, 2009, pp 45-7).

Method

The aim of our research was to study the role of grandparents in divorced and separated families in Ireland and obtained funding from the Family Support Agency of Ireland.[1] The focus on interpretations and meanings that grandparents attach to their experiences, in a poorly understood and under-theorised field, led us to adopt a qualitative research approach.[2]

Gender and lineage are highlighted in the literature as key variables that influence contact and support provision between (grand)parents and (grand)children following marriage breakdown in the middle generation (Amato and Cheadle, 2005). These variables were used to guide the sampling and are reflected in the sample composition (Table 8.1). As this was the first study of grandparenting in divorced and separated families in Ireland, we opted to sample for heterogeneity with the aim of gaining a broad understanding of the variety of grandparents' experiences. The 31 participants came from both affluent and deprived areas and ranged in age from early fifties to early eighties. Half of them lived in close proximity to their grandchildren. There was a preponderance of grandmothers in the sample (23 out of 31) due to the difficulty of attracting men to participate in the study. Most of the men were interviewed as part of a couple; six interviews were conducted jointly with both partners in a couple participating; in one case the partners were interviewed separately; and there were 17 individual interviews. The sample contains more paternal (19) than maternal (11) grandparents; we surmise that this is because paternal grandparents in Ireland are somewhat more dissatisfied with their position and hence were more motivated to take part in a study that sought to understand and highlight grandparents' experiences.

Table 8.1: Characteristics of grandparents interviewed: gender and lineage

	Maternal	Paternal	Both*	Total
Grandfathers	2	6	0	8
Grandmothers	9	13	1	23
Total (n =)	11	19	1	31

Note: *One grandmother had a son and a daughter who had experienced relationship breakdown.

We obtained 15 participants with the help of community and support agencies, and interest groups, and after this used newsletters and a newspaper advertisement in *The Irish Times*, which yielded 16 participants. The research team conducted the semi-structured interviews between August and October 2008. The interview guide consisted of open-ended and non-directive questions; respondents were prompted to a minimal degree to follow up interesting or incomplete lines of thought. The interviews ranged from 30 to 120 minutes in duration. All respondents granted permission to audio-record the interviews, which were professionally transcribed. In analysing the data, we applied the grounded theory method (La Rossa, 2005; Corbin and Strauss, 2008). 'Support' was the initial major category that emerged through open coping; axial coding led to deeper understanding of types of support, reasons for providing support and experiences of support provision; and selective coding gave rise to the overarching, core categories of 'compensation', 'boundaries' and 'strategies' as outlined below. These categories were then examined in the light of the literature on grandparenting in divorced and separated families. In the following sections, we have used pseudonyms to ensure anonymity.

Compensation for perceived losses

On the basis of our findings, we argue that in the context of divorce or separation of their adult children, grandparents seek to:

- *compensate* for perceived material and emotional losses that their adult children and grandchildren have experienced;
- *draw boundaries* around the support that they provide in order to compensate for these losses; and
- *develop and implement strategies* aimed at optimising the level of contact with their grandchildren.

We have discussed the first of these (compensation for perceived losses) elsewhere (Doyle et al, 2010; Timonen et al, 2011), so in this section we confine ourselves to a brief outline of what we mean by compensation in order to provide the necessary background to our analysis of the second and third points.

Grandparents seek to compensate for a range of perceived losses in their adult children's and grandchildren's lives following divorce or separation. These include *material* losses and setbacks associated with the loss of the family breadwinner (for daughters) or high expenses associated with legal proceedings and maintenance payments (for sons). *Emotional* losses and setbacks that the grandparents sought to compensate for included the perception that their child had been mistreated by their former spouse or partner, was the victim in the relationship, was emotionally vulnerable, or missing out on normal parental experiences as a result of the divorce or separation. Grandparents also felt that they needed to counteract the material, emotional and social losses experienced by their grandchildren. Monetary gifts towards a wide range of material goods (house, holidays, cars, hobbies) were motivated by the grandparents' desire to enable their adult children and grandchildren to maintain a lifestyle that they had become accustomed to, or were expected to reach, despite the challenges posed by the divorce or separation. Several paternal grandparents compensated for a perceived inadequacy of their sons' parenting skills, or compensated (either periodically or in the long term) for the complete absence of their son in their grandchildren's lives. Some paternal grandparents also felt the duty to compensate for losses that the son had in their view caused for his former partner and children (by, for instance, abdicating from parenting).

We argue that the boundary drawing and strategising outlined earlier are manifestations of grandparental agency, and discuss them in detail below.

Drawing boundaries around support provision

When called on to respond to the distress and needs (for money, housing, emotional support, childcare and advice) generated by their adult child's relationship breakdown, grandparents initially responded largely on the terms of their children and grandchildren (for a more detailed analysis of grandparents' perceptions of different types of support provided, see Timonen et al, 2011). Following their response to the crisis period, grandparents sought to gain greater control over their role and to adjust their involvement to a level that they regarded as manageable and suitable, and also thought it important to encourage their adult children to regain control over their own lives. In our sample, boundary drawing was more evident among grandmothers than grandfathers, which reflects the heavier involvement of grandmothers in grandchild care. Many had become aware of the negative consequences of heavy involvement in co-parenting and decided to pull back from extensive involvement:

> 'For a while I felt I was trying to compensate for their lack of parenting and now I'm not doing that any longer. I've withdrawn from that and I think the danger is that you would get hooked into that role and stay with it.' (Maev, maternal grandmother)

> 'At the very beginning we [respondent and spouse] did plan our lives around it.... If we were going out for dinner, we'd say, "No, we won't, we'll leave it to the weekend, [when the grandchild] is not here." But you can only do that for so long ... now we don't plan our lives around it [any more].' (Sinead, paternal grandmother)

Barbara, a maternal grandmother who had made a decision to reduce her involvement, had been heavily involved in supporting her daughter following divorce, allowing her daughter and her children to move in with her for a period of four years. Her reduction in involvement was motivated both by the increasing support needs of another close family member (her husband) and by determination to have her 'own life':

'I have pulled back a little in the last year. Well, now last year, my husband had a very serious ... operation.... Normally when I'm here I collect the children from school, and feed them and that, but I just said to [daughter] that this year I was going to try and do more for myself.... Talking to friends would be the same, to try and have some time for yourself, because if you do get involved, before you know where you are, you're very involved.... The children when they're older will be off doing their own thing, and you've missed out on your own life and your own friends.' (Barbara, maternal grandmother)

The grandmothers quoted above had reduced their involvement over time, or after some critical juncture or milestone (such as husband's illness or the perception that son had 'learned how to parent'). However, some grandparents signalled that they had *always* drawn a boundary around their involvement:

'I have always said ... if I can't [babysit], I am not going to feel guilty about it and if you ring me say on Friday night, and it suits me, no problem, and if I have plans, my plans have been made and so that is it.' (Alva, paternal grandmother)

'[A] good grandmother would be baking fairy cakes and taking children on expeditions every second week and *I don't do that*.... [Husband] sometimes says – when he gets tired of his beloved grandchildren – "Go home, it's time to go home now."' (emphasis added) (Pearl, paternal grandmother)

However, not all grandmothers found it easy to draw this boundary. Extensive involvement out of line with the grandmother's wishes did sometimes continue, giving rise to varying degrees of exasperation and even resentment that in turn could lead to more determined attempts to regain control of their level of involvement. This pattern was particularly strongly evident in relation to childcare support provided by paternal grandmothers who in many cases struggled to limit their involvement and felt that they had to continue their involvement in order to secure continued access to their grandchildren.

Strategies to optimise level of contact with grandchildren

We now present case studies of three grandparents (one paternal grandparent couple and one paternal grandmother) to illustrate the strategising that grandparents can engage in to optimise level of contact with grandchildren. These cases were selected for in-depth analysis here because they are particularly clear examples of grandparental agency. The fact that all three are paternal grandparents is not meant to imply that only paternal grandparents strategise; but they often have a greater need to strategise in order to ensure contact with grandchildren after divorce in the middle generation. Our later discussion shows that maternal grandparents also strategise and exercise their agency. As will become evident from these examples, strategising can lead to boundary (re)drawing, and tensions between strategising and boundary drawing can easily arise.

Hazel and Tom are paternal grandparents whose son had not been married to his former partner. They had *compensated* strongly for their son's initial lack of parenting skills and 'taught him how to parent'. Although they had been able to *draw the boundary* by reducing their involvement in grandchild care over time as their son gained confidence in parenting, the demands for childcare from the grandchild's mother sometimes became excessive. Despite this, Hazel and Tom continued to provide grandchild care 'on demand' because they felt that this fostered a positive relationship with the child's mother (the custodial parent) and helped to ensure access to their grandchild (for a similar pattern in a maternal grandparent's behaviour see Chapter Seven). Their *strategising* in the interest of maintaining contact with the grandchild is strongly evident in the extract below, and outweighs their evident desire to draw a boundary around involvement in grandchild care:

> Hazel: 'Sometimes when [grandchild's] mum goes away like at weekends, and she travels a fair bit for part of her job, that could be a bit ... touch and go.... In the sense that we would feel that we're imposed upon.'

> Tom: 'We're slightly imposed upon. Yes, oh yes.... At times we would have that feeling.'

> Hazel: 'I suppose we have gone with her because ... we don't confront her too much *because it's a very kind of delicate situation*.... But I think it has been worth it ... I think

[grandchild's mother] feels that we have really been there with her.' (emphasis added)

Tom: 'It has, yeah; it has kept relations good between us.'

Hazel: 'I think it really is now with the new partner there, you know, and as well as that the child is getting older.'

Interviewer: 'Yes, okay. So, you'd be quite aware of the fact then that you should keep relationships with her as positive as possible?'

Tom: 'Oh yeah, very much.'

Hazel and Tom had put considerable effort into keeping their grandchild's mother involved in family festivities. Their kin-keeping motivation was very strong and strategies around how to do this were carefully planned in advance:

Tom: 'This Christmas now I was just thinking, we'll invite herself and [name] her new boyfriend, if he's here. But like I think it's so important ... the more normal....'

Interviewer: 'Okay, so you still keep it within the family as much as you kind of ...'

Hazel: 'Oh yeah. She is family, she is family. She has to be family.'

Tom: 'She's the child's mother.'

This discussion concludes with a strong affirmation of the son's former partner as a member of the family, albeit the tone is somewhat forced ('she *has to be* family') and the centrality of the child is stressed ('she's the *child's mother*'). Hazel and Tom felt that their strategising had paid off as they attributed the relative ease of their own and their son's contact with the (grand)child to their own efforts:

Hazel: 'Oh [son] would be quite lucky, yeah, because I mean access isn't a problem.'

Tom: 'I do think ... that if we didn't have such a close relationship with [son's former partner] that would have been more difficult.... I think we had a kind of a mediation role.... I think we always saw her as a person and I think she liked that.'

Hazel: 'Yes and she is aware, she would be aware of that.'

Tom: 'We always helped her and I think she liked that....'

Hazel: 'I mean we would both find quite often that with her you'd have to bite your tongue, but we have always succeeded and she would see us as being supportive....'

Tom: '*You have to have a vision of where you're going.* You have to have some sort of, now I'm not saying that you're controlling, but you have to kind of know like what's good in a sense for the child ... like the thing about [grandchild's mother] coming to family things.' (emphasis added)

Hazel and Tom acknowledged that they had had to be very compromising and understanding, and exercise great self-control, in the interest of the greater good of their grandchild's wellbeing, and their ongoing contact with the grandchild. They went on to describe the sacrifices that they had made in the interest of 'being there' to support their son and his former partner:

'It [looking after grandchild] certainly would have lowered our quality of life, which we were sort of really looking forward to, as I say travelling and doing a lot of things.... When you retire you expect to have time for each other ... it would have interfered with that to some extent.' (Tom, paternal grandfather)

Another example of very conscious strategising, which was reported as an 'insurance' against future difficulties in access, is found in this account by maternal grandparents whose daughter lived in continental Europe:

'Every time we go over to visit my daughter and the children, we make a point of calling into [ex-son-in-law] in his office and saying, "Hello, how are you?" Absolutely, because we're very aware, and it's very selfish, if anything happens to our daughter, he's going to be the only means of seeing our grandchildren.... I think it's terribly important to stay friendly because I mean if [daughter] is killed in a car crash today, how then are we going to see our granddaughters?' (Clodagh, maternal grandmother)

This strategising may seem far-fetched, but our sample did contain another maternal grandmother who had lost all contact with her grandchildren following the death of her daughter after which the father took the children into his custody.

Other grandparents (for instance, Tara, who had both a separated son and a divorced daughter) had no need to be strategic in this sense because they felt they had already secured adequate contact with their grandchildren:

Interviewer: 'In terms of the relationship now with the [former] son-in-law and your son's ex-partner, what would that be like now? Would you have a relationship with them?'

Tara: 'No, we haven't. We don't see each other at all.'

Interviewer: 'Okay, so it kind of stopped after the break-up.'

Tara: 'It stopped. [But] I didn't care once I had the children.... Once I have access to the children, it doesn't bother me.'

The second case study of strategising and strong grandparental agency is a paternal grandmother, Elsie. Elsie is divorced, in her early sixties and working full time in an office. Her son had moved abroad for a year after his separation:

'And in that year, I made my arrangements with my daughter-in-law ... I asked her if I could see the children. And she said "yes." And she allowed me to see the children every weekend ... it became a more formal arrangement with *me*. So that was fine, but then my son came back. And ... she said that she wouldn't allow me to have ... the children anymore because my son was there and she didn't want their dad seeing the kids.... So she stopped all contact completely.... So, I decided that I would go to court to get my own rights as a grandparent ... so I went to court ... and I got rights ... I would see them once a week every weekend.'

However, Elsie soon started to struggle with drawing a boundary around her involvement, as she discovered that she had to shoulder full responsibility for maintaining contact with her grandson:

> 'I've developed a very good relationship with [son's former partner] and I see [grandchild] once a month ... we have very good ... arrangements, which exclude my son, though.... Now, I'm getting older, I work full time and I'm not really happy with the scenario I have at the moment, which is that my son now has remarried, okay, and has another family and it's almost like I'm responsible for his relationship with this child because he will ring me and he will say to me, "Are you seeing [name of grandson] this week? ... Isn't this the week that you are meant to have him?", and I'd say, "Well, yeah, but I was thinking of maybe doing something different", and he'd say "Well, yeah, but I have it all arranged now, I'm coming up to [name of city]...." So ... he'll still do what he did as a young man, he uses my home.... And ... my other sons and nephews and all meet up that day as well ... so it's a lot for me.... And I'm now getting to the stage where [grandson] now is 12 ... and I'm wondering do I need to be doing this at all.... Is it doing him [grandson] any good, is it doing me any good?...And I am wondering, did I make the right decision?'

Despite her son's lack of initiative, Elsie felt under a lot of pressure from him to maintain a relationship with her grandson, which led to resentment and deteriorating relationship quality with her adult son:

> Elsie: 'There's a lot of pressure on me from my son ... that I *have* to do this.'

> Interviewer: 'And how has that affected your relationship with your son?'

> Elsie: 'Em, well I get angry. I get annoyed with him ... saying to myself ... who does he think he is? He needs to be looking after his own child, his own arrangements.'

Elsie had started to reflect on ways out of the situation, which was a very difficult undertaking because exiting from the role of the facilitator of family contact (kin keeper) was in stark contradiction to everyone's expectations:

> Elsie: 'I've always had a big strong role in the family ... I can't seem to get out of that place, even though I know I'm trying really hard.... My own children is raised now and I'd like my freedom, but it's very difficult to get out ... I don't like being tied down any more.... They get very annoyed with me, all my family ... "Why aren't you a real nanny [granny]?" '

> Interviewer: 'And you don't want to be that?'

> Elsie: 'I don't want to be a real nanny like the way my nanny was years ago. And it's not practical.... I have a job that's quite heavy going and ... I need a break, and I want to keep going, developing myself.'

Elsie is here making a passionate plea to be 'liberated', or to have the courage to free herself from the expectations of grandparenting and other family rituals that take a huge proportion of her leisure time and energy. In addition to reducing her time commitment, Elsie also wanted a different quality of relationship: "I would like to have more quality time, more quality contact with my grandkids". It seems that by 'quality contact' Elsie means both more 'fun' activities outside the family gatherings and more scope for exercising her own choice over when and how the contact takes place. Later on in the interview she made a surprisingly frank statement about having developed an aversion to children. She also reflected on the change that has taken place very recently in the degree of freedom that grandmothers have in Irish society and appeared frustrated that she had not yet mustered the courage to seize it herself:

> 'I'm just sick of kids, I'm sick of looking at them. I hate them now and that's the truth [laughs].... I just can't bear another child now and ... that's affecting now the next ones coming along because that's my daughter's ... dying to have a baby. And I'm saying, "Oh my God, how am I going to drum up enthusiasm for this one?" ... I think that there's more opportunities for grannies nowadays, like I've a lot

more money than my mother ever had in her life. I've a lot more security, a lot more independence. So *I've a lot more choices* than my mother ever had and *I want to use them.*' (emphasis added)

Like Hazel and Tom, Elsie was adamant that her choice to facilitate contact had been crucial, and that in its absence her adult sons would have had no contact at all with their own children:

'I don't think that [sons] would have had any relationship with their children at all ... if I hadn't done what I did ... I don't think they'd even know anything about their children.'

Elsie had first exercised her agency to ensure ongoing contact with her grandchild, and was at the time of the interview seeking to exercise her agency in the other direction, that is, towards reduced involvement. It is therefore important to note that the aim or purpose of agency can shift over time, for instance from greater involvement to reduced involvement. Elsie was also on the cusp of making the stark choice not to invest time and effort into maintaining contact with the other grandchild from her second son who had divorced, despite the fact that this would mean loss of all contact between paternal kin and this grandchild:

'I stepped in there with good intentions, back then, because I was thinking about the grandchild but I'm not sure if I made the right decisions, I'm not sure if I *would* do that again. Actually, I won't do that again, and funnily enough now, I have another. You know I said both my ... other son ... split up ... I don't see that child. Because my son doesn't pick her up. The mother is very willing, but my son is not ... I certainly wouldn't go to the same extremes to see her as I did for the other [grand]child.'

In other words, Elsie was planning to *draw the boundary* in advance to such a degree that she has ruled out engagement in the compensatory behaviour of kin keeping for her second divorced son's child. Elsie's feelings contrast with those of another paternal grandmother who had also been highly strategic in cultivating a good relationship with her son's former partner (primarily by offering flexible childcare) and who was very happy with the result:

'[Son's ex-partner] and I have a great relationship.... She has always been more than.... Any time I wanted the kids, I had the kids.... Her and I go to Spain or go on holidays once a year. I have great input and I hope it's a very positive input.' (Niamh, paternal grandmother)

Strategising can be motivated by the wish to *increase* contact or to *decrease* responsibility – both paternal and maternal grandparents engage in both types of behaviour, but paternal grandparents are more likely to employ strategies that seek to increase contact. Examples of the use of agency and strategising emerged both in situations where the grandparent was determined to ensure continued access to their grandchildren, and in situations where the grandparent wished to reduce involvement. In our sample, grandmothers exercised agency more frequently and explicitly than grandfathers. Most of the complex emotional and practical work involved in negotiating to get access to grandchildren or to set boundaries to involvement was done by grandmothers; grandfathers exercised agency as part of a 'joint strategy' that was led by grandmothers.

In some cases there was no scope at all for strategising in relation to the custodial parent because of extreme animosity between the parties involved. Mary was aware of the impossibility of negotiating access with her son's former girlfriend and consequently directed her efforts at other possible 'gatekeepers' such as the ex-girlfriend's parents, and, when this avenue proved unsuccessful, various organisations helping fathers without access to their children, and, ultimately, the courts:

'[I had a] good relationship [with son's girlfriend] while she was here and just when they broke up she just cut off completely from us altogether.... So I rang her parents ... and they wanted to leave it up to her, what she wanted.... So, there was just no communication at all, she didn't want anything to do with us.... So I went through social services, tried everything, rang places in Dublin even ... I even contacted, we'll say, her social worker ... and they couldn't make her do what she didn't want to do. So, I was just left out of the loop. So then we had to go, well [son] had to go to court ... to actually see [grandchild].' (Mary, paternal grandmother)

However, increasing or decreasing contact was not the only manifestation of agency; our data contained examples of agency used for a multitude of purposes. The use of agency to cease all contact with one's own adult child was very rare and difficult, yet this custodial grandfather felt that it was a step he had to take in the interest of his grandson's and his own wellbeing:

> 'I just hadn't got the energy to give my son anymore, I had to concentrate on [grandson] because I was in hospital and I had to get myself right because of stress, I've two sons at the moment on drugs.... [I am not in contact with my sons, only with my grandson] ... but that's all I want, though.'
> (Alan, paternal grandfather)

There are therefore a range of different manifestations of grandparental agency, which include compensating for losses and disadvantages that follow divorce; affirming a grandchild's position in their kin network; acting as a mediator between the separated couple in order to ensure continued contact with grandchildren; and decisions to reduce involvement or even to cease all contact as in Alan's case.

Discussion and conclusion

The findings in this chapter are consonant with many arguments and theories in the literature on grandparenting, but also give rise to new theorising. Our data are in line with the argument that paternal grandparents experience greater difficulties than maternal grandparents in securing what they see as an adequate level of contact with their grandchildren following divorce (the 'matrilineal advantage' or the 'matrifocal bias' in families). The influence of the middle generation was strongly evident in our data, hence corroborating the parent-as-mediator theory. The grandparents' feelings of affective solidarity; their protective parenting style (manifest in, for instance, frequent phone calls and exhortations to their divorced child's siblings to check that all was well with the divorced child); and unstinting practical support of their adult children lend support to the argument that following a child's divorce some grandparents revert to earlier 'parenting' roles (Gray and Geron, 1995).

Our findings also lead us to formulate the following conclusions that are novel and in some cases run counter to arguments in the existing literature:

- Divorce calls for the reorganising of relationships within families; the extent and manner of grandparents' engagement in this reorganising behaviour is under-appreciated in the existing literature.
- Grandparents seek to actively influence the extent to which they are involved in the lives of their grandchildren and the middle generation following divorce or separation. Grandparents make choices and develop strategies to shape their involvement in the lives of younger generations. Where contact is perceived to be inadequate, grandparents may adopt strategies to increase it and where demands for support are considered excessive, grandparents may seek to adopt strategies to reduce it.
- The importance of the middle generation in influencing the grandparent–grandchild relationship is significant, but not determining. For instance, some grandparents are able to use their agency to forge a positive relationship with their former in-law, the custodial parent (and hence secure adequate contact with their grandchild), even where extreme conflict persists between the separated couple (see also Doyle et al, 2010). Characterising paternal grandparents as 'invisible' facilitators (Bradshaw et al, 1999) in the maintenance of divorced sons' relationship with their children underestimates the very active role that grandparents can play in affirming their grandchildren's position in the kin network; which in turn has important long-term implications for family relationships across the generations. Maternal grandparents also engage in active relationship maintenance, with a view to ensuring ongoing contact with grandchildren and maximising their grandchildren's sense of wellbeing and family cohesion.
- The main motivation for grandparental agency is the wellbeing of and contact with their grandchildren, but agency can also be directed at the grandparent's own wellbeing, for instance where extensive involvement in grandchild care is seen as diminishing opportunities to pursue their own interests and spend time with other people.

Some grandparents make considerable personal sacrifices in order to maintain contact with their grandchildren and to provide different kinds of support to their adult children and grandchildren following divorce or separation. Despite this, grandparents should not be seen as victims or as lacking agency. As Ferguson (2004, p 3) argues, 'the choices that grandparents make about the future path of their own lives do not always sit comfortably with policies aimed at mobilising them nationally as supporters of the wider family', for instance as custodial grandparents, or as providers of childcare.

We hope that further research will uncover and characterise different types of agency, which groups of grandparents are most likely (or free) to exercise agency, and with what results. Among the factors and characteristics that influence grandparental agency, gender is very significant. In most societies, women are still expected to be available to provide (child)care throughout the adult life course, and they are socialised to act as kin keepers; hence grandmothers have a greater need, but perhaps also more ability to exercise agency than grandfathers. Education and wealth interact with gender, and we hypothesise that higher socioeconomic status enhances the ability and willingness of grandparents to exercise agency. Certain characteristics of the post-divorce family also play an important role – age at which the son or daughter divorces or separates, their socioeconomic status, and the quality of the relationship of the separated couple.

Grandparental agency is present but compromised in instances where the adult child's dependence on the grandparent is high, for instance when the adult child is young, economically insecure or has extremely fraught relations with the separated partner. We argue that all grandparents seek autonomy and independence, and the degree to which this can be exercised for those with more dependent adult children tends to increase once stability is achieved in the adult child's life. Boundaries around the extent of involvement in the post-separation family are also dependent on how heavily involved grandparents were during the immediate post-separation period – those who were heavily involved may have to subsequently exert greater agency to regain independence and autonomy.

Notes
[1] The authors acknowledge funding for this study from the Family Support Agency of Ireland; our analysis does not necessarily reflect the views of the agency. We also wish to acknowledge Ciara O'Dwyer's contribution to data collection.

[2] The Research Ethics Approval Committee of the School of Social Work and Social Policy, Trinity College Dublin, granted ethical approval to the project in February 2008.

References
Ahrons, C.R. (2007) 'Family ties after divorce: long-term implications for children', *Family Process*, vol 46, no 1, pp 53-65.
Aldous, J. (1995) 'New views of grandparents in an intergenerational context', *Journal of Family Issues*, vol 16, no 1, pp 104-22.

Amato, P. and Cheadle, J. (2005) 'The long reach of divorce: divorce and child well-being across three generations', *Journal of Marriage and Family*, vol 67, no 1, pp 191-206.

Bengtson, V.L. (2001) 'Beyond the nuclear family: the increasing importance of multigenerational bonds', *Journal of Marriage and Family*, vol 63, no 1, pp 1-16.

Bengtson, V., Giarrusso, R., Mabry, J.B. and Silverstein, M. (2002) 'Solidarity, conflict, and ambivalence: complementary or competing perspectives on intergenerational relationships?', *Journal of Marriage and Family*, vol 64, no 3, pp 568-76.

Bradshaw, J., Stimson, C., Skinner, C. and Williams, J. (1999) *Absent fathers*, New York, NY: Routledge.

Bridges, L.J., Roe, A.E.C., Dunn, J. and O'Connor, T.G. (2007) 'Children's perspectives on their relationships with grandparents following parental separation: a longitudinal study', *Social Development*, vol 16, no 3, pp 539-54.

Chan, C.G. and Elder, G.H. (2000) 'Matrilineal advantage in grandchild-grandparent relations', *The Gerontologist*, vol 40, no 2, pp 179-90.

Cherlin, A.J. and Furstenberg, F.F. (1992) *The new American grandparent*, Cambridge, MA: Harvard University Press.

Connidis, I. and McMullin, J. (2002) 'Sociological ambivalence and family ties: A critical perspective', *Journal of Marriage and Family*, vol 64, no 3, pp 558-567.

Corbin, J. and Strauss, A. (2008) *Basics of qualitative research: Techniques and procedures for developing grounded theory* (3rd edn), London: Sage Publications.

Dench, G. and Ogg, J. (2003) *Grandparenting in Britain: A baseline study* (2nd edn), London: Institute of Community Studies.

Doyle, M., O'Dwyer, C. and Timonen, V. (2010) '"How can you just cut off a whole side of the family and say move on?" The reshaping of paternal grandparent–grandchild relationships following relationship breakdown in the middle generation', *Family Relations*, vol 59, no 5, 587-98.

Ferguson, N. with Douglas, G., Lowe, N., Murch, M. and Robinson, M. (2004) *Grandparenting in divorced families*, Bristol: The Policy Press.

Gladstone, J.W. (1989) 'Grandmother–grandchild contact: the mediating influence of the middle generation following marriage breakdown and remarriage', *Canadian Journal on Aging*, vol 8, no 4, pp 355-65.

Gray, C.A and Geron, S.M. (1995) 'The other sorrow of divorce: the effects on grandparents when their adult children divorce', *Journal of Gerontological Social Work*, vol 23, no 3-4, pp 139-59.

Hagestad, G.O. (1985) 'Continuity and connectedness', in V.L. Bengtson and J.F. Robertson (eds) *Grandparenthood*, Beverly Hills, CA: Sage Publications, pp 27-30.

Hodgson, L.G. (1992) 'Adult grandchildren and their grandparents: the enduring bond', *International Journal of Aging and Human Development*, vol 34, no 3, pp 209-25.

Johnson, C.L. (1985) 'Grandparenting options in divorcing families: an anthropological perspective', in V.L. Bengtson and J.F. Robertson (eds) *Grandparenthood*, Beverly Hills, CA: Sage Publications.

Johnson, C.L. (1998) 'Effects of adult children's divorce on grandparenthood', in M.E. Szinovacz (ed) *Handbook on grandparenthood*, Connecticut, CT: Greenwood Press, pp 184-99.

Johnson, C.L. and Barer, B.M. (1987) 'Marital instability and the changing kinship networks of grandparents', *The Gerontologist*, vol 27, no 3, pp 330-5.

La Rossa, R. (2005) 'Grounded theory method and qualitative research', *Journal of Marriage and Family*, vol 67, no 4, pp 837-57.

Luescher, K. and Pillemer, K. (1998) 'Intergenerational ambivalence: a new approach to the study of parent–child relations in later life', *Journal of Marriage and Family*, vol 60, no 2, pp 413-25.

Lunn, P., Fahey, T. and Hannan, C. (2009) *Family figures: Family dynamics and family types in Ireland, 1986-2006*, Dublin: Economic and Social Research Institute.

Pierce, M. and Timonen, V. (2010) *A discussion paper on theories of ageing and approaches to welfare in Ireland, North and South*, Belfast and Dublin: Centre for Ageing Research and Development in Ireland.

Ross, N., Hill, M., Sweeting, H. and Cunningham-Burley, S. (2003) *Grandparents and teen grandchildren: Exploring intergenerational relationships*, Glasgow: Centre for Research on Families.

Rossi, A.S. and Rossi, P.H. (1990) *Of human bondings: Parent–child relations across the life course*, New York, NY: Aldine de Gruyter.

Spitze, G., Logan, J.R., Deane, G. and Sterne, S. (1994) 'Adult children's divorce and intergenerational relationships', *Journal of Marriage and Family*, vol 56, no 2, pp 279-93.

Szinovacz, M. (1998) 'Grandparent research: past, present, and future', in M.E. Szinovacz (ed) *Handbook on grandparenthood*, Connecticut, CT: Greenwood Press, pp 1-20.

Timonen, V., Doyle, M., O'Dwyer, C. and Moore, E. (2009) *The role of grandparents in divorced and separated families*, Dublin: Family Support Agency.

Timonen, V., Doyle, M. and O'Dwyer, C. (2011) '"He really leant on me a lot": parents' perspectives on the provision of support to divorced and separated adult children in Ireland', *Journal of Family Issues*, vol 32, no 12, pp 1622-46.

NINE

Grandfathering: the construction of new identities and masculinities

Anna Tarrant

Introduction

Men's roles and identities as grandfathers are insufficiently explored in social science literatures (Bates, 2009; Tarrant, 2010). There has been a proliferation of research on fathering and grandparenting in Britain (Clarke and Roberts, 2002; Dench and Ogg, 2002), but this has not resulted in further interest in grandfathers, whose roles, relationships, identities and practices remain inadequately theorised (Mann, 2007). However, some researchers have argued that grandfathers' involvement in the lives of their grandchildren is equal to that of grandmothers (Leeson and Harper, 2009). The gendered nature of earlier research on grandparenting has resulted in men being excluded from most analyses, based on assumptions that they are less interested in family life than women, who are deemed the key kin keepers (Harper, 2005). Despite insufficient attention to grandparent identities more generally (Reitzes and Mutran, 2004), it is evident that being a grandfather influences how men perform and construct their identities in later life (Ando, 2005; Mann, 2007) and that grandfatherhood is an important part of the everyday identities of middle-aged and older men.

Traditional constructions of grandfathering assign essentialist conceptualisations to men that reflect rigid gendered boundaries. Men, for example, have been found to prefer to adopt roles in the family that are task orientated (Hagestad, 1985) as opposed to caring, resulting in expectations that they perform a 'minister of the state', or 'head of the family' role (Roberto et al, 2001). However, recent research suggests that being a grandfather is an identity through which men negotiate multiple and intersecting positions of social difference in their family relationships. Davidson and colleagues (2003, pp 178-9) suggest that:

An important and potentially paradoxical new role for older men is that of grandfather. It is paradoxical because, on the one hand, men may be exhibiting a 'gentler', more nurturing relationship with a grandchild than they had with their own children but, on the other hand, may still be viewed, and view themselves, as having the traditional patriarchal role as 'sage' or 'wise man'.

The influence of generation as a social identity and intergenerational relationships with family members on how men perform grandfather identities has also received limited attention, and existing literature has largely ignored the implications of different societal contexts. In contemporary Britain, men are grandfathering in a social context where divorce and family fragmentation are increasingly prevalent and known to influence grandparent identities and grandparent–grandchild relationships (Uhlenberg and Kirby, 1998; Drew and Smith, 1999; King, 2003). Grandparents play a key role in informal childcare in urban Britain as women's labour market participation has dramatically increased (Wheelock and Jones, 2002) and this is particularly the case in families affected by divorce (Ferguson et al, 2004). Little is known about how these changes shape and influence grandfather involvement with their grandchildren and grandfather identities.

This chapter focuses on men who are grandfathering and includes the stories of men whose families have been affected and restructured by divorce, either their own divorce or the breakdown of their children's relationships. The analysis of the empirical data confirms that men do want to be involved in their grandchildren's lives and this is achieved through various practices. It further reveals that this form and functioning of grandfathering is regulated by the quality and character of intergenerational relationships (as conceptualised by Katz and Lowenstein, 2010), which influences how men perform and construct their identities in a variety of ways. A 'new' identities approach (Fairhurst, 2003) is suggested to make sense of how the contemporary context shapes the familial and intergenerational relationships of men in middle and old age, and gives rise to multiple grandfathering roles and experiences. The chapter therefore focuses on grandfathering, identity construction and masculinities, and the contradictions that some men face in resolving these.

Conceptual framework and method

Existing conceptualisations of grandfathers are limiting; this has prompted the author to develop an alternative conceptual framing. In seeking to understand how grandfathers construct their identities, this chapter applies a unique framework that includes Butler's (1990) theorisations of gender performance and performativity, and intergenerationality, as defined by Hopkins and Pain (2007). The everyday practices that the men engage in reflect how men perform their identities and how this in turn sustains or subverts constructions of masculinity. As Finch (2007, p 76) argues, Butler's 'performativity has more to do with individual identity than with the nature of social interactions'.

Intergenerationality is a concept that is gaining increased interest in social geography and is influencing understandings of identity construction as relational. In geography, however, it has mainly been applied to children and young people and rarely to older generational identities and relationships (Vanderbeck, 2007; Tarrant, 2010) despite the potential of its application. The intergenerationality approach views generation in the same way as social relations such as gender and age, namely as a social identity. It suggests that generational identities (such as being a grandparent) are based on similarity as well as difference (Hopkins and Pain, 2007). This means that being a grandparent is constructed in relation to significant others, typically from different generational groups. While this is important to studies of grandfather identities, intergenerationality also emphasises how these identities are constructed through intergenerational relations. As this chapter argues, this provides the perspective that relationships with other generations influence what men do as grandfathers, and therefore how they construct and perform a variety of new identities (Fairhurst, 2003) and masculinities. Together the concepts of masculinities and intergenerationality constitute a more comprehensive framework for understanding the ways in which men negotiate gendered performativities in grandfatherhood in the context of their intergenerational relations. In order to explore how this is experienced by men, the research analyses how men construct their grandfather identities through their practices and performances of grandfathering.

The study was designed to gain an understanding of how men construct and give meaning to their identities as grandfathers, as well as to gain insight into the social structures within which men are performing their identities and how this shapes their role and involvement. Thirty-one qualitative in-depth interviews were conducted with men living in the Lancaster District area of north-west England. The men were recruited using a variety of methods including direct contact targeted at social groups and local gatekeepers in the local area, and snowballing. The interviews were predominantly conducted in the men's homes, not only so that they could feel more comfortable in their surroundings, but also to allow the researcher to gain richer information and insight into their identities as grandfathers and their personal geographies (Elwood and Martin, 2000). Men's voices as grandfathers are rarely central in grandparent research and assumptions about grandfathers have been made based on the responses of grandmothers, usually as a gendered binary; a questionable practice considering that grandmothers are not a homogenous group about which generalisations can be made.

While the men interviewed for this study were largely middle-class, retired professionals, there is some variation in their demographic profiles and social characteristics. As Table 9.1 shows, the majority of the men had retired from public sector and professional occupations and some were still employed. There was no great variation in ethnicity or ability (although Steve is Jamaican and Charles is visually impaired). There was a range of men of different ages and variation in familial circumstances relating to experiences of divorce and co-habitation, and number of grandchildren. The men's work and family histories, which were discussed during the interviews, were more variable and revealed greater diversity in their personal and familial circumstances than their social and demographic characteristics. Of the 31 participants, at the time of the interviews, 18 were in first marriages (referred to as 'still married'), six had remarried, five were divorced and living with a new partner (referred to as 'co-habiting') and two were widowed. Several of the men also had divorced children. Gerald was an interesting example of a recent grandfather who also had a young daughter from his second marriage, of a similar age to his grandchildren, an increasingly likely scenario for men in contemporary societies (Mann et al, 2009).

The age range of the sample was from 51 to 88, reflecting how grandfathering is increasingly bridging middle age in the UK but is also differentiated by age. The interviews ranged from 30 to 150 minutes in length and each participant granted permission for the conversations to be recorded. Because of the quantity of data generated, Atlas. Ti was used as a management tool and to code the data. The analysis process was iterative in that the interviews were transcribed, and the transcripts then read and re-read to gain familiarity with the data. Through this process, key themes were identified and a coding framework generated and applied.

Table 9.1: Sample characteristics

Pseudonym	Age	Marital status	Occupation
David	86	Still married	Retired engineer
Ted	66	Still married	Retired station foreman
Colin	68	Co-habiting	Retired private sector manager
Steve	51	Co-habiting	Local authority officer
Mervyn	72	Still married	Retired university professor
Duncan	70	Remarried	Retired teacher
Paul	58	Still married	University professor
Sam	51	Still married	University reader
Fred	74	Remarried	Retired (unknown)
Charles	65	Still married	Retired product developer
George	63	Co-habiting	University professor
Arthur	73	Still married	Retired engineer
James	62	Remarried	Retired surveyor
Robert	62	Still married	Part-time administrator
Andrew	70	Co-habiting	Retired teacher
William	88	Still married	Retired teacher
Arnold	65	Still married	Retired teacher
Roger	74	Widowed	Retired (unknown)
Wally	56	Still married	Self-employed
Gerald	63	Remarried	Self-employed
Percy	73	Co-habiting	Retired (unknown)
Reg	66	Still married	Retired teacher
Bill	70	Still married	Retired lawyer
Philip	61	Still married	Retired teacher
Ed	63	Still married	Retired (unknown)
Ray	69	Remarried	Retired psychologist
Jim	71	Still married	Retired sctor
Timothy	70	Still married	Retired garmer
Alan	72	Still married	Retired (unknown)
Peter	65	Remarried	Retired (unknown)
Jonah	84	Widowed	Retired (unknown)

The men's narratives, presented in the next section, are not intended to be representative of the experience of grandfathering as a whole; rather, they provide empirical data that can be used to explore how trends in contemporary Britain, including the increased prevalence of divorce, can influence men's sometimes contradictory performances of their grandfather identities. All of the men were assigned pseudonyms to protect their identities and the names of their family members and any identifiable places were anonymised.

Grandfathering and involvement with grandchildren

Perhaps unsurprisingly, most men's narratives reveal that they want to be involved in the lives of their grandchildren, hence supporting the findings of several recent qualitative studies (Roberto et al, 2001; Ross et al, 2005; Leeson and Harper, 2009). Regardless of familial and personal circumstances, across the sample, the men describe engaging in a range of different practices with their grandchildren that reflect their identities as men. These tend to be instrumental tasks such as accompanying grandchildren to appointments, playing together, educating, and taking them out to do various activities:

> 'We do all sorts of things with them you know, I mean, I've done woodwork with the kids, made them painting boards and sledges and things like that.' (Charles, age 65, still married)

> 'Sometimes we go and stay at their house, and when we do that we find various things to do, sometimes we play games or I read them books and stories, I've always had the feeling that grandparents, one of the useful things is to do reading with their kids, with their grandchildren, we've always tried to encourage them.' (Mervyn, age 72, still married)

> 'I take her to the dentists, the doctors, things like that you know.' (Arthur, age 73, still married)

According to the participants, grandfathering is about engaging in various practices with grandchildren that reflect their identities as men and also adhere to various constructions of masculinity, including being active, playing sports and going out. Some men suggested that these practices reflect fundamental differences between grandfathering and grandfather identities, compared with grandmothering and grandmother identities:

> 'I'm the man figure, aren't I? [My wife is] more involved I suppose in the domestic side of things. She'll do ... mending for my daughter-in-law, she's got a particular gift, she'll do some cooking, if needed, yeah, I'm much more [into] taking them and playing football with [grandson] or at the moment [granddaughter] likes being picked up and cuddled by me, which all little girls love, you know (laughs). I'm aware we're partly setting role models for them.' (Bill, age 70, still married)

It is important not to be essentialist about the differences between grandfathering and grandmothering, although gender underpinned the participants' responses with the men adopting clearly defined roles and practices that constructed their identities as grandfathers as different from their wives, partners and former wives. Regardless of their marital status, some of the men labelled their role in the family through specific masculine performativities, for example, one defining himself as 'Mr Fix it!' of the family, another as a 'cheeky-chappy clown' and another as the 'fun Butlin's redcoat'. Each of these performances of masculinity reflects the informal, fun-seeking style grandfathering that was predominant in the men's interviews and more prominent than the the informal, fun-seeking style of grandfathering that was predominant in the men's interviews and more prominent than the formal, distant style found by Neugarten and Weinstein (1964). However, as Davidson et al (2003) suggest, being a grandfather is more complex than this and men actually negotiate contradictory identities that on the one hand reflect being masculine, such as being a 'sage', but on the other hand are more nurturing.

As well as defending traditional masculine behaviours through their grandfathering practices, some of the men also discussed their involvement in more nurturing and caring tasks. In Bill's case, this relates to the genders of his grandchildren. In the context of his intergenerational interaction with his granddaughter, he performs nurturing tasks by cuddling her, although he explains how he does this in a masculine way by also picking her up. With his grandson, however, his performance of care is about playing football and being a male role model. Some of the men were also conducting more intimate childcare practices such as nappy changing, reflecting how the men are performing an 'alternative discourse of masculinity' in grandfatherhood (see Mann, 2007). This reflects transformations to their male identities in that they are adopting what has been constructed as 'women's work' (Aitken, 2000). For divorced and remarried grandfather James, this adoption of a new identity is a result of his wife's life-course experiences, and for Arnold it is a result of his intergenerational interactions with his son and son-in-law:

> 'My wife, she's on a learning curve because she's never had any children, and she's adapting to it, I must say, incredibly well, she does exceedingly well.... She performs some of the functions and I do the others, so for instance, [my wife] won't change nappies (laughs) so that immediately becomes my job, but yes, yeah we do different things and I'll keep [granddaughter] occupied while [my wife] goes and does things and she'll keep [granddaughter] occupied while I go and do things.' (James, age 62, remarried)

> 'It was put to me ... I think that it was a generational thing ... I was hopeless, as a father in terms of babies, absolutely hopeless. I didn't avoid it, it was just kind of, not my area of expertise, and I watched our son and our son-in-law, the way they just got stuck in, and was amazed.... They never gave it a thought ... but in my day, we had our children in our early twenties and had finished our family by our mid- twenties and I just had no idea. My wife was a star and didn't seem to have any expectations that I would help, except, of course, I had to feed them and take them out in pushchairs.... Now you have strollers; pushchairs and prams in those days ... but when our grandchildren were babies, I had far more to do with them, far more to do with them, and I was the one who would be saying "Look, you all go out, I will deal with them." [Wife said] "You can't change a nappy." "Oh well ... just let me try, I can do it." So it felt, I suppose I'd become kind of modernised a bit, by watching the way, younger people today behave.' (Arnold, age 65, married)

These examples highlight the differences between the men's reasoning for conducting more nurturing tasks. James's remarriage to a woman who has no children of her own means that he has become involved in intimate childcare practices such as nappy changing, challenging traditional constructions of men as uninvolved in the more intimate elements of family life. What is particularly interesting about James's narrative is that despite being divorced, he still takes regular care of his granddaughter. His remarriage to a woman who does not have children of her own influences his ability to adopt these nurturing practices and encourages them. For Arnold, intergenerational interactions with his children are important for facilitating the performance of these new identities because it is through this interaction that he responds to generational differences in parenting. For Arnold, this reflects a transition in his identity as he situates this change in relation to his life-course experiences as a father. This suggests not only that grandfather involvement leads to the construction of new identities and masculinities, but also that it is a result of the men's personal and familial circumstances. These circumstances are a product of the men's individual and familial life-course experiences, and the positive quality and character of their intergenerational relations.

The maintenance of these positive intergenerational relationships between the men and their children results from the men's adherence to paradoxical norms that reflect a desire to support but not to interfere with their children's wishes for their grandchildren; 'being there' but 'not interfering' (see Chapter Seven in this volume). This was particularly true of the grandfathers who were not divorced, as illustrated in the following quotation:

> 'I think when you're a father you're probably closer, aren't you, to your own father?... But when you're a grandfather you've got to remember that [the grandchild] has a father as well, so we've been very careful that we don't overrule anything that his dad wants to do. We'll discuss it, but we don't overrule, so I think that that's where the difference is ... I think when you're grandparents as well, you've got to pull towards helping them anyway but you've got to stand off a bit sometimes you know, because I know some grandparents can be very frustrating ... and domineering in some ways so we've always tried to step back and have a look. Now, if [grandson] wants to ask us something, we've got to think about this. What's his dad been saying, you know, because we're close to his dad as well, so he tells us what's going on, same as my daughter obviously, and I've got the same relationship with my daughter, so it's pretty fantastic.' (William, age 88, still married)

This adherence to the paradoxical norms of involvement and non-interference is predominantly characteristic of the men who are either still married, have children who remain married, or have managed to maintain positive relationships with their adult children despite the grandfathers being divorced. William highlights that he wants to be involved with his grandson but that he also considers it important to remember that his son-in-law has a role in fathering that he must negotiate in order to maintain positive relationships. These findings are not representative of the diversities across the sample, however. There are differences across the sample concerning men's attitudes to involvement with grandchildren. Some of the men explain that in the absence of their son-in-law they feel it necessary to adopt a male role for their grandchildren, as a direct consequence of conflictual relations caused by the separation of the parents in the middle generation. This is particularly evident in families affected by divorce, as the following section explores.

Divorce and its effect on family structures and intergenerational relations

The quality and character of the men's intergenerational relationships were not always positive and this is related not only to the men's personal circumstances, but also to the situations of their children. While James's divorce and subsequent remarriage led him to engage in nappy-changing practices and to perform new masculinities, he also has positive relationships with his daughter and son-in-law that facilitate this involvement and performance of new masculinities. The majority of the men discussed being able to sustain practices of masculinity by taking their grandchildren out to do various activities, particularly when their grandchildren visited their homes. However, Steve's divorce had had a negative impact on his relationship with his daughter, and Steve could only see his grandchildren at his daughter's home:

> 'I play with [grandchildren] in their house ... the odd thing with me and my daughter is that, you know, there's this sort of, you just don't feel like you can say sort of say, "Oh can I take them to the zoo for the day?" I'd love to, but you just don't get that vibe where you think, you just don't feel like you can ask.' (Steve, age 52, remarried)

Steve's daughter and the quality of their relationship influence the spaces in which he can perform his grandfathering identity. Earlier in his narrative, Steve attributes the quality of his relationship with his daughter to the displeasure he expressed when she first revealed she was pregnant at a young age, and also to his divorce from her mother in the past, which resulted in conflict in their relationship. While many of the men in the sample emphasised taking grandchildren out and frequenting outdoor spaces, reflecting how fathers in particular re-establish their male identities in a spatial way once their identities become divorced from work (Brandth and Kvande, 1998), Steve's daughter prevents him from doing this. George, another divorced grandfather, also explains how his divorce has resulted in differences in his parenting practices and those of his daughter, consequently influencing the quality and character of his relationship with his daughter, and also the frequency of face-to-face contact with his grandsons:

> '[Being a grandad] it's nice, it's nice, yeah, yeah, no I like, I now understand why my parents didn't want to look after my kids, though (laughs) and I was always sort of, I could do with a bit of time off you know.... They [George's parents] were happy to see them but they were happy to see them off as well and, well partly it has to do with, I mean, I wouldn't, I didn't bring up my kids the way my daughter is bringing up hers, and I certainly don't want to get into arguments about how you bring up your kids, obviously. I mean they should get on with their life ... but I find it is a little strained to be honest; she lets them do anything, so you know instead of teaching them the word "no", she never says the word "no", so they start screaming instead, and then, so what she does is divert their attention, it drives me crazy.... It's also actually quite difficult time wise, you know staying in touch is difficult, given that, you know, I don't want to disturb them when she's with the kids, when it's too late, I don't want to wake them up or, wake her up.' (George, age 63, has a partner)

Divorce influences the quality and character of intergenerational relations, or the affectual solidarity (Katz and Lowenstein, 2010) between grandfathers and their children and grandchildren, which is central to whether or not men can actually be involved in the lives of their grandchildren, and who controls this. The fact that George and Steve do not wish to impose their involvement with their grandchildren, and try to engage in practices they deem non-interfering, complicates matters but also corroborates the argument that grandparents try to maintain positive relations with their children and grandchildren by not interfering with the parenting practices of their children (Ross et al, 2005; Chapter Seven in this volume). As King (2003) argues, divorce also tends to result in greater geographical distance and weaker bonds with adult children, as is the case for George, whose daughter lives in Glasgow. In each of these cases, the quality and character of intergenerational relations are a result of divorce of the grandparents, but are also influenced by gendered and generational differences between the men and their daughters.

Gender is important for structuring men's involvement with grandchildren and this is particularly evident when considering the narratives of paternal grandfathers. For the men whose sons have divorced in particular, there are more significant and often negative impacts on the relationships men can have with their grandchildren. Some paternal grandfathers found that when their sons divorced, their lack of rights of access to their grandchildren and the breakdown of relationships meant they were restricted from seeing them altogether:

> 'Going through the divorce was very difficult and [son's] ex has decided that she's going to be vindictive and, part of that is her behaviour with the children. He [son] did have access to them, but she would pepper the children with all sorts of discreditable details about his behaviour before they went to see him. So they went to see him in the wrong frame of mind, which caused him endless problems, so currently they're not actually seeing their father, because it makes things ... well, it just creates too many rows and too many difficulties. So we are actually currently, debating, we do relate after a fashion, we're not terribly fond of his ex-wife, but the way she's behaving, but we can relate to her and, we were debating actually whether in the last few days, whether we ought to contact her, and go, arrange to go and see them direct, without my son being involved, and then at least we can report back to my son and say, well, you know, "We've seen them, they're OK, they're doing this, they're doing that".... We're trying to find a way around by possibly seeing them in her company ... which will maintain contact of sorts, but not the sort we want.' (Peter, age 65, remarried)

As Peter's narrative reveals, the divorce of his son has resulted not only in the decline of his son's and ex-daughter-in-law's relationship, but has also restricted the contact he can have with his grandchildren.

While previous literature suggests that grandparents are more likely to be involved in childcare in situations of divorce (Wheelock and Jones, 2002; Ferguson et al, 2004), for Peter, this has resulted in an intergenerational relationship characterised by conflict that has filtered through the generations. An important point to note in this narrative is that Peter is considering making direct contact with his former daughter-in-law. This resonates with Timonen and Doyle's discussion on grandparental agency in Chapter Eight in this volume.

Peter's familial circumstances were not an isolated incidence in the study sample. Arthur, a dedicated paternal grandfather who was very involved with his local grandchildren, described a similar situation when his son divorced his wife:

> 'Before [eldest son] emigrated to Australia ... he had a daughter, just his son was born in Australia. He used to bring his daughter and his daughter used to stay with us at weekends and that and, she used to like that you know, because there was a strained relationship between my eldest son and his wife. I won't say what we call her, but anyway, they're divorced now (laughs), and then that granddaughter is in Australia, she's now 24, I think ... but ... no relationship with them really. It's hard to say. His mother probably told him [Arthur's grandson] a lot of "porky pies" [lies] about our family; I know she did, and so he had a defence mechanism against us.' (Arthur, age 73, still married)

What these narratives reveal is that divorce in the middle generation can significantly influence the quality of intergenerational relationships that men have with their grandchildren as well as the frequency of face-to-face contact with their grandchildren. As such, family fragmentation in the middle generation is also significant in relation to whether or not involvement with grandchildren is facilitated. A common theme in each of these narratives is how the men's daughters and daughters-in-law act as key gatekeepers to grandchildren and exercise power over the men's relationships with their grandchildren. Thus gender, intergenerational relations, the social context and the men's personal and familial circumstances all intersect and have multiple and complex outcomes that can either facilitate or restrict men's performance of new identities and masculinities when grandfathering.

The variations in the men's practices of grandfathering are significantly influenced by (inter)generational relations to the extent that some of the men are evidently engaging in nappy changing practices, construed as 'women's work' (Aitken, 2000), while others adhere to more masculine practices. The narratives further reveal that as a result of divorce, paternal grandfathers in particular must negotiate the contradictions of their identities because both their gender and generational identities, and also the generational structures of their families, position them in a way that has the potential to restrict access to their grandchildren and consequently their practices and performances of grandfather identity. While they may want to be involved and to conduct nurturing practices, this is contingent on the quality of multiple (inter)generational relationships.

Clearly, the quality and character of the men's intergenerational relations with their children influence men's access to their grandchildren and structure their ability to perform grandfathering. Another participant, previously mentioned, illustrates a scenario that Mann and colleagues (2009) argue is increasingly likely to occur in the British context, namely that fathers who leave their first family as a result of divorce (Kay, 2006) become fathers to children in a second family later in life, while also becoming grandfathers when children in their original family become parents. Thus, they simultaneously have to balance being both a father to young children and a grandfather, as well as, in many cases, still being in employment. The implications of this are yet to be explored in the literature, but maternal grandfather Gerald, whose personal circumstances match this pattern, explained how this made him feel about his new identity as a grandfather:

> 'When my middle daughter became pregnant, I just didn't feel as though I was ready to be a grandfather, because I had [youngest daughter, age seven] and because of some of what we went through to have [youngest daughter] ... I've always been the main carer for [youngest daughter], because [second wife] works, almost full time.... I'm self-employed, so I've always been the one who's been here and been the main carer for [youngest daughter], so that made me really very much a dad, you know; very active and involved dad. So when I realised that [grown-up daughter] was going to have a baby, I just didn't feel ready to be a grandad, like when she said "So what do you want him, [grandson] to call you?"... "I don't know, Gerald, I want him to call me Gerald," [She said] "He's not going to call you Gerald, it'll have to be something to do with you being his grandad, that's what you're going to be," and it did take me a few months to get used to it. I was quite resistant, and it was to

do with being so much involved with [youngest daughter], as a dad.' (Gerald, age 63, remarried)

Interestingly, while being a grandfather may represent a new identity for many men and allow them to adopt more nurturing, softer masculine identities, having multiple generational identities can be the cause of some resistance and conflict for men. Gerald in particular highlights the added complication of still being a father to a seven-year-old daughter from his second marriage and having an older daughter of 32 who has her own children. Generational positions in the family and the signifiers of father and grandfather are evidently associated with expectations of how these should be practised and clearly influence how men construct their identities.

Technology and new grandfathering geographies

In the examples discussed in the previous section, there is an assumption that adult children always have complete control over whether or not men can be involved in their grandchildren's lives. However, there are examples in the men's narratives that suggest that while divorce can result in reduced frequency of face-to-face contact with grandchildren, the increased use of communication technologies can create new geographies of contact between grandfathers and their grandchildren that bypass the middle generation, as Ray and Duncan suggest:

Interviewer: 'With your older grandchildren, then, you said that they contact you every now and again ...'

Ray: '[Eldest granddaughter] does, the boys don't, but [eldest granddaughter] does, yeah.'

Interviewer: 'Is that by phone or email?'

Ray: (Shows phone sign) '"I'm alright grandad, I'm living with my boyfriend now, are you OK?" "Yes, love, what you doing?" "Well, I've got the manager's job." "Oh right, yeah, OK," that type of stuff ... because, like I say, they went through a very difficult time.' (Ray, age 69, remarried)

'The thing where I could ... influence him [grandson] or, communicate with him, I think I could communicate with him on an intellectual level, but now he's moved house he's

not, I just got to writing emails to him, but I don't know if
he's got the same email address, I'd rather not ask (laughs).'
(Duncan, age 70, remarried)

While Quadrello and colleagues (2005) suggest that communication
technologies are complementary, as opposed to compensatory, in
situations of divorce, geographical distance between grandfathers
and their grandchildren can increase. The introduction of new
technologies can reduce this impact, providing new spaces that facilitate
interaction and relationships with grandchildren, and performances of
grandfathering. This is reflected in the finding that family members
develop alternative expressions of support (Katz and Lowenstein, 2010).
Ray, for example, feels that it is important to maintain contact with his
grandchildren because they went through a difficult time when their
parents divorced. As a grandfather he is therefore involved in practices
of intergenerational support that are emotional and nurturing in the
context of his daughter's divorce (Hoff, 2007). While he does not see
them face-to-face, he is in telephone contact with them, overcoming
issues of negative intergenerational relations and geographical distance.
Interestingly, however, both gender and age are important here because
he only speaks to his granddaughter; she is older and has access to the
telephone, he speaks to her and learns about her life. With younger
grandchildren, using technologies may be more difficult. For Duncan,
his own divorce and that of his daughter means his grandson has had
to move further away so he tries to contact him via email. However,
his involvement is restricted by lack of knowledge about his grandson's
email address and a lack of willingness to find out what it is. Duncan
feels that he should still be involved, but his performance of masculinity,
manifest in his lack of initiative to make contact, creates a barrier to
re-establishing contact.

Discussion and conclusion

This chapter has examined contemporary grandfathering in north-
west England, and explored the potential for men to perform new
identities in a dynamic social context that is creating multiple and
varied personal and familial circumstances for men. Men negotiate
their complex and often contradictory gendered and generational
identities in the context of variable intergenerational relations, shaped
by specific personal and familial circumstances. The married men in
the sample construct their identities as grandfathers through a norm
of involvement with grandchildren. Their practices reveal that they

construct and perform new grandfather identities reflecting 'softer', more nurturing masculinities as Davidson and colleagues (2003) suggest. Nappy-changing practices in particular highlight the potential for men to adopt more nurturing and caring tasks in grandfatherhood, thereby challenging existing constructions of masculinities as distant and uninvolved (Cunningham-Burley, 2001) and suggesting that grandfathering may allow men to subvert traditional expectations of male identities (Butler, 1990).

The multifaceted and diverse nature of grandfathering practices revealed in this study suggests that instead of conventional grandfatherhood defined by essentialist conceptions of grandfathering, men are adopting new identities and masculinities. However, these cannot be fully explained without understanding the context of family and intergenerational relations. The intergenerationality approach (Hopkins and Pain, 2007) views generation as a social identity (that grandfathers perform in gendered and aged ways), but, unlike past conceptualisations, it suggests that generational identity is also shaped by interactions with other generational groups. The interconnectedness of generational identities and intergenerational relations is evident in the men's narratives. For example, Arnold explains that his involvement in nappy changing is a result of observing his son's fathering roles. Consequently, his grandfathering and his performance of new masculinities are constructed based on certain gendered possibilities presented by other generations, suggesting that intergenerational relations may have a transformative influence on masculine behaviours. This highlights the interdependent nature of grandfather identities (Holdsworth, 2007) in that gender positions that are normally assumed to be transmitted from fathers (Brannen and Nilson, 2006) are also transmitted from younger to older generations.

This process, however, is only facilitated when relationships with children are positive and cohesive. Family dynamics are changing and this has implications for men's intergenerational relationships in everyday life. The increased prevalence of divorce has significant effects on the intergenerational dynamics between grandfathers, their children and grandchildren, which in turn influences how men perform new identities and masculinities when grandfathering in this context. The data go beyond this finding, showing that there is also variation depending on which generation divorce affects. In situations where divorce and family fragmentation occur in the middle generation, relationships characterised by conflict, particularly with (former) daughters-in-law, are more likely and may disrupt how men perform grandfathering, if they are allowed to at all. There is further evidence to suggest that paternal grandfathers in particular may be restricted in their grandfathering because they lack rights and former daughters-in-law control access to grandchildren (for example, Arthur and Peter). While this is not a new finding, it is evident that this affects how masculinities and male identities are performed in grandfatherhood.

Acknowledging the diversity of grandfather identities is also useful because being a paternal grandfather does not always mean that divorce results in losing involvement with grandchildren (see Chapter Eight in this volume). The maternal (and divorced) grandfather Steve also finds that his practices are restricted and he is unable to take his grandchildren to activities outside their home because he does not feel that his daughter would let him. James, however, who has divorced in the past but has managed to maintain a positive relationship with his daughter, has gone on to marry a woman without children of her own. This set of circumstances has resulted in his involvement in more nurturing performances of childcare. This highlights how the generation in which divorce occurs, and the effect this has on intergenerational relations, can have differential and diverse outcomes for the identities that grandfathers perform.

These empirical examples suggest that generational structures and relationships that are gendered may act to marginalise men who are grandfathers, reduce their power and restrict their ability to create new identities in family life. This is not a straightforward process and has diverse outcomes for men dependent on their personal and familial circumstances. The use of new technologies, however, suggests that there may be potential for men to overcome these structures, leading to the argument that there are new social geographies of grandfathering that may allow men to facilitate involvement with grandchildren. As Duncan's example shows, however, this is dependent on the age of grandchildren and whether or not men choose to subvert traditional masculine behaviours. The men's personal geographies and access to resources do provide opportunities to perform an involved grandfatherhood, but this may also require agency (see Chapter Eight in this volume).

The findings from the empirical data reveal variations in what men do with their grandchildren, and show that their engagement with grandchildren is influenced by whether intergenerational relations are conflicting or cohesive. The nature of relationships between grandfathers and their children and grandchildren is also influenced by divorce. This highlights that a diverse range of grandfather identities exists and that there is room for negotiation and redefinition of the grandfather identity, made evident through the performance of multiple ageing masculinities. These findings have much broader implications for the ways in which grandfather identities are theorised and conceptualised.

Theorising about grandfathers is currently inadequate (Hagestad, 1985; Roberto et al, 2001), which led the author to develop a theoretical framework incorporating intergenerationality (Hopkins and Pain, 2007) and performativity (Butler, 1990). Application of this framework has provided a better understanding of the intersection of gender and intergenerational relations, and how grandfathers' personal and familial circumstances shape their masculinities and grandfather identities. Further work is required to understand diversity in grandfather identities. This chapter has suggested a conceptual framework for future research on men's experiences of family relationships and their influence on identity construction.

Acknowledgements

This study was conducted for the author's doctoral research, which was funded by Lancaster University.

References

Aitken, S.C. (2000) 'Fathering and faltering:"Sorry, but you don't have the necessary accoutrements"', *Environment and Planning A*, vol 32, no 4, pp 581-98.

Ando, K. (2005) 'Grandparenthood: crossroads between gender and aging', *International Journal of Japanese Sociology*, vol 14, no 1, pp 32-51.

Bates, J. (2009) 'Generative grandfathering: a conceptual framework for nurturing grandchildren', *Marriage and Family Review*, vol 45, no 4, pp 331-52.

Brandth, B. and Kvande, E. (1998) 'Masculinity and child care: the reconstruction of fathering', *Sociological Review*, vol 46, no 2, pp 293-313.

Brannen, J. and Nilsen, A. (2006) 'From fatherhood to fathering: transmission and change among British fathers in four-generation families', *Sociology*, vol 40, no 2, pp 335-52.

Butler, J. (1990) *Gender trouble: Feminism and the subversion of identity*, London: Routledge.

Clarke, L. and Roberts, C. (2002) 'Policy and rhetoric: the growing interest in fathers and grandparents in Britain', in A. Carling, S. Duncan and R. Edwards (eds) *Analysing families: Morality and rationality in policy and practice*, London: Routledge.

Cunningham-Burley, S. (2001) 'The experience of grandfatherhood', in A.J. Walker, M. Manoogian-O'Dell, L.A. McGraw and D.L.G. White (eds) *Families in later life: Connections and transitions*, Thousand Oaks, CA: Sage, pp 92-96.

Davidson, K., Daly, T. and Arber, S. (2003) 'Exploring the social worlds of older men', in S. Arber, K. Davidson and J. Ginn (eds) *Gender and ageing: Changing roles and relationships*, Maidenhead: Open University Press, pp 168-85.

Dench, G. and Ogg, J. (2002) *Grandparenting in Britain: A baseline study*, London: Institute of Community Studies.

Drew, L.A. and Smith, P.K. (1999) 'The impact of parental separation/divorce on grandparent–grandchild relationships', *International Journal of Aging and Human Development*, vol 48, no 3, pp 191-216.

Elwood, S. and Martin, D. (2000) '"Placing" interviews: location and scales of power in qualitative research', *The Professional Geographer*, vol 52, no 4, pp 649-57.

Fairhurst, E. (2003) 'New identities in ageing: perspectives on age, gender and life after work', in S. Arber, K. Davidson and J. Ginn (eds) *Gender and ageing: Changing roles and relationships*, Maidenhead: Open University Press, pp 31-46.

Ferguson, N. with Douglas, G., Lowe, N., Murch, M. and Robinson, M. (2004) *Grandparenting in divorced families*, Bristol: The Policy Press.

Finch, J. (2007) 'Displaying families', *Sociology*, vol 41, no 1, pp 65-81.

Hagestad, G.O. (1985) 'Continuity and connectedness', in V.L. Bengtson and J.F. Robertson (eds) *Grandparenthood*, London; Sage Publications, pp 31-48.

Harper, S. (2005) 'Understanding grandparenthood', in V.L. Bengtson and M.L. Johnson (eds) *Cambridge handbook of age and ageing*, Cambridge: Cambridge University Press.

Hoff, A. (2007) 'Patterns of intergenerational support in grandparent–grandchild and parent–child relationships in Germany', *Ageing and Society*, vol 27, no 5, pp 643-65.

Holdsworth, C. (2007) 'Intergenerational inter-dependencies: mothers and daughters in comparative perspective', *Women's Studies International Forum*, vol 30, no 1, pp 59-69.

Hopkins, P. and Pain, R. (2007) 'Geographies of age: thinking relationally', *Area*, vol 39, no 3, pp 287-94.

Katz, R. and Lowenstein, A. (2010) 'Theoretical perspectives on intergenerational solidarity, conflict and ambivalence', in M. Izuhara (ed) *Ageing and intergenerational relations: Family reciprocity from a global perspective*, Bristol: The Policy Press, pp 29-56.

Kay, T. (2006) 'Where's Dad? Fatherhood in leisure studies', *Leisure Studies*, vol 25, no 2, pp 133-52.

King, V. (2003) 'The legacy of a grandparent's divorce: consequences for ties between grandparents and grandchildren', *Journal of Marriage and Family*, vol 65, no 1, pp 170-83.

Leeson, G.W. and Harper, S. (2009) 'Oxford Institute highlights increasing role of grandfathers in caring for grandchildren', www.ageing.ox.ac.uk/news (accessed 30 March 2010).

Mann, R. (2007) 'Out of the shadows? Grandfatherhood, age and masculinities', *Journal of Aging Studies*, vol 24, no 1, pp 271-81.

Mann, R., Khan, H.T.A. and Leeson, G.W. (2009) *Age and gender differences in grandchildren's relations with their maternal grandfathers and grandmothers*, Working Paper 209, Oxford: Oxford Institute of Ageing, University of Oxford.

Neugarten, B.L. and Weinstein, K.K. (1964) 'The changing American grandparent', *Journal of Marriage and Family*, vol 26, no 2, pp 199-204.

Quadrello, T., Hurme, H., Menzinger, J., Smith, P.K., Veisson, M., Vidal, S. and Westerback, S. (2005) 'Grandparents' use of new communication technologies in a European perspective', *European Journal of Ageing*, vol 2, no 3, pp 200-7.

Reitzes, D.C. and Mutran, E.J. (2004) 'Grandparent identity, intergenerational family identity, and well-being', *The Journal of Gerontology*, vol 59B, no 4, pp 213-9.

Roberto, K.A., Allen, K.R. and Blieszner, R. (2001) 'Grandfathers' perceptions and expectations of relationships with their adult grandchildren', *Journal of Family Issues*, vol 22, no 4, pp 407-26.

Ross, N., Hill, M., Sweeting, H. and Cunningham-Burley, S. (2005) *Grandparents and teen grandchildren: Exploring intergenerational relationships*, Glasgow: Centre for Research on Families.

Tarrant, A. (2010) 'Constructing a social geography of grandparenthood: a new focus for intergenerationality', *Area*, vol 42, no 2, pp 190-7.

Uhlenberg, P. and Kirby, J.B. (1998) 'Grandparenthood over time: historical and demographic trends', in M.E. Szinovacz (ed) *Handbook on grandparenthood*, Westport, CT: Greenwood Press, pp 23-39.

Vanderbeck, R. (2007) 'Intergenerational geographies: age relations, segregation and re-engagements', *Geography Compass*, vol 1, no 2, pp 200-221.

Wheelock, J. and Jones, K. (2002) '"Grandparents are the next best thing": informal childcare for working parents in urban Britain', *Journal of Social Policy*, vol 31, no 3, pp 441-63.

TEN

Understanding adolescent grandchildren's influence on their grandparents

Alice Delerue Matos and Rita Borges Neves

Grandparent–grandchild relationships have been studied in the social sciences for over 50 years, with traditional perspectives emphasising the importance of grandparents as agents of socialisation for grandchildren (Neugarten and Weinstein, 1964; Denham and Smith, 1989). Most studies have adopted the grandparents' perspective while neglecting the grandchild's viewpoint (Dellmann-Jenkins et al, 1987; Attar-Schwartz et al, 2009). Research has demonstrated that grandparents are a key element in grandchildren's socialisation by transmitting to them core values, by representing a role model and through companionship (Robertson, 1976; Denham and Smith, 1989). Nonetheless socialisation is not limited to childhood but occurs throughout the life course (Putney and Bengtson, 2002) and influences are mutual between parties within interactions (Tomlin, 1998; Putney and Bengtson, 2002). Both grandparent and grandchild have the potential to transmit knowledge to and influence each other.

Given recent rapid changes in social norms, knowledge and technology, we assume that the younger generation can provide a 'linkage' with new developments. Grandchildren can contribute to their grandparents' integration by socialising them into new ideas and practices, by providing support and by enhancing social engagement. Previous research (Neugarten and Weinstein, 1964; Cherlin and Furstenberg, 1985; Franks et al, 1993) has shown that grandparents can take on diverse styles of grandparenting and exert greater or lesser influence on their grandchildren (for example, on religiosity). We also propose that a grandchild can undertake different roles while interacting with their grandparent and that the youngster's influence will vary in nature and intensity according to the characteristics of the grandparent–grandchild relationship.

This chapter focuses on the connection between non-adjacent generations and therefore needs to be seen within the broader family dynamics. The parent–grandparent tie affects the grandparent–grandchild relationship (Robertson, 1976; Monserud, 2008; Doyle et al, 2010, also see Chapter Eleven). However, given increasing life spans in western countries, long-lasting intergenerational relationships across three and even four generations are now a frequent and relevant phenomenon (Harper, 2005; Hoff, 2007). The possibilities of long-term connections between grandchildren and grandparents are greater than ever and family ties other than those established within nuclear households are assuming greater importance (Bengtson, 2001). A key issue is whether contemporary relationships between grandparents and adolescent grandchildren can become more direct, and less mediated by the parent generation.

Little previous research attention has been given to the potential capacity of grandchildren to change their grandparents' attitudes and behaviours. There is a need for an in-depth understanding of the areas in which a grandchild can exert influence over their grandparents.

This chapter examines the nature of the bond between adolescent grandchildren and their emotionally closest grandparent in order to understand the potential beneficial effects of grandchildren for the elder person, and considers the grandchild's perception regarding their influence on their grandparent. First, the chapter outlines some previous relevant findings on grandparent–grandchild relationships in relation to the influence process and intergenerational solidarity; second, it describes and discusses findings from the authors' empirical research conducted with children aged from 12 to 18 years old in Portugal.

Mutual influence within grandparent–grandchild relationships

Influence can be understood as complying with the expectations of significant others (normative influence) or adopting their perspectives on important issues (informational influence) (Turner, 1991). Traditional perspectives on family influences have focused on socialisation and on the internalisation of roles and cultural norms by children. Socialisation has been used to describe a unidirectional learning process that serves the continuity of a given social system (Parsons, 1955). This approach emphasises how adults influence youngsters and research within grandparent–grandchild dyads has focused primarily on the older party as a socialisation agent.

Either through face-to-face interaction with their grandchild or by influencing the parent's childrearing practices, grandparents can directly or indirectly influence the grandchild's development (Denham and Smith, 1989; Franks et al, 1993; Roberto and Skogland, 1996; Tomlin, 1998). It has been shown that grandparents can influence their grandchildren within areas as broad as morals, religion, politics, education, work ethic, family ideals, sexuality and personal identity (Franks et al, 1993; Lawton et al, 1994; Tomlin, 1998). Influences vary according to the characteristics of the individuals involved, such as their age, gender, ethnic background or health status. Family configuration, geographical distance and the parents' relationship with the grandparents can all affect the grandparents' role (Neugarten and Weinstein, 1964; Barranti, 1985; Denham and Smith, 1989; Tomlin, 1998; Monserud, 2008; Attar-Schwartz et al, 2009; Doyle et al, 2010).

A considerable body of literature has been published on grandparenting styles with the assumption that different styles will be associated with varying types of influence on grandchildren. The grandparent can relate to the grandchild in various ways, as a fun seeker (Neugarten and Weinstein, 1964), buddy or playmate, storyteller, or confidant (Franks et al, 1993). Cherlin and Furstenberg (1985), focusing explicitly on the influence of grandparents on grandchildren, argued that active grandparents are emotionally closer to their grandchildren and can either be caregivers and provide support to grandchildren (supportive), or they can undertake a more parental-like influence (authoritative) or both (influential).

As mentioned earlier, within social interaction, individuals can learn from one another, as both parties are open to influence (Tomlin, 1998; Putney and Bengtson, 2002). Mutuality also applies to grandparent–grandchild relationships: the elders may conform to the expectations of a loving grandchild or adjust their behaviour or attitudes in the light of information provided by the youngsters. Since grandparents assume a variety of styles of interaction with their grandchildren, we take as a corollary that youngsters can also act in different ways as influential grandchildren.

The nature of intergenerational solidarity

Emotional closeness, service exchange, frequency of contacts and role expectations have all been identified as underlying dimensions of grandparent–grandchild relationships that provide understanding of the way grandparents act and exert influence over grandchildren. These dimensions were described by Bengtson and colleagues (Bengtson and Roberts, 1991; Silverstein and Bengtson, 1997) in the intergenerational solidarity model (see Chapters One, Five, Six and Eleven). This model has been very significant in research within the sociology of the family in studies of older parent–adult child relationships, and was later applied to grandparent–grandchild dyads.

According to these authors, the dynamics of intergenerational relations within the family group are based on solidarity or the lack of it (Bengtson and Roberts, 1991; Silverstein and Bengtson, 1997). They argue that different generations are brought together within families by positive feelings, such as affection and trust (affectual solidarity); contacts, either formal/ritualistic or informal and shared activities (associational solidarity); consensus in beliefs (consensual solidarity); financial, physical and emotional assistance (functional solidarity); and obligations felt towards family members (normative solidarity). Being able to interact with family members also depends on the opportunity structure, for instance residential proximity, gender, age and health (Bengtson and Roberts, 1991) (also see Chapter Eleven).

However, the intensity and quality of solidarity can vary. Silverstein and colleagues (1994) distinguished different types of parent–adult child relations: the 'tight-knit' (all aspects of solidarity are ranked high); the 'detached' (all aspects of solidarity are ranked low); the 'sociable' (high on opportunity, and on associational, affectual and normative solidarity, but low functional solidarity); the 'intimate-at-a-distance' (low opportunity, associational and functional, but high on affectual and normative); and the 'obligatory' (high opportunity, associational and instrumental, but low affectual and normative solidarity). Silverstein and colleagues' (1998) suggestion to test this typology on grandchild–grandparent relationships was considered by the current authors. However, some aspects of grandparent–grandchild relationships that feature within the typology are not applicable to this study, namely lack of geographical propinquity and low levels of affective solidarity (because the study sampled only grandchildren who indicated affection towards at least one grandparent living nearby). The grandparent–grandchild dyads used in this study are characterised by both physical and emotional closeness and therefore are similar only to Silverstein and colleagues' (1994) tight-knit and sociable dyads. Geographical propinquity and emotional closeness can enhance the frequency of contact (Taylor et al, 2005). Consequently they are critical for direct influence to take place.

In order to apply the solidarity model, Silvertstein and colleagues (1998) suggest that distinctive aspects of grandparent–grandchild relationships must be considered: role expectations; mediation of relationships between grandparent–grandchild dyads; each individual's developmental stage; and historical contexts. Each of these aspects is discussed here.

Grandchildren roles have been variously described in research literature and include acting as caregivers who provide instrumental and emotional support to grandparents, especially adult grandchildren (Even-Zohar and Sharlin, 2009). The care provided can be explained by a sense of filial duty and gratitude towards grandparents. Filial norms and behavioural patterns learned from parents also affect the likelihood of grandchildren acting as caregivers. However, children's rights and responsibilities towards their grandparents are not closely prescribed in western societies (Silverstein et al, 1998). This raises the question of which roles an adolescent can play as a grandchild.

The parent-as-mediator theory stresses the relevance of the middle generation as a link between the two non-adjacent generations (Robertson, 1975). Both contact and emotional closeness between grandparents and young grandchildren tend to vary according to the quality of the parent–grandparent relationship (Whitbeck et al, 1993; Connidis, 2001). Women (mothers) as primary kin keepers have a particular impact on the grandparent–adult grandchild tie leading to a matrilineal bias (Matthews and Sprey, 1985; Monserud, 2008). Chan and Elder (2000) point out that the maternal grandparents tend to be more involved with grandchildren than paternal grandparents, since mothers are privileged mediators of the non-adjacent generations' relationship. From another viewpoint, grandchildren may enhance the contact between the parent and grandparent generations (Bucx et al, 2008).

The grandparent–grandchild tie changes across the life course of each party (Connidis, 2001) and a number of studies have found that adolescent grandchildren tend to become less involved with grandparents (Kahana and Kahana, 1970). However, others argue that this does not happen (Dellmann-Jenkins et al, 1987; Roberto, 1990) and conclude that grandparents remain relevant figures of attachment (Dellmann-Jenkins et al, 1987; Creasey and Koblewski, 1991).

Nowadays grandparent–grandchild relations are mainly explained by emotional attachment and do not depend as much on obligation as they traditionally did (Barranti, 1985; Kivett, 1985), which is also shown in Chapter Eleven. This emotional bond is an important characteristic of European family relationships, despite some differences between countries that can be explained by cultural and structural factors (Torres et al, 2008). Grandchildren can be an important resource for older adults while providing emotional support, instrumental help and promoting social contact (Armstrong, 2005), which can help grandparents regain a sense of purpose and direction in the face of role loss (Jerrome, 1990).

In summary, grandchildren's influence on grandparents is an underexplored topic despite its potential benefits for older women and men. This chapter addresses adolescents' influence over their grandparents' behaviours and/or attitudes, as well as some of the mechanisms underlying this process. To understand these influences, we choose to study emotionally close adolescent grandchild–grandparent dyads, taking the grandchild's standpoint. We apply the intergenerational solidarity framework and consider the role of the middle generation as a mediator. We analyse our findings in terms of a typology of 'grandchilding' roles.

Methods

This qualitative study involved interviews with 34 youngsters ranging from 12 to 18 years old (average age 15; 16 boys and 18 girls) conducted in the northern region of Portugal. First, 130 students responded to a short questionnaire that asked about gender, age, number of living grandparents and geographical distance to their grandparents. Second, 34 interviewees were selected from the completed questionnaires according to the following criteria: having at least two grandparents alive, which allowed a choice (preference) of a reference grandparent based on affection; not residing with grandparents; and living within a short distance of at least one grandparent (under 15 km away) to allow regular personal contact.

The semi-structured interviews focused on several aspects of the youngster's relationship with who they considered to be their 'emotionally closest' grandparent. The in-depth interviews probed about levels of affection, assistance and grandchildren's obligations to their closest grandparent, degree of agreement concerning values and beliefs, extent and nature of interaction, expectations about the relationship, and perceived behavioural and attitudinal changes of their grandparents as a result of their interaction.

Interviews lasted between 30 and 120 minutes and were conducted privately without the presence of grandparents or parents. They were audiotaped, transcribed and their content subjected to open coding followed by axial coding where categories were related through inductive and deductive reasoning involving intensive comparison. At a final stage, selective coding allowed the integration of the categories into core, broader ones (Corbin and Strauss, 2008). Codes and interpretations were compared and discussed between the authors. Pseudonyms are used to preserve confidentiality with the grandchild's age in brackets.

Grandchild–grandparent interactions

The majority of the interviewees lived with parents and siblings, while a minority lived only with both parents. Almost half of the children referred to the maternal grandmother as being their 'emotionally closest' grandparent; the rest referred either to the paternal grandmother or the maternal grandfather. This stated preference seemed to be mediated by geographical propinquity as they interacted more often and felt more attached to the nearest grandparent: "This grandmother is very special because I spend a lot more time with her than with the others. She lives nearby" (Carla, 18).

The age of the chosen grandparents ranged from 63 to 86 years old. Nearly all had little or no schooling. They had previously been blue-collar employees, agricultural workers or housewives, and therefore were similar to the majority of older people from the northern region of Portugal (Delerue, 2007). Generally, they did not need assistance with activities of daily living.

The teenagers considered that they had a responsibility towards their grandparents. They felt obliged to maintain frequent contact and assist them when needed. All the teenagers kept the grandparent company, cheered him/her up and spent time together. More than half went for walks with their closest grandparent and helped them with domestic errands or with grocery shopping; a smaller proportion accompanied them to appointments (like the doctor, bank and hairdresser). They stated that they were reciprocating the grandparents' love and care over the years:

> 'I keep him company ... help him with food.... He spent the day in bed, didn't have proper meals and I feel I must be around to help him.... Now I feel that it is my turn to help, to keep him company and visit him not to feel lonely.' (Julia, 16)

Interaction led to the grandchild directly influencing their grandparent, who was reported to have changed some of their behaviour and even attitudes. According to the grandchildren, grandparents were more willing to learn IT skills and coped better with technology as a result of their interaction. Teenagers helped grandparents to become more autonomous using mobile phones, small electrical appliances (such as microwaves) and TV remote controls. They constantly insisted on their grandparent using this technology, persuading them of its advantages. When the younger generation were aware of the importance of being environmentally friendly, they tried to change their grandparents' behaviour. Grandchildren reported that some elders adopted new environmental attitudes once they became aware of these issues through their grandchild.

Some youngsters also influenced their grandparent's dietary routines. They made them aware of the benefits of having a healthy diet, informing them about nutrition and aiding with the preparation of some meals. Grandchildren were particularly zealous when the elder had to comply with strict dietary routines due to health problems. However, they were not always successful despite all efforts, as their grandparent often resisted changing their food habits:

> 'I say, "Grandma take it easy, you don't need to eat all that, you can leave it for tomorrow." ... But I know it only works when I am there. When I'm not, she overeats.' (Ana, 14)

Grandchildren encouraged grandparents to participate in social events and leisure activities, as they were conscious of the importance of social interaction for wellbeing. Some grandparents also became less critical of the younger generation when they came to understand their grandchildren's lifestyles and preferences:

> 'She was always telling me to cut my hair, but because I kept arguing my side, she is more and more persuaded that a boy can let his hair grow long.' (Daniel, 17)

Some of the grandchildren also encouraged their grandparents to become more open-minded and talk about 'taboo' issues, such as homosexuality, divorce and non-married couples living together. However, grandchildren reported that despite these conversations the elders were not very likely to change their opinions, especially regarding homosexuality.

Overall, the research found different types and degrees of influence of grandchildren according to the nature of the grandchild's relationship with their closest grandparent.

'Grandchilding' roles

Since this study focused solely on the 'emotionally closest' grandparent, affectual solidarity was paramount, and in some cases affection was especially strong. When grandparents and adolescent grandchildren were living a short distance from one another, the opportunity for interaction was relatively high. From our analysis of this non-adjacent generation's bond, and drawing on the various dimensions of intergenerational solidarity (Bengtson and Roberts, 1991), we developed a fourfold typology of 'grandchilding' roles.

Buddies had a very close relationship with their grandparent based on exceptional levels of associative and functional solidarity, and these grandchildren had the most influence on their grandparents' attitudes and behaviour. *Companions* established more formal relationships and had the least influence on the elders. They were present in grandparents' lives, but mainly through a sense of obligation. *Carers* had a strong attachment to their grandparent and assisted them when needed. They were particularly sensitive to grandparents' wellbeing and to the importance of undertaking leisure activities to attain it, and transmitted this understanding to their grandparents. *Playmates* were mainly the younger children (12-14 years old), who engaged in various leisure activities with grandparents, indicating relatively high levels of association. They were particularly influential regarding IT and encouraging environmentally friendly attitudes. The number of grandchildren in each category and their gender are shown at the base of Table 10.1.

Differences in relationships were particularly obvious among the most contrasting groups: buddies and companions. Buddies built a daily routine with the grandparent and felt a part of several dimensions of the elder's life, whereas interactions between companions and their grandparents were scarcer and almost ritualistic. For grandchildren, the emotional support they gave to their closest grandparent was most obvious within more intimate relationships. We now describe each of the four types of grandchild–grandparent relationships in turn (see Table 10.1).

Table 10.1: 'Grandchilding' roles, solidarity relationships and the influence of adolescent grandchildren on grandparents

		Typology of 'grandchilding' roles			
		Buddies	Companions	Carers	Playmates
Solidarity dimensions	Affectual	●●●	●●	●●●	●●●
	Associational	●●●	●	●●	●●
	Functional	●●●	●	●●●	●
	Normative	●●	●●●	●●	●●●
	Consensual	●	●	●	●●●
Areas of influence on grandparents	Technology	●●	●●	●●	●●●
	Eco-friendly behaviours	●●	O	●	●●●
	Youth lifestyles	●●●	●●	●●●	●
	Contemporary social phenomena	●●●	●	●	●
	Social activities	●●	O	●●●	●
	Dietary routines	●●	●	●●●	●
Mediator generation	Grandparents (mediating parent–child relation)	●●	O	O	O
	Parents (mediating grandparent–grandchild relation)	O	●	●	●●
	Grandchildren (mediating grandparent–parent relation)	●●	●	O	O
n = 34 (grandchildren)	Male (n = 16)	5	4	4	3
	Female (n = 18)	4	6	5	3

Key: O absence of the attribute; ● attribute of low intensity; ●● attribute of intermediate intensity; ●●● attribute of high intensity.

Buddies

The first group, buddies, were the most influential. Within this group of interviewees, only grandmothers were chosen as the preferred grandparent, both from the maternal and the paternal line. The grandchildren nurtured a special bond with them and described a trusting and warm relationship. Both parties were committed to an intimate relationship, as they relied heavily on each other and saw themselves as friends. These grandchildren helped their grandmothers with chores, especially when they became too physically onerous for the elder. When grandmothers were in need of emotional support they received it from their grandchild: "I listen to her when she needs it ... when something is troubling her she comes to me for advice" (Carla, 18). The youngsters considered themselves as equals in the relationship and did not see their grandparent as an authority figure. In addition, grandparents were often seen as mediators with parents, as they might intervene in aspects of the parent's childrearing and try to defend the grandchild's cause or point of view:

> 'Sometimes my parents don't allow me to go out in the evening with friends and my grandmother persuades them otherwise. She argues that I can sleep at her house. She is a great friend. I share everything with her, more than with my parents.' (David, 15)

Parents in fact rarely seemed to mediate the relationship. These adolescents did not depend on parental initiative to contact their grandparents. The grandchildren took the initiative and saw the elder almost every day. Although parents as primary socialisers might have originally transmitted feelings about kin to their children, the grandparent–grandchild relationship now displayed autonomy.

This buddy relationship could be reinforced by frank conversations. Despite not always reaching consensus, grandchild and grandparent debated all sorts of topics, from religion to marriage, from homosexuality to abortion, in a straightforward fashion. Discrepancies in beliefs and values were explained by interviewees as a consequence of the 'natural' generation gap. Dialogue and persuasion resulted in grandchildren having significant potential influence over their grandparents. The elders' perceptions about homosexuality, religion, new lifestyles and the importance of social activities or dietary routines were challenged by their grandchildren: "I brought to her knowledge about the modern world and the changes that have been occurring" (Daniel, 17). The elders accepted talking about controversial issues, but were less willing to adopt new attitudes regarding religion and sexuality.

Companions

Companions exerted the least influence on their grandparents. These grandchildren felt more attached to their maternal grandparents. Companions saw grandparents less frequently than those in other groups, sometimes less than once a week. Nonetheless they had a sense of family duty and were concerned with maintaining some regularity in personal contact. In this group it was particularly obvious that familism (internalised obligations towards the family) was the basis of their affectual relationship: "I believe that we [grandchildren] have an obligation to make them feel better, not to allow them to feel lonely and to keep them company" (Maria, 13). In half of the cases the parents mediated the relationship and encouraged grandchildren to spend time with the elders.

Companions and their grandparents shared meals and watched TV together. The youngsters ran some errands and helped the grandparent with mobile phones. However, the relationship was not considered to be one of intimacy as they kept conversations at the level of small talk. They maintained between themselves a formal distance, avoiding delicate or controversial subjects, and did not rely on each other for emotional support: "I try my best to be with him and talk about many things, except personal stuff, either mine or his" (Ines, 15). Being in contact with their grandchildren, grandparents obtained more insights about the lifestyles of today's youth. Nevertheless, the interviewees stated that they did not influence the elder's mindset. Companions were less interested in interfering with grandparents and refrained from giving advice or guidance regarding social activities or environmental issues such as recycling. Regardless of the frequency of interaction, there was little influence exerted by the youngsters and little service exchange.

Carers

Carers tended to elect maternal grandparents as their emotionally closest. Perhaps for this reason, mothers occasionally influenced the relationship. These grandparents tended to be older (75 years and older) and had more health problems. The majority of the adolescents categorised as carers belonged to the oldest age group within the sample.

These grandchildren spent a substantial amount of time with their grandparent. They were genuinely concerned about the elders' physical, psychological and social wellbeing. The carers provided substantial assistance with shopping and errands, heavy household work and attending doctor's appointments. When their grandparent was feeling emotionally down or had a problem, they relied on their grandchild for encouragement. The elders' needs brought about functional solidarity: "My grandmother was diagnosed with diabetes. I stood for her. I helped her dealing with her illness, pushing [her] to stricter routines and extra care with [her] food" (Marcos, 17). This dimension of solidarity associated with feelings of nurture for the grandparent was prominent within this category.

This group of interviewees did not change their grandparents' perceptions of social issues, and rarely discussed controversial subjects. The grandchildren were not interested in debating these matters, as they recognised that they and their grandparent seldom agreed with each other. Their only concern was with the quality of life of their grandparent. This was apparent when they explained to elders how small home appliances worked or talked about the advantages of social interaction. The carers could instigate some changes regarding dietary routines and other behaviours, by persuading the grandparent to adopt healthier options:

> 'I managed to persuade him not to smoke that much.... He used to go out and drink ... but I always find some excuse for him to stay at home or to do something else.' (Luis, 14)

Playmates

Within this group, there were generally younger grandparents (less than 75 years old) as well as younger grandchildren. All the grandparents had good health, largely because of their younger age. Maternal and paternal kin were equally represented and all the grandparents except one were grandmothers. Both parents had an impact on this relationship and set the rhythm of contacts by stimulating and enabling them. Contact was very frequent, with grandparents and grandchildren in this category seeing each other almost every day or at least once a week, mostly for leisure activities. They were usually fond of short walks and playing games, and shared domestic chores for fun:

> 'We do not watch that much television as we prefer to do stuff outside the house. We go shopping together, to the park, to the movies; we do a lot of stuff together. We are very close.' (Maria, 14)

Notwithstanding their age, these youngsters represented an emotional support for their grandparent. Although the children did not discuss serious or intimate problems with their grandparent, they played an encouraging role in overcoming emotional distress: "I tell him not to think about his problem, to think about something else and he stops thinking and he plays with me" (Ricardo, 12).

This playmates style of interaction resulted in some forms of influence. The grandchildren raised grandparents' awareness of environmentally friendly attitudes, such as the value of recycling. Being a fun-oriented relationship, these children challenged the seniors to play some of their favourite electronic games. When playing these games, the elders became more familiar with technology and less resistant to handling new devices. These grandchildren did not openly discuss beliefs or values and stated that they normally agreed with their grandparents, implying a high level of consensus. Grandchildren did not consider that they influenced their grandparents' perspective on current social issues or on youth lifestyles.

Influential grandchildren

The bulk of research on grandparent–grandchild relationships has used a traditional perspective that focuses on grandchildren as being the sole party that is influenced. We support a new approach by exploring the mutuality of the influence process, as Tomlin (1998) and Putney and Bengtson (2002) suggest. We set out to understand the mechanisms by which an adolescent grandchild is able to change their grandparents' behaviours and/or attitudes.

Our first aim was to examine whether Portuguese adolescent grandchildren have the potential to exert beneficial influences on their 'emotionally closest' grandparent. We found that grandchildren were able to affect the way that close grandparents related with technology (IT, mobile phones and small domestic devices). This was in line with Armstrong's (2005) research in New Zealand on young grandmothers, which found that grandchildren transmitted knowledge to grandparents and assisted them with IT, as well as influencing their leisure and social activities. We also found that grandchildren may have beneficial effects on their grandparents' environmentally friendly behaviours, dietary routines, social activities and perception of societal changes (such as divorce and co-habitation). Many of the adolescents were zealous in trying to support their elders' best interests and persuaded their grandparents to make changes in areas they felt were important for general wellbeing. Influences were therefore mainly informational as alterations arose from the recognition of the validity of the grandchild's viewpoint (Turner, 1991).

However, the grandchild's influence seemed to be intentionally limited to more practical issues. They had no interest in intervening on more controversial issues regarding religion, politics and attitudes towards sexuality (for instance related to homosexuality). Even if the adolescents held different opinions, they still considered close grandparents to be an important reference concerning moral values, education, family ideals and work ethics (also shown by Franks et al, 1993; Lawton et al, 1994). They respected their grandparents' opinions and aimed to minimise disagreements. However, this non-interference might have been because they perceived little possibility of changing the elders' core values and beliefs. They acknowledged that the grandparents had a different cultural, social and material background from their own.

Our second aim was to delineate the characteristics of an influential adolescent grandchild–grandparent tie. Grandchildren were assumed to play different roles while interacting with their grandparents and exerted varying influence accordingly to those roles. Our analysis of intergenerational relationships was conducted using the intergenerational solidarity model as a framework (Bengtson and Roberts, 1991; Silverstein and Bengtson, 1997) to examine the types of solidarity associated with greater influence potential. The grandchildren designated as buddies had the highest solidarity levels and the greatest influence on their grandparents, followed respectively by carers and playmates, while companions were not only less solidary, but also had least influence on their grandparents' behaviour or attitudes.

Affection, association and functional support provided by grandchildren were higher among the most influential groups, leading to the conclusion that these dimensions of solidarity are central to the influence process. Vala and Monteiro (2002) point out that close relationships involving some degree of emotional or even physical dependency are foundational for influence. If there is a topic that the grandparent is not very familiar with (for instance IT, recent information about health and health-related behaviours), it is more likely that the elder's outlook will be affected by a grandchild whom he/she sees often. Regarding long-established values and beliefs (concerning, for example, religion and sexual mores), the elder, despite willingness to talk them over (with buddy grandchildren), is less likely to change his/her mind.

Other factors must be considered in order to fully understand the grandchild's influence within these relationships, namely gender and lineage (which may also structure opportunity for interaction and affection), role expectations from the grandchildren, mediation by the middle generation and the historical/cultural context. As discussed earlier, these aspects were considered by Silverstein and colleagues (1998) as relevant when applying the intergenerational solidarity model to grandparent–grandchild relationships. Each of these factors is briefly discussed here.

Within our sample, the adolescents' choice of favourite grandparent was the maternal grandmother in almost half the cases. These results are congruent with earlier research that found that grandchildren establish emotionally close relationships with grandmothers in particular (Eisenberg, 1988; Spitze and Ward, 1998) and that the maternal grandmother is the most important grandparent in their lives (Creasey and Koblewski, 1991). In the case of playmates, a maternal 'bridge' (Monserud, 2008) can explain the grandchild preference for maternal grandparents. However, the most relevant aspect that seems to affect emotionally close relationships is geographical propinquity. The youngsters feel more attached to the nearest grandparent with whom they interact more often. However, in northern Portugal there is a matrilocal tradition and young couples tend to live near the women's parents, which might not occur in other cultures. These findings are consistent with the intergenerational solidarity model: both gender and geographical distance comprise an opportunity structure that enhances or reduces the possibilities for association (Bengtson and Roberts, 1991; Silverstein and Bengston, 1997; Hammarström, 2005). Furthermore, frequent contacts and diversity of shared activities (association) favoured emotional closeness.

In order to understand the meaning that these adolescents gave to being a grandchild (role expectations), we cannot overlook their strong sense of filial responsibility, which has also been found among adult grandchildren (Robertson, 1976; Even-Zohar and Sharlin, 2009). Regardless of their sense of duty, the major booster to functional solidarity was emotional attachment combined with the senior's need (in the case of carers) provided that grandchildren were old enough to support these needs. Companions, despite having a strong sense of obligation, established less intimate relationships with their grandparent, which resulted in less expressive emotional support (functional solidarity).

The greater importance of affection compared with norms in contemporary grandparent–grandchild relationships is also a conclusion in Barranti's (1985) and Kivett's (1985) work. However, normative obligation remained the paramount driver within the least influential group, in contrast to the other three groups. This leads to the inference that relationships solely sustained by a sense of obligation are ones in which grandchildren have less influence on their grandparents. Within grandparent–grandchild relationships it was noticeable that lack of consensus over key values did not impair feelings of affection nor influence. Bengtson and Roberts (1991) also argue that affection is not necessarily linked to consensus over social values.

Limited role of the middle generation as mediator

A third aim was to consider the parent's role as mediator, which has been emphasised by several authors since seminal work by Robertson (1975). As the grandparents and grandchildren in our sample had long-standing bonds and frequently interacted with each other, leading to possible gain in generational autonomy, we expected that parental mediation would be low in many cases.

Our results suggest that parents do not play a prominent role as facilitators of the non-adjacent generations' association. Although younger adolescents (playmates) were somewhat more dependent on the middle generation, the other groups did not rely on parents to contact grandparents. They took the initiative to be with their grandparents and did not need parents' encouragement. Companions took their grandchilding responsibilities further and reminded parents of their obligations towards the elders. Within this group, the adolescents' interaction with their grandparents was mainly set by norms of family duty rather than by affection. Buddies' relationships with their grandparents were emotionally so strong that both buddies and grandparents defended each other's positions against parents. Grandparents were in this case mediators between parent and child and could be seen as stress buffers (Hagestad, 1984, 1985; Bengtson, 1985) or arbitrators (Bengston, 1985; Hagestad, 1985).

Our findings suggest that age of the grandchild is an important factor that must be considered while analysing the mediator role of parents. We might assume that as children grow older they gain autonomy and, motivated either by affection or responsibility, they interact with their grandparents without relying as much on their parents' mediation. On the other hand, in a society with a high proportion of working women, mothers (the traditional primary kin keepers) may have less available time, not only to mediate this tie but also to provide care. This may result in the solidarity between non-adjacent generations gaining in importance, relative to the solidarity displayed by the middle generation (Even-Zohar and Sharlin, 2009). Grandchildren may also encourage their parents to strengthen the bonds with the older generation. This grandchild mediation is mainly visible in relationships of great intimacy (buddies). We conclude that each generation has the potential to reinforce the ties among the other two generations and to strengthen intergenerational family solidarity.

Conclusion

This chapter provides novel insights regarding not only the areas of grandchildren's influence on their grandparents, but also the channels by which this influence is exerted. Grandchildren are indeed able to affect grandparents' attitudes through providing information and persuasion, especially concerning practical matters such as technology, environmentally friendly practices and dietary routines, but also influence their social activities and perceptions of societal changes. The elders were susceptible to these influences, despite some resistance to changing their core values and beliefs.

This bond between adolescent grandchildren and their grandparents may be empowering for the latter. It can represent a source of 'decoded' information, a bridge to overcome a generational gap that facilitates adjustment to contemporary societal changes and minimises grandparents' risk of social exclusion. The potential of grandchildren as agents of socialisation must be considered while designing policies for the social integration of older people. Any future research could be enriched by exploring family dynamics and considering the perspectives of all three generations.

Our research has contributed to knowledge of non-adjacent generations by identifying that the combination of shared activities (associational solidarities) and the provision of emotional support and assistance (functional solidarities) might explain variation in the influence of adolescent grandchildren over grandparents. Youngsters are more influential over grandparents with whom they have emotionally close relationships, where intense interaction takes place, diverse activities are shared, and support is given. Adolescent grandchildren may help grandparents interpret societal changes, encourage social engagement and healthier behaviours, and strengthen ties with other family members such as parents. They vary in how they engage with their grandparents and assume diverse styles while 'acting' as grandchildren.

Grandchildren privilege the relationship with grandmothers or with maternal grandparents. This is consistent with the 'grandmother theory' that emphasises how older women play a key role in raising their daughters' children (Harper, 2005). It is also noticeable that the closest and more influential relationships (buddies) are established with grandmothers. In most of the cases, the younger grandchildren (playmates) also have a privileged relationship with grandmothers. In this sense, older women are more prone to be influenced than older men, as they have more contact with grandchildren as 'influential' agents.

We also found that the mediation performed by the middle generation may be less significant. Adolescent grandchildren who maintain close connections with their grandparents display autonomy and rely less on parents' intervention to preserve that bond. Grandparent–grandchild relationships will be better understood if the mutual nature of influences and the potential autonomy from the parents' generation is considered.

References

Armstrong, M. (2005) 'Grandchildren's influences on grandparents: a resource for integration of older people in New Zealand's aging society', *Journal of Intergenerational Relationships*, vol 3, no 2, pp 7-21.

Attar-Schwartz, S., Tan, J.-P. and Buchanan, A. (2009) 'Adolescents' perspectives on relationships with grandparents: the contribution of adolescent, grandparent, and parent–grandparent relationship variables', *Children and Youth Services Review*, vol 31, no 9, pp 1057-66.

Barranti, C. (1985) 'The grandparent/grandchild relationship: family resource in an era of voluntary bonds', *Family Relations*, vol 34, no 3, pp 343-52.

Bengtson, V. (1985) 'Diversity and symbolism in grand-parental roles', in V. Bengtson and J. Robertson (eds) *Grandparenthood*, Beverly Hills, CA: Sage Publications, pp 11-25.

Bengtson, V. (2001) 'Beyond the nuclear family: the increasing importance of multigenerational bonds', *Journal of Marriage and Family*, vol 63, no 1, pp 1-16.

Bengtson, V. and Roberts, R. (1991) 'Intergenerational solidarity in aging families: an example of formal theory construction', *Journal of Marriage and Family*, vol 53, no 4, pp 856-70.

Bucx, F., van Wel, F., Knijn, T. and Hagendoom, L. (2008) 'Intergenerational contact and the life course status of young adult children', *Journal of Marriage and Family*, vol 70, no 1, pp 144-56.

Chan, C. and Elder, G. (2000) 'Matrilineal advantage in grandchild–grandparent relations', *The Gerontologist*, vol 40, no 2, pp 179-90.

Cherlin, A. and Furstenberg, F. (1985) 'Styles and strategies of grandparenting', in V. Bengtson and J. Robertson (eds) *Grandparenthood*, Beverly Hills, CA: Sage Publications, pp 97-116.

Creasey, G. and Koblewski, J. (1991) 'Adolescent grandchildren's relationships with maternal and paternal grandmothers and grandfathers', *Journal of Adolescence*, vol 14, no 4, pp 373-87.

Connidis, I. (2001) *Family ties and aging*, Thousand Oaks, CA: Sage Publications.

Corbin, J. and Strauss, A. (2008) *Basics of qualitative research: Techniques and procedures for developing grounded theory* (3rd edn), London: Sage Publications.

Delerue, A. (2007) 'Cohabitation, "intimité à distance" ou isolement familial? Les rapports familiaux intergénérationnels aux âges élevés dans la société portugaise', Unpublished thesis presented for the title of Docteur en Sciences Sociales (Démographie), UCL, Louvain-la-Neuve.

Dellmann-Jenkins, M., Papalia, D. and Lopez, M. (1987) 'Teenagers' reported interaction with grandparents: exploring the extent of alienation', *Journal of Family and Economic Issues*, vol 8, no 3-4, pp 35-46.

Denham, T. and Smith, C. (1989) 'The influence of grandparents on grandchildren: a review of the literature and resources', *Family Relations*, vol 38, no 3, pp 345-50.

Doyle, M., O'Dywer, C. and Timonen, V. (2010) '"How can you just cut off a whole side of the family and say move on?" The reshaping of paternal grandparent–grandchild relationships following divorce or separation in the middle generation', *Family Relations*, vol 59, no 5, pp 587-98.

Eisenberg, A. (1988) 'Grandchildren's perspectives on relationships with grandparents: the influence of gender across generations', *Sex Roles*, vol 19, no 3-4, pp 205-17.

Even-Zohar, A. and Sharlin, S. (2009) 'Grandchildhood: adult grandchildren's perception of their role towards their grandparents from an intergenerational perspective', *Journal of Comparative Family Studies*, vol 40, no 2, pp 167-85.

Franks, L., Hughes, J., Phelps, L. and Williams, D. (1993) 'Intergenerational influences on midwest college students by their grandparents and significant elders', *Educational Gerontology*, vol 19, no 3, pp 265-71.

Hagestad, G. (1984) 'The continuous bond: a dynamic multigenerational perspective on parent–child relations between adults', in M. Perlmutter (ed) *Parent–child interaction and parent–child relations in child development*, The Minnesota Symposium on Child Psychology, vol 17, Hillsdale, NJ: Lawrence Erlbaum Associates, pp 129-58.

Hagestad, G. (1985) 'Continuity and connectedness', in V. Bengtson and J. Robertson (eds) *Grandparenthood*, Beverly Hills, CA: Sage Publications, pp 31-48.

Hammarström, G. (2005) 'The construct of intergenerational solidarity in a lineage perspective: a discussion on underlying theoretical assumptions', *Journal of Aging Studies*, vol 19, no 1, pp 33-51.

Harper, S. (2005) 'Grandparenthood', in M. Johnson (ed) *Handbook of age and ageing*, Cambridge: Cambridge University Press, pp 422-8.

Hoff, A. (2007) 'Patterns of intergenerational support in grandparent–grandchild and parent–child relationships in Germany', *Ageing and Society*, vol 27, no 5, pp 643-65.

Jerrome, D. (1990) 'Intimate relationships', in J. Bond and P. Coleman (eds) *Ageing in society*, London: Sage Publications.

Kahana, E. and Kahana, B. (1970) 'Grandparenthood from the perspective of the developing grandchild', *Developmental Psychology*, vol 3, no 1, pp 98-105.

Kivett, V. (1985) 'Grandfathers and grandchildren: patterns of association, helping, and psychological closeness', *Family Relations*, vol 34, no 4, pp 565-71.

Lawton, L., Silverstein, M. and Bengtson, V. (1994) 'Affection, social contact, and geographic distance between parents and their adult children', *Journal of Marriage and Family*, vol 56, no 1, pp 57-68.

Matthews, S. and Sprey, J. (1985) 'Adolescents' relationship with grandparents: an empirical contribution to conceptual clarification', *Journal of Gerontology*, vol 40, no 5, pp 621-6.

Monserud, M. (2008) 'Intergenerational relationships and affectual solidarity between grandparents and young adults', *Journal of Marriage and Family*, vol 70, no 1, pp 182-95.

Neugarten, B. and Weinstein, K. (1964) 'The changing American grandparent', *Family Relations*, vol 26, no 2, pp 199-204.

Parsons, T. (1955) 'Family structures and the socialization of the child', in T. Parsons and R. Bales (eds) *Family, socialization, interaction process*, Glencoe, IL: Free Press, pp 35-131.

Putney, N. and Bengtson, V. (2002) 'Socialization and the family revisited', in R.A. Settersten and T.J. Owens (eds) *New frontiers in socialization: Advances in life course research*, London: Elsevier, pp 165-94.

Roberto, K. (1990) 'Grandparent and grandchild relationships', in T. Brubaker (ed) *Family relationships in later life* (2nd edn), Newbury Park, CA: Sage, pp 100-12.

Roberto, K. and Skogland, R. (1996) 'Interactions with grandparents and greatgrandparents: a comparison of activities, influences, and relationships', *International Journal of Aging and Human Development*, vol 43, no 2, pp 107-17.

Robertson, J. (1975) 'Interaction in three generation families, parents as mediators: toward a theoretical perspective', *International Journal Aging and Human Development*, vol 6, no 2, pp 103-10.

Robertson, J. (1976) 'Significance of grandparents perceptions of young adult grandchildren', *The Gerontologist*, vol 16, no 2, pp 137-40.

Silverstein, M. and Bengtson, V. (1997) 'Intergenerational solidarity and the structure of adult child–parent relationships in American families', *American Journal of Sociology*, vol 103, no 2, pp 429-60.

Silverstein, M., Giarrusso, R. and Bengtson, V. (1998) 'Intergenerational solidarity and the grandparent role', in M. Szinovacz (ed) *Handbook on grandparenthood*, Westport, CT: Greenwood Press, pp 144-58.

Silverstein, M., Lawton, L. and Bengtson, V. (1994) 'Types of relations between parents and adult children', in V.L. Bengtson and R.A. Harootyan (eds) *Intergenerational linkages: Hidden connections in American society*, New York, NY: Springer, pp 43-76.

Spitze, G. and Ward, R. (1998) 'Gender variations', in M. Szinovacz (ed) *Handbook on grandparenthood*, Westport, CT: Greenwood Press, pp 113-27.

Taylor, A., Robila, M. and Lee, H. (2005) 'Distance, contact, and intergenerational relationships: grandparents and adult grandchildren from an international perspective', *Journal of Adult Development*, vol 12, no 1, pp 33-41.

Tomlin, A. (1998) 'Grandparents' influences on grandchildren', in M. Szinovacz (ed) *Handbook on grandparenthood*, Westport, CT: Greenwood Press, pp 144-58.

Torres, A., Mendes, R. and Lapa, T. (2008) 'Families in Europe', *Portuguese Journal of Social Science*, vol 7, no 1, pp 49-84.

Turner, J. (1991) *Social influence*, Buckingham: Open University Press.

Vala, J. and Monteiro, M.B. (2002) *Psicologia social*, Lisboa: Fundação Calouste Gulbenkian.

Whitbeck, L., Hoyt, D. and Huck, S. (1993) 'Family relationship history, contemporary parent–grandparent relationship quality, and the grandparent–grandchild relationship', *Journal of Marriage and Family*, vol 55, no 4, pp 1025-35.

ELEVEN

Social contact between grandparents and older grandchildren: a three-generation perspective

Katharina Mahne and Oliver Huxhold

Introduction

The study of the relationships between grandparents and grandchildren is important for various reasons. Being a grandparent is generally a central role in later life (Hodgson, 1992; Mahne and Motel-Klingebiel, 2012). Relationships with grandchildren are reported by the majority of grandparents as among the most important relationships they have (Reitzes and Mutran, 2002; Clarke and Roberts, 2004) and grandparent identity is positively related to wellbeing (Reitzes and Mutran, 2004a). Despite its obvious centrality, the opportunities for the enactment of the grandparental role are subject to change over time.

The transition to grandparenthood is no longer a self-evident life event since fertility rates are declining in most EU countries (Frejka and Sobotka, 2008; Harper et al, 2010). Uhlenberg and Cheuk (2010, p 449) even predict that grandchildren will be in 'short supply' in the near future. Moreover, shifting family patterns indicated by greater geographical distance between family members and higher rates of female employment and marital disruption have repeatedly been shown to influence the quality of grandparent–grandchild ties (Uhlenberg and Hammill, 1998; Lussier et al, 2002). Thus, family systems become more complex and the framework for the grandparent–grandchild tie has to be renegotiated throughout the life course (Hagestad, 1985).

The quality of relations with grandchildren is likely to vary among grandparents, and some grandparents may have no or very little contact with their grandchildren. Since grandparenthood is often described as emotionally rewarding and the grandparent role provides important subjective meanings to the majority of grandparents (Kivnick, 1982;

Silverstein and Marenco, 2001), the way grandparent–grandchild ties are experienced is a crucial criterion for the quality of later life. The frequency of contact is a tangible indicator of how the relationship between a grandparent and a grandchild is enacted.

While there is consensus on *why* it is important to study grandparent–grandchild contact, the issue of *how* to study grandparent–grandchild contact needs further development. Research to date has suggested that the middle generation plays a crucial role as a gatekeeper or facilitator of the grandparent–grandchild connection (Drew and Smith, 1999; Kemp, 2007). It is therefore important to take a three-generation approach when studying the relations between grandparents and grandchildren (Hagestad, 2006). Nevertheless, only a few previous studies have simultaneously considered the specific impact of grandparents, adult children and grandchildren on the frequency of contact between grandparents and grandchildren (Geurts et al, 2009).

Grandparent–grandchild relations are varied, even in the context of the same family (Davey et al, 2009). Often, however, studies are based on grandparent–grandchild dyads that have been selected by a predetermined pattern. For example, reports on only 'the closest' grandparent or grandchild will be biased towards the positive (Brussoni and Boon, 1998; Taylor et al, 2005) (see also Chapter Ten). Equally, using a composite measure relating to all grandchildren or categorising grandparents into different groups on the basis of specific styles of grandparenting (Neugarten and Weinstein, 1964; Mueller et al, 2002) cannot capture the complexity of family relations. In order to account for within-family variation as well, it is vital to examine different individual grandparent–grandchild ties in one family. The approach to the grandparent–grandchild relationship applied in this study thus takes a three-generation perspective on randomly selected relationships of grandparents and their grandchildren both within and between families.

This chapter analyses how often grandparents in Germany interact with their grandchildren aged 16 and over. Analyses are based on data from the German Ageing Survey (DEAS), a nationally representative survey of the population aged 40 and older. This dataset provides information on individual grandparent–grandchild relationships as well as the respective adult children of the grandparents. With regard to the concept of intergenerational solidarity, we explore the individual contributions of all three generations involved in the association between grandparents and grandchildren. First, this chapter discusses the intergenerational solidarity model and its applicability for the study of grandparenthood. Next, the existing literature on contact between grandparents and grandchildren is outlined. The formulation of several hypotheses guides the empirical analyses. After a description of the data set, measures and method employed, the findings are presented. The chapter concludes with a discussion of the results.

Grandparenthood and the intergenerational solidarity model

The intergenerational solidarity model was originally developed as a conceptual and empirical instrument to describe and analyse the relations between parents and their adult children (Bengtson and Schrader, 1982; Roberts and Bengtson, 1990; Bengtson and Roberts, 1991) (see also Chapters One, Six and Ten). The model builds on the assumption that the strength of bonds between the generations in a family – intergenerational solidarity – can be described within a framework comprising the following six dimensions. *Associational solidarity* relates to the frequency of contact and shared activities between the generations. This dimension depicts an important aspect of the actual enactment of intergenerational relations and is the dependent variable in this chapter. *Affectual solidarity* refers to the positive sentiments towards family members and the perceived reciprocity of these sentiments. It deals with the emotional bonds between family members. *Consensual solidarity* involves shared values, attitudes and beliefs among the generations. This dimension quantifies the degree of agreement on these aspects. *Functional solidarity* refers to helping behaviour and the exchange of various forms of support. *Normative solidarity* is the strength of commitment to intergenerational obligations. It describes the importance of family roles and norms like familism. *Structural solidarity* indicates the opportunity structure for intergenerational relationships, and the various factors that can enhance or hinder the development of intergenerational interaction.

Associational solidarity has been labeled 'the most idiosyncratic characteristic of family solidarity' (Bengtson and Roberts, 1991, p 861) as it is subject to the opportunity structure, norms of familism, and affection, which all influence the extent of association between the generations in a family. The frequency of interaction between family members is theorised as a manifest behavioural outcome of intergenerational solidarity. In empirical research on the intergenerational solidarity model, the frequency of contact between family members is therefore often operationalised as the dependent variable reflecting associational solidarity.

Although primarily designed and used for the analysis of adjacent intergenerational parent–child relations, Silverstein and colleagues

(1998) argue that the solidarity concept can be equally applied to the study of non-adjacent intergenerational relations, such as those of grandparents and grandchildren. They argue that most studies on grandparent–grandchild ties in fact apply the intergenerational solidarity model, but do this more implicitly than explicitly. This chapter therefore keeps to the overall framework and terminology of the solidarity model, but identifies the influence of the middle generation as a distinctive feature in the relationships between grandparents and grandchildren (Silverstein et al, 1998). Nevertheless, the solidarity concept has not been developed theoretically by including the moderating or mediating effects that the middle generation has on the grandparent–grandchild connection. This theoretical enhancement is needed in order to extend the original intergenerational solidarity model for the study of non-adjacent family generations.

Dimensions of grandparenthood

This chapter focuses on the contributions of grandparents, adult children and grandchildren to the frequency of social contact between grandparents and older grandchildren. We pay special attention to the changing opportunity structures for grandparent–grandchild interaction, and the specific role of the middle generation in relation to the different dimensions of intergenerational solidarity.

Frequency of contact (associational solidarity)

The frequency of contact has been labelled a 'manifest' form of intergenerational solidarity within families (Silverstein et al, 1998). How often grandparents and grandchildren are in contact with each other provides a solid behavioural outcome of this relationship. The impact of age, gender and lineage is discussed in many studies on the grandparent–grandchild association. Regarding age, or – to be more precise – stage of the family life course, studies in general report less frequent contact in older dyads and declining interaction as both generations age (Uhlenberg and Hammill, 1998; Silverstein and Long, 1998; Silverstein and Marenco, 2001; Geurts et al, 2009; Hurme et al, 2010).

Geurts and colleagues (2009) point out that differences in contact according to age of grandchild are mainly explained by grandchildren's patterns of co-residence with their parents. Leaving the parental home reduces parents' influence on regulating or instigating grandparent–grandchild interaction. Hurme and colleagues (2010) investigated several traditional and new forms of interaction and found less contact with older grandparents only in relation to landline and mobile phone calls, whereas the frequency of meeting grandchildren and writing letters to them was not age related. However, grandchildren in the same study report the use of text messaging less often with older grandparents. In Uhlenberg and Hammill's (1998) study of grandparent–grandchild contact, age and gender of the grandparent interact. For grandmothers they found a small age effect on contact frequency, but not for grandfathers. Using longitudinal data, Silverstein and Long (1998) found a constant decrease of face-to-face contact with grandchildren over the grandparent's life course. As grandchildren grow older, not only does parents' influence diminish, but also grandchildren's focus on peers and partners increases.

Some studies identify a gender pattern in grandparent–grandchild interaction. Silverstein and Marenco (2001) find grandmothers to be more involved in any kind of interaction with grandchildren such as babysitting, talking about problems or meeting at family gatherings. Similarly, other studies found grandfathers to have less contact with their grandchildren (Reitzes and Mutran, 2004b; Pollet et al, 2007; Geurts et al, 2009). Uhlenberg and Hammill (1998, p 281), however, state that the influence of gender should be 'neither neglected nor exaggerated'.

Lineage, however, seems to be an important influence on the grandparent–grandchild association. Contact frequency is usually higher for grandchildren who descend from daughters than for the offspring of sons (Uhlenberg and Hammill, 1998; Pollet et al, 2007). One explanation for this matrilineal preference suggested by evolutionary biology is the relational uncertainty that only exists for fathers (Bishop et al, 2009). According to this approach, this uncertainty leads to grandparents investing more in daughters' than in sons' offspring (Michalski and Shackelford, 2005). From a sociological standpoint, this matrilineal preference is seen as due to the kin-keeping role that is still mainly provided by female family members (Lye, 1996). The close and intense relations between mothers and daughters usually translate into more intimate relations with daughters' grandchildren. This becomes especially relevant in the case of divorce in the middle generation (Kruk and Hall, 1995; Cooney and Smith, 1996; Drew and Smith, 1999). Since mainly mothers remain the custodial parent following divorce or break-up, paternal grandparents may have more difficulty enacting the grandparent role (see also Chapter Eight in this volume).

Opportunities for contact (structural solidarity)

The intergenerational connection is highly dependent on a range of different opportunities, which can be characterised as the structural component within the model of intergenerational solidarity. Geographical proximity is beneficial for maintaining frequent interaction, especially face-to-face contact. Several studies support the thesis that greater spatial distance between grandparents and grandchildren is associated with less contact (Uhlenberg and Hammill, 1998; Mills, 1999; Mueller and Elder, 2003). Hurme and colleagues (2010) find distance to be responsible only for a decrease in face-to-face contact, whereas other forms of contact are not affected and writing letters is, for example, more frequent among grandparents and grandchildren who live at a greater distance.

In this chapter, we also examine other opportunity factors. Although previous studies provide no evidence that grandparents' employment status affects contact frequency with grandchildren (Uhlenberg and Hammill, 1998; Silverstein and Marenco, 2001), it seems reasonable to expect that grandparents who are actively participating in the labour market experience time restrictions that might reduce their interaction with grandchildren. Evidence for the influence of grandparents' health status is mixed. Whereas Uhlenberg and Hammill (1998) do not find contact frequency to vary with grandparents' health, Silverstein and Marenco (2001) show that better health is associated with higher involvement in 'fun' activities. Reitzes and Mutran (2004b) report an interaction with the grandparent's gender and health – namely that for grandmothers, poor health is positively related to contact with grandchildren, but for grandfathers the opposite is true. The authors theorise that the generally closer relations with grandmothers encourage grandchildren to intensify contact during difficult times, whereas grandfathers might find it more problematic to engage in grandparenting when facing health problems.

Well-educated grandparents are in less frequent contact with grandchildren than their less educated counterparts (Uhlenberg and Hammill, 1998; Reitzes and Mutran, 2004b). Since higher education is associated with higher levels of engagement in paid work and volunteering, these grandparents probably experience several competing roles to their grandparent role and greater demands on their time. However, Mueller and Elder (2003) found that higher educated grandparents are more likely to act as influential and supportive types of grandparents. They suggest that better opportunities for travelling in order to see the grandchild, that are associated with the higher socioeconomic status of well-educated grandparents, could be responsible for this finding.

Finally, grandparents' marital status can also influence the opportunity structure for contact with grandchildren. Especially for grandfathers, being married enhances interaction with grandchildren (Reitzes and Mutran, 2004b) due to the kin-keeping role of their wives. Divorce in the grandparent generation, however, is often associated with less frequent grandchild contact (Uhlenberg and Hammill, 1998), which is especially true for grandfathers (Kruk and Hall, 1995; King, 2003) (also see Chapter Eight). Reasons for this are related to the predominantly negative influence of divorce on the quality of the parent–child relation (Lye, 1996; Ahrons, 2006; Daatland, 2007). Although both mothers and fathers can experience weakening ties with adult children following divorce, it is mainly the fathers who are affected by less contact or support (Tomassini et al, 2004, 2007; Lin, 2008).

Emotional bonds (affectual solidarity)

Emotional bonds between family members and their frequency of interaction are closely linked, with a positive association found between affectual and associational solidarity (Bengtson and Roberts, 1991). Grandparents and grandchildren who feel close to each other interact more often (Silverstein and Marenco, 2001; Davey et al, 2009). Rather than assuming a clear direction of effects of emotional closeness on contact frequency, the relationship between the affectual and associational components of intergenerational solidarity may change over time. Silverstein and Long (1998) find diverging patterns of contact frequency and emotional closeness over the life course. As grandparents and grandchildren age, interaction decreases while the emotional bonds remain close. In the present cross-sectional study, however, emotional closeness between grandparents and grandchildren is understood as a predictor of their contact frequency. At a given point in time, the relationship between both components cannot be modelled as mutually dependent. Furthermore, emotionally close relations within the family can compensate for the usually negative effects of divorce or greater geographical distance (King, 2003; Engstler and Huxhold, 2010).

Family role importance (normative solidarity)

The impact of family values and filial obligations has mainly been studied in the context of intergenerational helping behaviour (Kohli and Künemund, 2003; Silverstein et al, 2006; Lowenstein et al, 2007).

Personal values and norms about family roles – normative solidarity – are theorised as shaping the evaluation of a situation and the resulting behaviour. Silverstein and colleagues (2006) consider filial obligations as a latent resource that becomes manifest in triggering situations such as 'parental need'. Regarding the grandparent–grandchild relationship, it has been shown that the perceived importance of the grandparental role is positively related to how often grandchildren and grandparents interact (Silverstein and Marenco, 2001; Mahne and Motel-Klingebiel, 2012).

The middle generation: gatekeepers and facilitators

This chapter analyses the association between grandparents and older grandchildren and focuses on the influence of the middle generation of adult children. In particular, studies on the effects of divorce in the middle generation have highlighted the important gatekeeper function that the middle generation plays (Cooney and Smith, 1996; Drew and Smith, 1999; Lussier et al, 2002; Kemp, 2007; see also Chapter Eight in this volume). The history and the present quality of the grandparent–adult child relationship leave their imprints on the grandparent–grandchild tie (Whitbeck et al, 1993).

Aims and hypotheses

Building on our literature review, this chapter analyses German data on the frequency of contact between grandparents and grandchildren aged 16 years and above to examine the following hypotheses.

Life course hypotheses: The frequency of grandparent–grandchild interaction decreases over the life course. It is assumed that older grandparents have less contact than younger ones (hypothesis 1a) and that older grandchildren have less contact than younger grandchildren (hypothesis 1b).

Kin-keeper hypothesis: Because women generally display more intimate relationships with kin and because female role expectations are related to the maintenance of family life, it is assumed that grandmothers have more contact with grandchildren than grandfathers (hypothesis 2).

Lineage hypotheses: Based on the primary involvement of women in kin-keeping obligations and according to evolutionary theorising, it is expected that grandparents will have more contact with daughters' children – that is through the maternal lineage (hypothesis 3a). In addition, it is expected that there will be greater contact with biological grandchildren than step-grandchildren (hypothesis 3b).

Opportunity hypotheses: The frequency of contact is dependent on several aspects of the opportunity structure. It is expected that geographical distance decreases contact frequency (hypothesis 4a). Marital disruption often leads to strained relationships with family members. Therefore it is assumed that divorced or separated grandparents have less contact than others (hypothesis 4b). Due to the kin-keeping role of women, this is expected to be especially true for divorced grandfathers (hypothesis 4c). Potentially competing working-life roles of grandparents may impact on the grandparent–grandchild association. Employed grandparents are expected to have less contact than non-working grandparents (hypothesis 4d). Since bad health limits the ability to travel or engage in meetings with grandchildren, we assume that healthier grandparents will have more contact with their grandchildren (hypothesis 4e). Higher education usually implicates higher income and better resources for traveling to see grandchildren. Well-educated grandparents are therefore expected to have more contact than their less educated counterparts (hypothesis 4f).

Family role importance hypothesis: Personal attitudes are assumed to guide grandparent behaviour. We expect that grandparents who rate their role as a grandparent as more important will have more contact with grandchildren (hypothesis 5).

Middle generation hypotheses: Higher contact frequency with the adult child (middle generation) should be associated with higher contact frequency with the grandchild (hypothesis 6a). Marital disruption of the adult child may reduce the opportunities for contact, so we expect grandparents to have less contact with a grandchild if their adult child is divorced or separated (hypothesis 6b). Due to the impact of lineage and female kin keeping, this should be especially true for grandchildren of sons (hypothesis 6c).

Emotional bonds hypotheses: Associational and affectual components of intergenerational solidarity are linked. Grandparents who experience emotionally closer relations with grandchildren are assumed to have more contact (hypothesis 7a). Moreover, emotionally close relations with grandchildren are expected to buffer the negative effects of greater geographical distance and divorce or separation (hypothesis 7b).

Method

The analyses use data from DEAS, a nationwide representative cross-sectional and longitudinal survey of the population aged over 40 in Germany. It is funded by the Federal Ministry for Family Affairs, Senior Citizens, Women and Youth and examines a large spectrum of themes:

current occupational status and living conditions after retirement, social participation and leisure activities, economic and housing situation, family ties and other social contacts, as well as issues regarding health, wellbeing and life goals. The first DEAS survey took place in 1996, and the second wave in 2002. The chapter analyses the most recent wave conducted in 2008, which covers detailed information on grandparenthood.

Data were collected on all of the respondents' children and grandchildren. Detailed information on the intergenerational relationship is available for all the children and for one randomly selected grandchild per child (this applies to the first four children). The procedure of selecting one random grandchild per child avoids biased information on the grandparent–grandchild relationship. Contact frequency with a grandchild is not asked if the particular grandchild is younger than 16 years. For grandchildren aged 16 years and older in the sample, it is likely that the measure of contact frequency relates primarily to interaction that is initiated by grandparents and grandchildren themselves.

We analyse a sub-sample of first-time and panel participants in 2008 who reported having at least one grandchild aged 16 years and older. The sub-sample consists of 1,754 grandparents and a corresponding 2,601 observations of grandparent–grandchild relations. Where a grandchild lived within the same household as the grandparent, this particular observation was omitted from the sub-sample.

Measures and analytic strategy

The question on contact frequency in DEAS does not differentiate between face-to-face and remote contact. Contact frequency therefore indicates a single and overall measure of frequency of interaction. Contact frequency with children and grandchildren was assessed by answering options ranging from (1) 'never' to (7) 'daily'. Emotional closeness was rated using five-answer options ranging from (1) 'not close at all' to (5) 'very close'. Geographical proximity ranged from (1) 'in the neighbourhood' to (5) 'further away, abroad'. Family role importance was assessed using the question: 'On the whole, how important is your role as a grandmother/grandfather to you?'. Participants were given four answer options, ranging from 'completely unimportant' to 'very important'. Self-reported health status was measured on a five-point scale ranging from (1) 'very bad' to (5) 'very good', and educational level was coded as (1) 'low', (2) 'middle' and (3) 'high'. All eligible variables are T-standardised[1] in order to achieve comparability of effects.

The dataset contains a hierarchical structure with data on up to four grandchildren per grandparent. Due to the nested nature of the data, a multilevel regression was conducted. The analyses distinguish two levels: the grandchildren and adult children (on level 1 – depicting within-family variation) and the grandparents (on level 2 – depicting between-family variation). Information on the grandchildren and children are on the same level, since we use the information on one randomly selected grandchild per adult child only. This procedure allows us to differentiate variation between grandparents (or families) from variation within grandparents (or families). Variation in the dependent variable of contact frequency can be attributed to the two different levels of the data by allowing for random intercept and slopes.

We run two different models. The first model tests hypotheses 1 to 6. In the second model, we additionally include information on affectional solidarity in order to test hypotheses 7a and 7b on the distinct and moderating influences of emotional closeness. In both models, all variables are entered simultaneously. This means that every reported coefficient is adjusted for all other variables in the model.

Results

The results in Table 11.1 clearly show the value of adopting a multilevel, multigenerational approach. Characteristics of all three generations involved do have an independent impact on the frequency of contact between grandparents and older grandchildren, which varies not only between families but also within families. The Intraclass Correlation (ICC = 0.355) shows that about 35 percent of the variation in contact is attributable to characteristics that differ between families (level 2). The larger part, about 65 per cent of all variation, however, originates from different relations that grandparents experience with their different grandchildren within the same family (level 1). This indicates the value of using an approach that incorporates information on several grandchildren per grandparent.

Model 1 (in Table 11.1) shows a negative relationship between age of grandparent ($\beta = -0.06, p < .001$)[2] and amount of contact between grandparent and grandchild, supporting the *life course hypothesis* that older grandparents have less contact than younger grandparents (hypothesis 1a). Similarly, there is a negative association with age of grandchild ($\beta = -0.16, p < .001$), indicating that older grandchildren interact less often with their grandparents (hypothesis 1b). The stages of the life course of both grandparents and grandchildren therefore have independent effects on how often they communicate. Since Model

1 controls for cohort-related differences in grandparental educational attainment and health, we have some support for the assumption that the effects for age may represent a life-course phenomenon.

Table 11.1: Multilevel model results predicting the frequency of grandparents' social contact with their grandchildren aged 16 years and older

		Model 1	Model 2
		β	B
Level 2 (between family variation)			
Grandparent			
	Age	–0.06***	–0.06***
	Grandfather	0.31	0.49
	Divorced	–2.26**	–2.14**
	Grandfather* Divorced	–3.27*	–2.87*
	Employed	–1.45*	–1.67**
	Subjective health status	0.02	0.01
	Education level	0.29	0.17
	Role importance	0.25***	0.18***
Level 1 (within family variation)			
Grandchild			
	Age	–0.16***	–0.10***
	Geographical distance	–0.30***	–0.28***
	Biological child	3.73***	0.85
	Emotional closeness	–	0.52***
Adult Child			
	Son	–1.23***	–0.74*
	Divorced	–0.75	–0.47
	Son* Divorced	–2.42*	–0.07
	Contact between grandparent and adult child	0.41***	0.25***
Intraclass correlation		0.355	0.355

Notes: * $p < .05$; ** $p < .01$; *** $p < .001$.
n = 1,754 grandparents, 2,601 grandchildren.

There is no evidence for the *kin-keeper hypothesis*. The coefficient for being a grandfather ($\beta = 0.31$, NS) rather than a grandmother is not statistically significant, indicating that grandmothers and grandfathers do not differ in their contact frequency (hypothesis 2) when the influence of all other variables in the model is controlled. This is probably due to the age structure of the grandchildren in the sample. Grandchildren aged 16 and older no longer need childcare, a form of help that grandmothers provide more often than grandfathers. Other forms of interaction or activities are more likely to be shared with both grandparents alike. In an initial model, the gender of the grandchild was also controlled for, but it had no effect at all.

In contrast, there is strong support for both *lineage hypotheses*. Grandparents interact less often with their grandchildren if they are offspring of their son ($\beta = -1.23, p < .001$) (hypothesis 3a). Thus, the less close bonds that exist between (grand)parents and sons may influence the grandparents' relationships with their grandchildren. Lineage has a far stronger effect on grandparent–grandchild interaction than grandparents' and grandchildren's gender or age. Changing patterns of socialisation in terms of a weakening of traditional gender roles – that later cohorts may experience – could affect and diminish the effects of lineage in the future.

When we analyse the impact of whether the grandchild is a biological child of the adult child or a step-child, grandparents interact more often with grandchildren who are biological children ($\beta = 3.73, p < .001$) of their own adult children, which supports hypothesis 3b. Since relationships with step-grandchildren usually start later in the life course, it could be that the shorter period of shared lifetime between step-grandparents and step-children is responsible for the lower contact frequency. In an earlier version of the model, we also included the number of siblings of the grandchild. However, being an only child did not affect the frequency of contact.

Evidence for the *opportunity hypotheses* is mixed. Geographical distance – the classic indicator of structural solidarity – does have an effect. Grandparents interact less often with grandchildren who live further away ($\beta = -0.30, p < .001$) (hypothesis 4a). Since we are analysing a global measure of contact, we do not know whether residential propinquity mainly provides opportunities for certain forms of interaction such as face-to-face contact. However, the impact of geographical distance is relatively small.

The most important 'opportunity factor' is grandparents' marital status. Grandparents who are divorced or separated have less contact with their grandchildren ($\beta = -2.26, p < .01$) (hypothesis 4b). Obviously, marital disruption in one generation alters family relations in a wider context. As predicted by hypothesis 4c, there is lower contact with grandchildren for divorced or separated grandfathers ($\beta = -3.27, p <$

.05). One potential explanation could be that grandmothers in their role as kin keepers are mainly responsible for initiating contact with grandchildren and that they – through their own communication with grandchildren – encourage their partners to interact with grandchildren as long as the marriage is intact. When grandfathers lose their wives as the kin keeper due to divorce or family break up, this has a negative impact on the grandfather–grandchild association.

Grandparents who actively take part in the labour force interact less often with their grandchildren ($\beta = -1.45, p < .05$) than grandparents who do not work (hypothesis 4d). Time restrictions and competing roles connected with employment therefore affect the grandparent–grandchild association. Contrary to our expectations, neither the subjective health status (hypothesis 4e) nor the educational level (hypothesis 4f) of grandparents uniquely accounts for variation in frequency of interaction with grandchildren.

Normative and associational solidarity interact. According to the *family role importance hypothesis*, grandparents, who derive greater meaning from grandparenthood, are in more frequent contact with their grandchildren than grandparents who rate their role less important ($\beta = 0.25, p < .001$) (hypothesis 5). Whether grandparents' value orientations guide action and therefore provide a basis for their association with grandchildren or whether grandparental role meaning is mainly an outcome of the frequency of contact, can only be unravelled using longitudinal analyses. Thus, future studies should examine the dynamic interrelation of values and behaviour over time.

As well as lineage playing a crucial role in the associational component of grandparent–grandchild solidarity, contact frequency of the grandparent with their adult child (the middle generation) also influences the extent of interaction between grandparents and grandchildren ($\beta = 0.41, p < .001$). As predicted by the *middle generation hypothesis*, higher contact frequency with an adult child is associated with higher contact frequency between grandparents and the respective older grandchildren (hypothesis 6a).

Although there is no main effect of divorce or separation in the children's generation on contact between grandparents and grandchildren ($\beta = -0.75$, NS) (hypothesis 6b), there is a strong interaction of gender and marital status (hypothesis 6c). Only where a son experiences marital or union dissolution do grandparents have less contact with their grandchildren ($\beta = -2.42, p < .05$). The fact that contact is less frequent for offspring of a son is amplified if a divorce occurs – a finding that is consistent with the results of earlier studies focusing on the impact of marital breakdown on intergenerational contact (see Chapters Eight and Nine in this volume).

Finally, we are interested in the impact of affectual solidarity, namely the emotional closeness that grandparents experience with their grandchildren (see Table 11.1, model 2). In line with the *emotional bonds hypothesis*, the level of emotional closeness itself has a discrete influence on contact frequency in the predicted way. Grandparents interact more often with those grandchildren for whom they feel more affection ($\beta = 0.52, p < .001$) (hypothesis 7a). However, the assumption of a buffer function of strong emotional bonds against the negative effects of geographical distance (hypothesis 7b) is not supported. In contrast, if 'emotional closeness' is included in model 2, the influence of a son's marital breakdown on the grandparent–grandchild association completely disappears (the effect becomes statistically insignificant, $\beta = -0.07$, NS) (hypothesis 7c). Having an emotionally close relationship with grandchildren may act as a safeguard for maintaining contact even during difficult times. The finding that emotional closeness eliminates the effect of divorce of a son on contact frequency is also more in line with the notion that lineage effects might be a consequence of the generally closer relationships between mothers and daughters.

Discussion and conclusion

The aim of this chapter has been to analyse the frequency of contact between grandparents and older grandchildren within the framework of intergenerational solidarity theory and using a three-generation perspective. By doing so, it is possible to take into consideration simultaneously the influences of characteristics of grandparents, their adult children and their grandchildren on the frequency of contact between grandparents and older grandchildren (aged at least 16 years). Given changing family and work patterns, it is pertinent to consider the effects that social changes, such as higher rates of divorce or employment, could potentially have on the opportunity structures for grandparent–grandchild contact. Since being a grandparent is a rewarding and valued role for many older people, the factors supporting or hindering the enactment of the grandparent role can provide important insights into the conditions for the quality of later life.

The results clearly show that the relationships between grandparents and older grandchildren cannot be understood as independent of or isolated from other family relationships, but are embedded in a complex family network. The multilevel approach showed that aspects of the family structure and the living situation of grandparents, grandchildren and adult children can all influence how often grandparents and grandchildren interact. Moreover, the enactment of the grandparent role varies even within the same family. Since each grandparent may experience differing relationship qualities with his or her different grandchildren, it is advisable to take into account several grandparent–grandchild ties per grandparent in order to capture the variability and complexity of the grandparent–grandchild association.

Although the results in many respects affirm our knowledge on the correlates of grandparent–grandchild contact frequency from earlier research, the study also adds to the existing literature. For the first time, grandparents' contact with their older grandchildren was studied in Germany using representative data on both grandmothers and grandfathers from varying social backgrounds and from different regions within the country.

The opportunities for interaction – the structural aspects of family solidarity – were found to play a crucial role. In line with other studies, divorce or separation in either the grandparent or the middle generation was associated with less contact with grandchildren. Divorced grandparents – and especially grandfathers – showed less frequent contact with grandchildren than other grandparents with similar characteristics. However, if a divorce had occurred in the middle generation, decreased contact was only observable among paternal grandparents (whose sons had divorced). These results imply differing grandparent–grandchild relationships according to lineage following divorce. One reason for this finding could be that kin-keeper functions are still associated with female role expectations. Given the increasing rates of divorce, remarriage and step-families, being a divorced or a step-grandparent will become more prevalent in the future. It is therefore possible that increasing numbers of future cohorts of grandfathers may experience less frequent contact with their grandchildren – at least if gender role expectations in terms of kin keeping do not change (see Chapter Nine).

In this context, the findings on the emotional bonds between grandparents and grandchildren – the affectual component of intergenerational solidarity – are especially noteworthy. Besides the positive influence of a close emotional relationship on the frequency of contact with the respective grandchild, we found a protective function of affection against the negative effects of an adult child's union dissolution and step-grandparenthood. Grandparents who experience an emotionally close relationship with their grandchild may be able to maintain their frequency of interactions despite disrupting family events.

It is not only the findings on divorce that corroborate the central role of the middle generation in facilitating or hindering grandparent–grandchild interaction. The positive effects of the grandparent–adult child association on grandparent–grandchild contact also show the importance of the middle generation in shaping ties with older grandchildren. High contact frequency with an adult child was associated with high contact frequency with the respective grandchildren. This finding is particularly interesting, because the analyses examined relationships with grandchildren who were at least 16 years or older and therefore in most cases no longer living in the same household with their parents (the middle generation). Since there is an independent effect for contact frequency of grandparents with the middle generation, the results may speak for intergenerational transmission of family interaction patterns. Thus, the relationship between a (grand)parent and an adult child prepares the ground for the relations between grandparents and grandchildren.

Grandparents who are still active in the labour force report less frequent contact with their older grandchildren. In the face of rising employment rates for people in their fifties and sixties – especially for women – it is assumed that future grandparents will more often experience coexisting and competing roles that may have a negative impact on the amount of contact between grandparents and grandchildren. However, the affectual and associational components of solidarity are not perfectly correlated. This implies that although being employed restricts the opportunities for grandparents to meet with or talk to their grandchildren, this may not necessarily be at the cost of an emotionally rewarding relationship.

The generalisation of our results to all possible grandparent–grandchild relationships is limited for two reasons. First, the analyses examine the relations with older grandchildren, who are at least age 16. On the one hand, this ensures that grandparent–grandchild interactions are less biased by the direct influence of the middle generation. Teenage and adult grandchildren are likely to decide on their own whether to talk to or to meet grandparents. On the other hand, frequency and forms of interaction between grandparents and grandchildren differ according to their age. If contact with grandchildren of younger ages had been considered, it would have been more likely to find evidence for the kin-keeper hypothesis. This is because contact with young grandchildren is often associated with childcare arrangements, and babysitting is more common among grandmothers. Furthermore, grandparents of young grandchildren are more likely to experience competing roles due to their engagement in paid work, which might also affect the frequency of contact with younger grandchildren. Second, the measure of contact frequency does not differentiate between face-to-face and remote contact. Geurts and colleagues (2009) have shown that, for example, divorce in the middle generation decreases face-to-face contact only, but not remote contact.

In summary, the present study revealed that grandparenthood is embedded in a complex system of family ties across multiple generations. In particular, variability in grandparent–grandchild relationships can only be understood by considering the moderating role of the middle generation. Analyses of associational solidarity between grandparents and grandchildren should, therefore, take into account the respective and different contributions of all generations involved. Moreover, grandparents experience diverse relations with different grandchildren not only in terms of behaviour, but also in terms of emotional closeness. Thus, future studies that do not address this variability in relationships with grandchildren will ignore large parts of the social reality that constitutes the specific situation of grandparents.

The present study also points to potential enhancements of the model of intergenerational solidarity (Bengtson and Schrader, 1982) to make it applicable for non-adjacent family generations. The prevalent multigenerational bonds in today's families could be explicitly integrated into the model's basic assumptions. Most importantly, interaction between grandparents and grandchildren is affected by wider social changes, such as increasing divorce rates and higher levels of labour market participation. Both trends may hinder grandparents', and especially grandfathers', frequent interaction with their grandchildren. However, strong emotional bonds with grandchildren can buffer against disruptions in the family structure. Thus, early investments in relationships with grandchildren could cushion the potentially detrimental effects of changes in family structure. When considering the conditions for the quality of later life, future research should pay more attention to the grandparenting experience and its consequences. Given the high subjective meaning of the grandparental role, unequal chances for the enactment of the role might affect older people's wellbeing in the future.

Acknowledgements

The authors would like to thank Dr Andreas Motel-Klingebiel for helpful comments and Wendy Marth for proofreading the manuscript. The data are from DEAS, provided by the Research Data Centre of the German Centre of Gerontology.

Notes

[1] The T-distribution is often used as a norm scale to overcome the different scaling of variables that are used in the same statistical procedure. The T-distribution has a mean of 50 and a standard deviation of 10. T-standardised values were obtained by the following equation: (10*((value-mean)/standard deviation))+50.

[2] The reported β values represent the regression coefficients obtained in the statistical model. A positive coefficient indicates a positive relationship between the predictor variable and grandparent–grandchild contact frequency. Vice versa, a negative coefficient indicates a negative relationship (for example, increased age is associated with decreased contact). The reported p values refer to the statistical significance (indicated by asterisks in Table 11.1); values above .05 are considered not significant, indicated by 'NS'.

References

Ahrons, C.R. (2006) 'Family ties after divorce: long-term implications for children', *Family Process*, vol 46, no 1, pp 53-65.

Bengtson, V.L. and Roberts, R.E.L. (1991) 'Intergenerational solidarity in aging families: an example of formal theory construction', *Journal of Marriage and Family*, vol 53, no 4, pp 856-870.

Bengtson, V.L. and Schrader, S.S. (1982) 'Parent–child relations', in D.J. Mangen and W.A. Peterson (eds) *Social roles and social participation*, Minneapolis, MN: University of Minnesota Press, pp 115-85.

Bishop, D.I, Meyer, B.C., Schmidt, T.M. and Gray, B.R. (2009) 'Differential investment behavior between grandparents and grandchildren: the role of paternity uncertainty', *Evolutionary Psychology*, vol 7, no 1, pp 66-77.

Brussoni, M.J. and Boon, S.D. (1998) 'Grandparental impact in young adults' relationships with their closest grandparents: the role of relationship strength and emotional closeness', *International Journal of Aging and Human Development*, vol 46, no 4, pp 267-86.

Clarke, L. and Roberts, C. (2004) 'The meaning of grandparenthood and its contribution to the quality of life of older people', in A. Walker and C.H. Hennessy (eds) *Quality of life in old age*, Maidenhead: Open University Press, pp 188-208.

Cooney, T.M. and Smith, L.A. (1996) 'Young adults' relations with grandparents following recent parental divorce', *Journal of Gerontology: Social Sciences*, vol 51B, no 2, pp S91-S95.

Daatland, S.O. (2007) 'Marital history and intergenerational solidarity: the impact of divorce and unmarried cohabitation', *Journal of Social Issues*, vol 63, no 4, pp 809-25.

Davey, A., Savla, J., Janke, M. and Anderson, S. (2009) 'Grandparent–grandchild relationships: from families in contexts to families as contexts', *International Journal of Aging and Human Development*, vol 69, no 4, pp 311-25.

Drew, L.A. and Smith, P.K. (1999) 'The impact of parental separation/divorce on grandparent–grandchild relationships', *International Journal of Aging and Human Development*, vol 48, no 3, pp 191-216.

Engstler, H. and Huxhold, O. (2010) 'Beeinflusst die Beziehung älterer Menschen zu ihren erwachsenen Kindern die räumliche Nähe zwischen den Generationen? Wechselbeziehungen zwischen Wohnentfernung, Kontakthäufigkeit und Beziehungsenge im Längsschnitt', in A. Ette, K. Ruckdeschel and R. Unger (eds) *Intergenerationale Beziehungen: Bedingungen, Potentiale und Konflikte*, Würzburg: Ergon Verlag, pp 175-98.

Frejka, T. and Sobotka, T. (2008) 'Fertility in Europe: diverse, delayed and below replacement', *Demographic Research*, vol 19, no 3, pp 15-46.

Geurts, T., Poortman, A.-R., van Tilburg, T. and Dykstra, P.A. (2009) 'Contact between grandchildren and their grandparents in early adulthood', *Journal of Family Issues*, vol 30, no 12, pp 1689-713.

Hagestad, G.O. (1985) 'Continuity and connectedness', in V.L. Bengtson and J.F. Robertson (eds) *Grandparenthood*, Beverly Hills, CA: Sage Publications, pp 31-48.

Hagestad, G.O. (2006) 'Transfers between grandparents and grandchildren: the importance of taking a three-generation perspective', *Zeitschrift für Familienforschung*, vol 18, no 3, pp 315-32.

Harper, S., Smith, P. and Hagestad, G. (2010) 'Editorial and introduction', *Journal of Intergenerational Relationships*, vol 8, no 3, pp 207-18.

Hodgson, L.G. (1992) 'Adult grandchildren and their grandparents: the enduring bond', *International Journal of Aging and Human Development*, vol 34, no 3, pp 209-25.

Hurme, H., Westerback, S. and Quadrello, T. (2010) 'Traditional and new forms of contact between grandparents and grandchildren', *Journal of Intergenerational Relationships*, vol 8, no 3, pp 264-80.

Kemp, C.L. (2007) 'Grandparent–grandchild ties: reflections on continuity and change across three generations', *Journal of Family Issues*, vol 8, no 7, pp 855-81.

King, V. (2003) 'The legacy of a grandparent's divorce: consequences for ties between grandparents and grandchildren', *Journal of Marriage and Family*, vol 65, no 1, pp 170-83.

Kivnick, H.Q. (1982) 'Grandparenthood: an overview of meaning and mental health', *The Gerontologist*, vol 22, no 1, pp 59-66.

Kohli, M. and Künemund, H. (2003) 'Intergenerational transfers in the family: what motivates giving?', in V.L. Bengtson and A. Lowenstein (eds) *Global aging and challenges to families*, New York, NY: Aldine de Gruyter, pp 123-42.

Kruk, E. and Hall, B.L. (1995) 'The disengagement of paternal grandparents subsequent to divorce', *Journal of Divorce and Remarriage*, vol 23, no 1, pp 131-48.

Lin, I.-F. (2008) 'Consequences of parental divorce for adult children's support of their frail parents', *Journal of Marriage and Family*, vol 70, no 1, pp 113-28.

Lowenstein, A., Katz, R. and Gur-Yaish, N. (2007) 'Reciprocity in parent–child exchange and life satisfaction among the elderly: a cross-national perspective', *Journal of Social Issues*, vol 63, no 4, pp 865-83.

Lussier, G., Deater-Deckard, K., Dunn, J. and Davies, L. (2002) 'Support across two generations: children's closeness to grandparents following parental divorce and remarriage', *Journal of Family Psychology*, vol 16, no 3, pp 363-76.

Lye, D.N. (1996) 'Adult child–parent relationships', *Annual Review of Sociology*, vol 22, pp 79-102.

Mahne, K. and Motel-Klingebiel, A. (2012) 'Grandparenthood: a common aspiration for later life? On the subjective importance of the grandparent role in Germany', *Advances in Life Course Research*, vol 17, forthcoming.

Michalski, R.L. and Shackelford, T.K. (2005) 'Grandparental investment as a function of relational uncertainty and emotional closeness with parents', *Human Nature*, vol 16, no 3, pp 293-305.

Mills, T.L. (1999) 'When grandchildren grow up: role transition and family solidarity among baby boomer grandchildren and their grandparents', *Journal of Aging Studies*, vol 13, no 2, pp 219-39.

Mueller, M.M. and Elder, G.H. (2003) 'Family contingencies across the generations: grandparent–grandchild relationships in holistic perspective', *Journal of Marriage and Family*, vol 65, no 2, pp 404-17.

Mueller, M.M, Wilhelm, B. and Elder, G.H. (2002) 'Variations in grandparenting', *Research on Aging*, vol 24, no 3, pp 360-88.

Neugarten, B.L. and Weinstein, K.K. (1964) 'The changing American grandparent', *Journal of Marriage and Family*, vol 26, no 2, pp 199-204.

Pollet, T.V., Nettle, D. and Nelissen, M. (2007) 'Maternal grandmothers do go the extra mile: factoring distance and lineage into differential contact with grandchildren', *Evolutionary Psychology*, vol 5, no 4, pp 832-43.

Reitzes, D.C. and Mutran, E.J. (2002) 'Self-concept as the organization of roles: importance, centrality, and balance', *The Sociological Quarterly*, vol 43, no 4, pp 647-67.

Reitzes, D.C. and Mutran, E.J. (2004a) 'Grandparent identity, intergenerational family identity, and well-being', *Journal of Gerontology: Social Sciences*, vol 59B, no 4, pp S213-S219.

Reitzes, D.C. and Mutran, E.J. (2004b) 'Grandparenthood: factors influencing frequency of grandparent–grandchildren contact and grandparent role satisfaction', *Journal of Gerontology: Social Sciences*, vol 59B, no 1, pp S9-S16.

Roberts, R.E.L. and Bengtson, V.L. (1990) 'Is intergenerational solidarity a unidimensional construct? A second test of a formal model', *Journal of Gerontology: Social Sciences*, vol 45, no 1, pp 12-20.

Silverstein, M., Gans, D. and Yang, F.M. (2006) 'Filial support to aging parents: the role of norms and needs', *Journal of Family Issues*, vol 27, pp 1068-84.

Silverstein, M., Giarrusso, R. and Bengtson, V.L. (1998) 'Intergenerational solidarity and the grandparent role', in M.E. Szinovacz (ed) *Handbook on grandparenthood*, Westport, CT: Greenwood Press, pp 144-58.

Silverstein, M. and Long, J.D. (1998) 'Trajectories of grandparent's perceived solidarity with adult grandchildren: a growth curve analysis over 23 years', *Journal of Marriage and Family*, vol 60, no 4, pp 912-23.

Silverstein, M. and Marenco, A. (2001) 'How Americans enact the grandparent role across the family life course', *Journal of Family Issues*, vol 22, no 4, pp 493-522.

Taylor, A.C., Robila, M. and Lee, H.S. (2005) 'Distance, contact, and intergenerational relationships: grandparents and adult grandchildren from an international perspective', *Journal of Adult Development*, vol 12, no 1, pp 33-41.

Tomassini, C., Glaser, K. and Stuchbury, R. (2007) 'Family disruption and support in later life: a comparative study between the United Kingdom and Italy', *Journal of Social Issues*, vol 63, no 4, pp 845-63.

Tomassini, C., Kalogirou, S., Grundy, E., Fokkema, T., Martikainen, P., Broese van Groenou, M. et al (2004) 'Contacts between elderly parents and their children in four European countries: current patterns and future prospects', *European Journal of Ageing*, vol 1, no 1, pp 54-63.

Uhlenberg, P. and Cheuk, M. (2010) 'The significance of grandparents to grandchildren: an international perspective', *The SAGE handbook of social gerontology*, London: Sage, pp 447-458.

Uhlenberg, P. and Hammill, B.G. (1998) 'Frequency of grandparent contact with grandchild sets: six factors that make a difference', *The Gerontologist*, vol 38, no 3, pp 276-85.

Whitbeck, L.B., Hoyt, D.T. and Huck, S.M. (1993) 'Family relationship history, contemporary parent–grandparent relationship quality, and the grandparent–grandchild relationship', *Journal of Marriage and Family*, vol 55, no 4, pp 1025-35.

TWELVE

Grandparenting in the 21st century: new directions

Sara Arber and Virpi Timonen

Contemporary grandparenting is at the fulcrum of family relationships, but the nature and practices of grandparenting are very different in the 21st century than 50 years ago, and are very different today in the UK than in China or Africa. To fully understand grandparenting, it is critical to adopt a cross-national and temporal perspective, and be attuned to the impact of globalisation. The global focus of this book emphasises that cultural norms in different societies and broader societal changes have a profound impact on grandparenting. Thus, the practices of grandparenting and subjective meaning of being a grandparent vary markedly between societies and within the same societal context over time.

This book considers 'grandparenting' as an active and dynamic family practice, focusing on *doing* grandparenting. Recent literature on family practices (Morgan, 2011) points to the importance of studying everyday family behaviours. Chambers and colleagues (2009, p 6) emphasise 'that family relationships are constructed through interactive processes of negotiation and thus involve more than a simple following of culturally accepted rules'. Thus, grandparents and other family members exercise agency in constructing their relationships with one another. Although extensive research on 'doing family' has examined family practices among couples and their children (Ribbens, 1994), fewer studies consider family practices among extended (and non-co-resident) family members. An exception is Chambers and colleagues (2009) who examine older parent–adult child relationships focusing on negotiated exchanges and interdependencies.

Our relational perspective emphasises grandparenting as one part of a dynamic and changing network of family relationships, in contrast to studying grandparents using a traditional role framework. Such a role framework provides a more static image of grandparent roles, one that is often seen as substantially proscribed by cultural norms of appropriate behaviour (see Chapter One).

The perspectives adopted in this book are very different from dominant policy concerns about 'an ageing society' and the lack of carers and resources to pay for the 'burden' of older people. Such a 'social problem' or 'dependency' perspective sees older people as a 'burden' to be cared for by their family members, especially the adult child generation (Chambers et al, 2009). A counter to this has been research on intergenerational relationships and reciprocity between generations. The edited volume by Izuhara (2010) examines shifts in relationships between generations, and changes in family structure and support, that are occurring in diverse global contexts, focusing particularly on processes of transformation in intergenerational relations as a response to economic, social and demographic change, and to what extent new patterns of reciprocity are emerging.

Studies of 'intergenerational transfers' have examined the bi-directional flows between generations of financial resources and time devoted to caregiving, showing that the dominant direction of financial transfers is from the older to the middle and grandchild generations (Attias-Donfut et al, 2005; Albertini et al, 2007). This book has not addressed intergenerational transfers; the focus has been on one particular type of intergenerational relationship, namely that between grandparents and grandchildren. While this relationship may involve transfers of time (particularly in terms of caregiving for grandchildren), as chapters in this book show, these transfers reflect much more than 'time', including complex negotiated practices of support and emotional exchanges.

It is surprising that gender has not been more visible in research on grandparenting. Much research on grandparent care for grandchildren implicitly assumes that the primary caregiver is the grandmother. In many contexts, 'grandparenting' may be a euphemism for 'grandmothering'. Little previous research has explicitly examined family practices associated with grandmother and grandfather care in a nuanced way. For example, we know little about whether grandfathering practices largely support the grandmothers' practices, with his involvement dependent on her encouragement and support.

Our focus has been on the everyday practices of grandparenting, and how these are negotiated across both the dyadic grandparent–grandchild relationship and the triad of grandparent–adult child–grandchild. Underlying the family practices of 'doing' grandparenting, we recognise that family relationships are constrained by material and structural realities that face individual family members and the family as a whole. Although these structural constraints often operate within the bounded household context, research on grandparenting brings into sharp relief the need to consider how family relationships that transcend household boundaries are influenced by structural constraints.

This concluding chapter first reviews how demographic and societal changes, and cultural and generational changes, have influenced grandparenting. Since a key 21st century issue is the growth of dual-earner families and grandparents' involvement in grandchild care, we consider how welfare state policies are linked to this trend in different societal contexts, demonstrating the interconnections between families, labour markets and state policies, as well as between the public and private. We consider cultural norms about grandparenting and the agency of grandparents, and how clashes between norms and agency may result in ambivalence. Finally, we emphasise that grandparenting is part of a complex web of negotiated family relationships, within which the grandchild may influence the grandparents' attitudes and practices.

Social change and grandparenting

Many societal changes that shape the practices of grandparenting are associated with globalisation, including demographic changes, trends in paid employment, geographical mobility and the communications revolution. Although these will be reviewed separately, they are, of course, interconnected and interacting.

A fundamental demographic change is the rapid increase in longevity across the globe. For many Asian countries, over one generation, there have been gains in life expectancy of 20 years, which means that grandchildren will share a much longer period of life with their grandparents (Phillipson, 2010). Within the increasing number of three- and four-generational families, there is the potential for grandchildren to establish much longer-lasting relationships with their grandparents. Declines in fertility have been rapid, especially in southern Europe, China and Asia, resulting in fewer grandchildren and the development of 'bean-pole' families (Bengtson and Harootyan, 1994). Fewer grandchildren may mean that grandparents 'invest' more time and resources in their relationships with these grandchildren, developing stronger emotional bonds.

Other demographic changes include changing patterns of marriage, divorce and cohabitation. Divorce is increasingly prevalent in both the grandparent and the parent (middle) generation, often resulting in the establishment of reconstituted families. Divorce in the middle generation may increase the intensity of support provided by (particularly maternal) grandparents, while fracturing relationships with (particularly paternal) grandparents. Divorce and repartnering in the grandparent generation may potentially result in one grandchild having eight (step-)grandparents, while divorce and repartnering in the parent generation can have similar effects. Complexities of contemporary families include children within the same family having different sets of (usually paternal) grandparents. The prevalence of divorce and reconstituted families varies greatly between societies, being higher in the US, UK and northern Europe, very low in China and Asian countries, and at an intermediate level in the predominantly Catholic countries of southern Europe and Ireland. Chapters Eight and Nine consider the impact of divorce and the agency exercised by grandparents in contexts of divorce, but only scratch the surface of understanding the meaning of grandparenting in the context of divorce and cohabitation, while issues regarding grandparenting in reconstituted families remain unexplored.

A profound societal change affecting grandparenting relates to paid employment, particularly the growing labour force participation of women in western and Asian societies. However, societies differ in their policies regarding provision of childcare for children (when mothers are in paid work) and grandparents' (or more usually grandmothers') role in childcare (as discussed in Part One). Alongside increases in women's employment, trends towards earlier exit from the labour market in European countries have had the potential to 'free up' grandparents from paid employment, allowing them more 'opportunity' to act as grandchild carers. However, policy concerns internationally have recently emphasised the costs of the 'ageing population' leading to increases in retirement age and policy initiatives for workers to delay retirement and remain longer in the labour market. A key issue is therefore how grandparents' participation in paid employment affects their grandparenting practices. Chapter Four illustrates how grandmothers in the US 'juggle' their own paid work with providing intensive grandchild care, while Chapter Eleven finds that grandparents in paid employment in Germany have less frequent contact with their grandchildren.

Globalisation has resulted in major migratory flows *between* countries for paid employment (such as for domestic work, Chapters Five and Six), and rural to urban migration within countries (Chapter Three). Paid work opportunities are a major reason for moving *within* countries. All these migratory flows potentially severe or militate against contact between grandparents and grandchildren. However, following retirement, grandparents may move to live closer to grandchildren (Glaser et al, 2010). Geographical proximity of grandparents and grandchildren is crucial in providing 'opportunities' for interaction and thereby influencing grandparent–grandchild relationships (Cherlin and Furstenberg, 1992). Societal norms also influence geographical propinquity; Kohli and colleagues (2008) report marked differences across Europe in living near adult children, varying from about 30% of people aged 50 and over living within 1 km of a child in Sweden and Denmark to over 70% in Italy, Spain and Greece.

In parallel, societal changes associated with rapid developments in communications technology may reduce the barriers of geographical distance. Apart from mobile telephones and email, grandparents and grandchildren may increasingly communicate across countries and continents through Skype calls. Chapter Nine touches on how new communication technologies may facilitate links between grandparents and grandchildren. However, use of internet-based communication technologies is influenced by material and cultural resources that are more available or accessible to certain groups.

Alongside these macro-level societal and global changes, there are cross-cutting socioeconomic and material inequalities within any society that play a profound role in influencing interpersonal relationships within families. For example, where there is public provision or adequate financial resources to purchase high-quality daycare, grandparents' lives may *not* be constrained by daily grandchild care. While the employment of foreign domestic workers may be a 'solution' to support mothers' paid work within middle-/higher-income families in Singapore (Chapter Six), the domestic workers themselves may have left behind grandparents, parents, children or grandchildren in their native country, limiting these women's own family relationships. Thus, within any society there are patterned diversities in the practices of grandparenting, associated with gender, material circumstances, ethnicity, geographical propinquity and family structure.

Cultural and generational changes

Cultural norms regarding the appropriate roles of, and behaviour towards, grandparents have changed over time and vary markedly between societies. The changes in Asian societies have been particularly rapid, resulting in a 'profound generational gap regarding social norms, expectations and cultural practices' (Izuhara, 2010, p 3). Thus, the potential for conflict between generations regarding cultural norms may be greater in the East than the West. In China and East Asian societies, Confucianism has emphasised the importance of filial piety towards elders, wisdom of elders, and esteem of grandparents within the society.

Although the legacy of these Confucian ideals remains, other societal and cultural changes may lead to conflicts with these more traditional norms (Chapter Five).

Grandparenthood is often equated with 'old age' in the popular imagination, although grandparents can range in age from 35-year olds to centenarians. The age of a grandparent clearly influences practices of grandparenting (Chapters Ten and Eleven), both because of age per se (and its association with health and physical ability), and because of their birth cohort. Mannheim (1952) discussed 'historical generations' associated with particular 'birth cohorts', highlighting how generations have different historical experiences that shape their outlook and attitudes (Arber and Attias-Donfut, 2000). Grandparents who have lived through different historical periods and societal contexts enter later life with varying attitudes and expectations that influence their perspectives on grandparenting. The image of the grandmother knitting in a rocking chair, or the old widow dressed in black, no longer chimes in the 21st century. Contemporary grandmothers are less constrained by cultural expectations of passivity. The 'baby boomers', born in the late 1940s and early 1950s (Evandrou, 1997), are entering later life with different sets of cultural values, as well as being healthier, wealthier and more oriented to leisure than earlier cohorts. We can therefore expect that this generation will practise grandparenting in very different ways to their parents.

A key normative cultural change in contemporary western societies is the expectation that older people should be active and productive (Bowling, 2003; Katz, 2005). Grandparents may adopt the cultural norm of 'active ageing' and wish to be seen as ageing 'successfully', as exemplified by leading an active lifestyle and demonstrating agency over their activities. However, this contemporary cultural mandate to 'active' or 'successful ageing' may conflict with other cultural norms and expectations, such as to 'be there' for grandchildren (Chapter Seven), and to support and provide grandchild care when required by the middle generation (Chapters Two to Six). Thus, the norm of 'active ageing' may conflict with expectations of the parent generation that grandparents will be available to care for grandchildren while the mothers work. Conflict between these two cultural norms may lead to growing tensions or ambivalence between the desires of the grandparent generation for 'active ageing' and the requirements of the middle generation for grandchild care, which are likely to be most keenly felt by older women.

Grandparenting, by definition, involves a dyadic relationship with one or multiple grandchildren. Literature from the sociology of childhood over the past 20 years (James et al, 1998; Knapp, 1999) has emphasised the active ways that children influence relationships with their parents and other adults. Cultural changes in norms regarding childhood, and the expectations of being a grandchild, will also influence the nature of grandparent–grandchild relationships.

In summary, to understand grandparenting practices, we need to consider both the changing cultural scripts for older people as well as changing norms about children and childhood, in tandem with the societal changes discussed in the previous section. While it is important to emphasise diversity and the agency of both parties in the dyadic relationship of grandparent and grandchild, as well as the agency of the parent (middle) generation, we need to be mindful of how cultural and societal changes intersect with material and socioeconomic resources, which contribute to the everyday realities of grandparenting practices.

Grandparenting responses to mothers' paid employment

Since the 'dual-earner' family has become the norm in most developed societies, it is vital to consider childcare arrangements where both parents (and lone parents) are in paid work. Chapters in Part One showed how grandparents are central to supporting the increased employment of women, but in varying ways according to the welfare policy context, demonstrating the interconnections between families, labour markets and state policies.

From a macro perspective, Chapter Two contrasted the varied responses across European societies regarding women's increased labour force participation. In northern European countries, welfare policies support the provision of childcare and care for elders, with policies also encouraging greater gender equality in the domestic division of labour. Although the majority of grandparents provide support and 'babysitting' for their grandchildren, they rarely undertake daily childcare to enable daughters/in-law to work. Grandparents in these countries provide a back-up resource in temporary emergencies or times of need, and are characterised as 'family savers'. Grandparents therefore 'complement' the provision of state welfare services. In contrast, the countries of southern Europe provide very little welfare state provision for childcare (or elder care). This, together with very marked gender-segregated roles in the domestic arena, has resulted in employed women turning to their mothers (the grandmothers) for everyday childcare. Cross-national survey data show that a high proportion of grandparents in southern European countries provide daily childcare, characterised as 'mother savers', who play a vital role in supporting their daughters/-in-law to enter and remain in the labour market. They 'substitute' for the inadequacy of state childcare support. However, there are divisions by financial circumstances, with more affluent grandparents and higher-earning women better able to afford formal childcare, rather than relying on (and constraining the lives of) their grandmothers.

The UK exemplifies a combination of both systems and is profoundly class-divided. Lack of affordable childcare means that working-class parents in particular turn to grandparents for daily childcare (or a regular commitment of childcare on two or three days per week) (Dench and Ogg, 2002). Wheelock and Jones (2002) demonstrate the heavy reliance of employed mothers on grandparent care and that some grandparents give up paid work to provide regular grandchild care. Indeed, the UK Grandparents Plus report (Glaser et al, 2010) highlights the considerable involvement of grandparents in regular childcare in the UK and across Europe, arguing that policies should be in place to provide financial and other supports for grandparents in this role. Thus, it is important to consider the interdependence between formal and informal systems of childcare and how these differ across societal contexts.

Grandparents perform the greatest childcare role where the middle generation is absent because of migration (as in China; see Chapter Three), through HIV/AIDS (as in sub-Saharan Africa; see Oduran and Oduran, 2010) or because of inability to parent through mental health problems, drug or alcohol addiction (as in the US; see Minkler, 1999). However, as Chapter Three demonstrates, the routes are very different into each of these forms of 'custodial grandparenting' within 'skipped-generation' households, leading to diverse outcomes for the grandparents. In the US, custodial grandparents are disadvantaged on financial and health grounds prior to entry into custodial grandparenting, and their health and wellbeing then worsens, largely due to the accumulation of economic disadvantages. In contrast, grandparents in rural China are advantaged in their health and financial assets prior to entry into custodial grandparenting, and while in this role their health and wellbeing (measured by number of depressive symptoms) improves, both because of financial remittances from adult children and the psychological benefits of grandparenting within the Chinese cultural context. Custodial grandparents in the US are characterised as 'child savers', whereas in the Chinese context, they are characterised as 'family maximisers', since their role is part of a broader family strategy to improve the financial wellbeing of the whole extended family.

Chapters Two and Three provided a macro-level perspective to highlight the influence of societal contexts and welfare state policies on grandparents' role in providing 'substitute' or 'complementary' childcare. Less attention has previously been paid to the micro-level perspectives of grandparents themselves about providing childcare, especially to what extent they feel constrained by 'being expected' to provide grandchild care or ambivalent towards their role as regular caregivers for grandchildren. Three chapters adopt a micro perspective, examining grandchild care and intergenerational relationships in different societal contexts – Chapter Four (the US), Chapter Five (Hong Kong) and Chapter Six (Singapore).

Chapter Four provided in-depth case studies of three US grandmothers, who, while engaged in full-time paid work, also undertook very extensive grandchild care. They privileged their daughters' employment over their own, and accepted the priority of their daughter 'keeping her job' or pursuing educational qualifications. These grandmothers devoted nearly all of their time, while not working themselves, to providing grandchild care. Despite their very extensive time commitments, they expressed little ambivalence about their grandchild care practices, being motivated entirely by the wellbeing of their grandchildren and adult daughters (all of whom were single mothers). Although these women lived close to their grandchildren, they were not custodial grandparents, and could be characterised as 'mother savers'.

Asian societies exemplify rapid changes in cultural norms about the role of grandparents, declines in co-residence within three generational households, and acceptance of the contemporary norm of mothers' participation in paid work. The policy response in both Hong Kong and Singapore has been to support mothers' employment through 'importing' foreign domestic workers, mainly from the Phillipines. Chapter Five analysed the perspectives of grandparents in Hong Kong on their supportive relationships with adult children and adolescent grandchildren, both in co-residential and non-co-residential families. Although multigenerational co-residence is still seen as an act of filial piety and a virtue in traditional Chinese culture, this conflicts with newer cultural expectations that a successful son should be able to afford his own independent residence. Tensions and ambivalences were revealed, with grandparents expressing resentment that they were treated like 'domestic workers', and not accorded the traditional respect (as a manifestation of filial piety) that should be accorded to elders. Thus, grandparents experienced ambivalence generated from conflicts between different norms, as well as conflicts between norms and the realities of providing everyday functional support to their adult children and grandchildren.

Chapter Six probed the perspectives of young adults in Singapore about preferred carers for children under the age of three, illustrating that grandparents were the preferred childcarers, even though foreign domestic workers were usually employed. Grandparents played a key role in 'supervising' foreign domestic workers, and ensured that grandchildren would be taught morals and good behaviour. However, the feasibility of employing foreign domestic workers was divided by income, with those in lower-income households more reliant on grandparent care. As one participant stated, "When you get your parents, you get the real Singaporean deal, cheap and good". However, adult children expressed a sense of ambivalence that reliance on grandparental childcare may be 'unfair' to their parents whose lives were severely constrained, may result in adverse health consequences for their parents, or that care by less educated grandparents may not be in the best interests of the educational development of their child.

The chapters in Part One illustrate the vital role grandparents play in enabling the middle generation (mothers) to be employed, but that state policies differ in the nature of support provided for children during mother's employment. Grandparents perform a key role by undertaking grandchild care, and have been characterised in different societal contexts as 'child savers', 'mother savers', 'family savers' and 'family maximisers'. Another distinction that could be made is to what extent grandparents represent a 'regular army', providing grandchild care on a regular basis, as in the Mediterranean countries, China and Singapore, or act as a 'reserve army'[1], providing care only in times of crisis or emergencies and on their own terms, as in the Nordic countries. Grandparents within the 'reserve army' are much less constrained by grandchild care, more able to pursue an 'active ageing' later life, and experience less intergenerational ambivalence. In contrast, in contexts where grandparents are *expected* to be a 'regular army', there is greater potential for intergenerational tensions and ambivalence, and constraints experienced by the older generation. Cross-cutting this is gender; where grandparents form a 'regular army', the major childcare roles and responsibilities normally fall on grandmothers, although grandfathers often provide a supportive role to their wives.

Grandparenting norms, gender and complex family configurations

Micro-level perspectives were employed to tease out the realities of grandparenting practices, as well as the impact of cultural norms about grandparenting, based on in-depth qualitative research in Chapters Seven to Nine. These chapters documented the subtle ways that grandparents negotiate relationships and exercise agency, the nature of ambivalences within grandparents' relationships with the middle generation, and how gender intersects in these intergenerational dynamics.

Cultural norms about grandparenting may conflict with other norms and with everyday practices. Vanessa May and colleagues (Chapter Seven) reported the ubiquity of norms of grandparents 'being there' for their grandchildren and 'not interfering' with the middle generations' parenting practices in the UK. Using survey data, Katharina Herlofson and Gunhild Hagestad (Chapter Two) in Norway also found strong support for the norm of 'being there' among both the grandparent and adult child generations, showing very little gender difference in support for this norm. May and colleagues' relational approach highlights how grandparents negotiate competing norms within their everyday practices of grandparenting. The norm of grandparents being a 'good parent' to their own adult children implies allowing them to be independent and thereby 'not interfering', but this can conflict with responsibilities to their grandchildren. Another paradox and potential conflict relates to balancing the personal norm of 'self-determination' with 'being there' for grandchildren.

The clash of cultural norms may be greater in specific societal or material contexts, increasing the need for negotiations between competing understandings of different kin responsibilities, tensions and ambivalence. A pronounced generational gap in cultural norms exists in Hong Kong. Lisanne Ko (Chapter Five) highlighted substantial ambivalence in Hong Kong, where the filial norms of piety towards grandparents and current norms that grandparents provide extensive support to their grandchildren were in conflict.

Ambivalence and how grandparents negotiate contradictions between cultural norms were also highlighted in cases of divorce, especially in contexts where divorce is less normative, as in contemporary Ireland. Virpi Timonen and Martha Doyle's qualitative research (Chapter Eight) on grandparenting following an adult child's divorce in Ireland illustrated grandparents' key role in the process of reorganising relationships within families following divorce. They showed how grandparents use agency to maintain (and sometimes to reduce) contact with their grandchildren, and how they actively renegotiated boundaries around the expectations of others about their grandparenting practices. They argued that grandparental agency was primarily motivated by the wish to maintain their grandchild's wellbeing and to bridge formally dissolved family relations in order to secure contact with grandchildren. However, grandparents' own wellbeing could also be the driving consideration in situations where agency was used to reduce involvement that was experienced as onerous or excessive.

Gender remains unacknowledged in many studies of grandparenting with very little research on grandfathering, especially among divorced or widowed grandfathers. An exception is Anna Tarrant (Chapter Nine), who considered grandfathering practices in the UK, among 'still-married', 'repartnered' and widowed grandfathers. She examined the performance of masculinities among grandfathers following divorce and family reformation, shattering the myth that all divorced grandfathers have poorer relationships with their grandchildren. Her chapter showed how grandfathers were taking on new identities within their grandfathering role, and may be acting with agency to forge new caregiving relationships with their grandchildren, engaging more extensively in childcare practices than they did when their own children were young. She reminds us of the importance of taking into consideration generation, and the nature of generational influences on grandparenting, demonstrating how some grandfathers learn new grandparenting practices and behaviours by observing their adult sons' fathering practices. In addition, new technologies open new spaces for the performance of masculinities among grandfathers, who may be more likely to communicate with their grandchildren through internet technologies. Skype calls mean that grandparenting relationships can be co-constructed, when grandparents and grandchildren are divided by great geographical distances.

A number of chapters illustrate the negotiated nature of grandparenting relationships and the paradoxes and ambivalences within these relationships. However, there remains a lack of attention to the gendered nature of grandparenting practices, including among grandfathers who are divorced or widowed. Much more research is needed on grandparenting following divorce and in more complex family configurations, and on how grandparenting practices vary by the intersections of gender, lineage and step-grandparenting, as well as class and ethnicity. These chapters build on the perspectives of the grandparent generation, while neglecting the perspectives of grandchildren, to which we now turn.

A relational perspective and grandchildren's agency

The voices of grandchildren have been surprisingly absent in research on grandparenting. This is akin to assuming that the nature of couple relationships can be understood by only interviewing husbands (or wives). Clearly each party will have differing perspectives on the nature of the grandparent–grandchild relationship, as well as varying degrees of influence on different aspects of this relationship. Research in the sociology of childhood has emphasised that children have agency over their relationships and has pioneered new methodologies for researching and hearing the voices of children (James et al, 1998; Knapp, 1999; Greene and Hogan, 2005), but has not yet had a major influence on approaches within research on grandparent–grandchild relationships.

Earlier research on grandparents emphasised the importance of grandparents as socialisation agents for grandchildren (Neugarten and Weinstein, 1964), and portrayed a one-way influence of grandparents on grandchildren. Later work also emphasised the potentially mediating role of the middle generation in influencing grandparent–grandchild relationships (Robertson, 1976). This 'downward' model has neglected consideration of upward flows of influence from the grandchild to the grandparent, and that older grandchildren may influence the nature of the grandparent–adult child relationship; all three generations should be considered in order to fully understand grandparent–grandchild relationships (Hagestad, 1985).

The practices of grandparenting can only be understood through a broader relational approach that 'emphasises the individual's place within a dynamic and continuous set of transactional processes' (Hillcoat-Nallétamby and Phillips, 2011, p 212). Thus, grandparents must be seen within an interactional network that involves not only the grandparent and grandchild, but also the parent(s) and potentially other family members. Within a relational perspective, all three generations may be seen as having agency over the nature of the relationships.

Alice Delerue Matos and Rita Borges Neves (Chapter Ten) used qualitative interview data to illustrate how adolescent children in Portugal influenced the behaviour and opinions of their 'emotionally closest' grandparent. Grandchildren exercised agency in altering their grandparents' use of information technology and domestic appliances, altering their dietary behaviour and their attitudes towards contemporary social issues. The influence of grandchildren on their grandparents was greatest where the dyad shared activities and had an emotionally close relationship. In many cases, among these adolescent grandchildren, there was little mediation of the relationship by the middle (adult child) generation.

The importance of taking a three generational perspective was illustrated by Katharina Mahne and Oliver Huxhold (Chapter Eleven). Their methodologically innovative chapter simultaneously considered the impact of the grandparent, adult child and grandchild on the frequency of face-to-face contact between grandparents and older grandchildren. By using nationally representative German data on contact with a randomly selected grandchild within the family of *each* adult child, they disentangled within-family and between-family variation in grandparent–grandchild contact. The impact of social changes such as divorce was addressed, showing that divorced grandparents (especially grandfathers) had less contact with their grandchildren, while divorce among the middle generation only resulted in less contact with paternal grandparents. They demonstrated how the adult child generation moderated the nature of grandparenting even with older grandchildren who no longer lived in the parental home.

In their varying ways, these two chapters illustrate the agency of each party within the triad. Chapter Ten used qualitative research to focus on the 'grandchilding' practices of adolescent grandchildren and how they influenced their emotionally closest grandparent. In contrast, Chapter Eleven used sophisticated multilevel statistical analysis to analyse the triad of grandparent–adult child–grandchild, and simultaneously measured the independent influence of each party on the frequency of grandparent–grandchild contact.

Conclusion

This collection has brought to light novel findings, arguments and conceptualisations of grandparenting that provide a basis for advancing research on family relationships. However, we also wish to acknowledge limitations. Although this book covers a range of contexts (Europe, US, China, Hong Kong, Singapore), it is mainly about grandparenting in developed countries. Grandparenting may be of particular salience in developing countries where grandparents are often critical for the wellbeing of their grandchildren, adult children and indeed societies and economies as a whole (Oppong, 2006; Oduaran and Oduaran, 2010).

Globalisation has increased distance between family members, and distance matters (Cherlin and Furstenberg, 1992). However, we know little about grandparenting at a very long distance, for example in transnational families. In western countries, the increasing prevalence of divorce, repartnering and step-families means that step-grandparenting is a more common experience, yet remains poorly understood. New patterns in family reciprocity, including within step-families and transnational families, are examined in the edited collection by Izuhara (2010), but need further study. Great-grandparenting may also become more important with four or even five surviving generations in some families, and calls for research.

Gender often remains unacknowledged in both macro-level and micro-level studies of grandparenting. For example, where an older couple provide grandchild care, few studies analyse the divisions of grandchild labour in terms of the relative roles of each grandparent in grandchild care. We could draw an analogy with the lack of research on the gendered divisions of household work and childcare prior to feminist research from the 1970s onwards. Future studies should more explicitly tease out the gendered dimensions of grandparenting practices, including emotional aspects of relationships with grandchildren.

Divorce and family reconstitution throw into sharp relief issues of how gender is implicated in grandparenting practices. We need to better understand the constraints and possibilities associated with grandfathering following divorce and widowhood, and how this contrasts with grandmothering by divorced/widowed women. The growth of same-sex families (Heaphy, 2007) has not been matched by research on grandparenting in relation to same-sex couples within the parent (middle) generation or the grandparent generation. An exception is Oriel and Fruhauf (2012), who analyse lesbian, gay, bisexual and transgender (LGBT) grandparents. It remains fundamental to consider how gender influences grandparenting in the context of divorce and family reformation, as well as LGBT parents/grandparents, regarding the attitudes and practices of members of all three relevant generations.

This volume does contain chapters that take seriously the exhortation to employ a three-generational approach; for instance, Chapter Eleven and several other chapters are attuned to the role and impact of the middle generation. However, we adhere to Szinovacz's (1998) recommendation that triads and indeed broader family groups and horizontal family relationships call for more research. For instance, the impact of relationships between maternal and paternal grandparents within a family on the experience of grandparenting, and the experience of being a grandchild, remain poorly understood.

Contemporary grandparenting has illuminated some of the newer contours of grandparenting in a diversity of societal and cultural contexts. Chapters have examined how grandparenting is influenced by cultural norms and welfare policies, as well as global trends associated with demographic changes, migration and increases in women's employment. The importance of examining the *doing* of grandparenting has been emphasised, together with the value of using a relational perspective to understand the negotiated nature of grandparent–adult child–grandchild relationships and the agency of each party within these three-generational relationships. Key cross-cutting dimensions include the salience of gender, age (or generation), marital status and structured inequalities associated with class and material resources. Themes addressed in this book represent a rich arena for future research, given the rapid pace of global and societal changes, increased scope for agency in many contexts, and the fact that grandparenting is at the fulcrum of family relationships.

Note

[1] Gunhild Hagestad coined the concept of grandparents as a 'reserve army' (personal communication), which builds on her earlier discussion of grandparents in the US as the 'family National Guard' (Hagestad, 1985).

References

Albertini, M., Kohli, M. and Vogel, C. (2007) 'Intergenerational transfers of time and money in European families: common patterns – different regimes?', *Journal of European Social Policy*, vol 17, no 4, pp 319-34.

Arber, S. and Attias-Donfut, C. (eds) (2000) *The myth of generational conflict: The family and state in ageing societies*, London: Routledge.

Attias-Donfut, C., Ogg, J. and Wolff, F.C. (2005) 'European patterns of intergenerational financial and time transfers', *European Journal of Ageing*, vol 2, no 3, pp 161-73.

Bengtson, V. and Harootyan, R.A. (1994) *Intergenerational linkages: Hidden connections in American society*, New York, NY: Springer.

Bowling, A. (2003) 'The concepts of successful and positive ageing', *Family Practice*, vol 10, no 4, pp 449-53.

Chambers, P., Allan, G., Phillipson, C. and Ray, M. (2009) *Family practices in later life*, Bristol: The Policy Press.

Cherlin, A.J. and Furstenberg, F.F. (1992) *The new American grandparent*, Cambridge, MA: Harvard University Press.

Dench, G. and Ogg, J. (2002) *Grandparenting in Britain: A baseline study*, London: Institute of Community Studies.

Evandrou, M. (1997) *Baby boomers: Ageing in the 21st century*, London: Age Concern.

Glaser, K., Montserrat, E.R., Waginger, U., Price, D., Stuchbury, R. and Tinker, A. (2010) *Grandparenting in Europe*, London: King's College London and Grandparents Plus.

Greene, S. and Hogan, D. (eds) (2005) *Researching children's experience. Approaches and methods*, London: Sage Publications.

Hagestad, G. (1985) 'Continuity and connectedness', in V.L. Bengtson and J.F Robertson (eds) *Grandparenthood*, Beverly Hills, CA: Sage Publications.

Heaphy, B. (2007) 'Lesbian and gay families', in G. Ritzer (ed) *Blackwell encyclopedia of sociology*, Oxford: Blackwell.

Hillcoat-Nallétamby, S. and Phillips, H. (2011) 'Sociological ambivalence revisited', *Sociology*, vol 45, no 2, pp 202-17.

Izuhara, M. (ed) (2010) *Ageing and intergenerational relations: Family reciprocity from a global perspective*, Bristol: The Policy Press.

James, A., Jenks, C. and Prout, A. (1998) *Theorizing childhood*, Cambridge: Polity Press.

Katz, S. (2005) 'Busy bodies: activity, ageing and the management of everyday life', in S. Katz (ed) *Cultural aging: Life courses, lifestyles and senior worlds*, Peterborough, ON: Broadview Press.

Kohli, M., Kunemund, H. and Vogel, C. (2008) 'Shrinking families? Marital status, childlessness, and intergenerational relationships', in A. Borsch-Supan (ed) *First results from the Survey of Health, Ageing and Retirement in Europe (2004-2007)*, Mannheim: Mannheim Research Institute for the Economics of Ageing, pp 166-73.

Knapp, S.J. (1999) 'Facing the child. Rethinking models of agency in parent–child relations', in C.L. Shehan (ed) *Through the eyes of the child: Revisioning children as active agents of family life*, Stamford, CT: JAI Press Inc, pp 53-75.

Mannheim, K. (1952) 'The problem of generations', in K. Mannheim (ed) *Essays on the sociology of knowledge*, London: Routledge and Kegan Paul.

Minkler, M. (1999) 'Intergenerational households headed by grandparents: contexts, realities and implications for policy', *Journal of Aging Studies*, vol 13, no 2, pp 199-218.

Morgan, D.H.J. (2011) *Rethinking family practices*, Basingstoke: Palgrave Macmillan.

Neugarten, B. and Weinstein, K. (1964) 'The changing American grandparent', *Journal of Marriage and Family*, vol 26, no 2, pp 199-204.

Oduran, A. and Oduran, C. (2010) 'Grandparents and HIV and AIDS in sub-Saharan Africa', in M. Izuhara (ed) *Ageing and intergenerational relations: Family reciprocity from a global perspective*, Bristol: The Policy Press.

Oppong, C. (2006) 'Familial roles and social transformations: older men and women in Sub-Saharan Africa', *Research on Aging*, vol 28, no 6, pp 654-68.

Oriel, N.A. and Fruhauf, C. A. (2012) 'Lesbian, gay, bisexual and transgender grandparents', in A.Goldberg and K.R.Allen (eds) *LGBT parent families: Possibilities for new research and implications for practice*, New York, NY: Springer.

Phillipson, C. (2010) 'Globalisation, global ageing and intergenerational change', in M. Izuhara (ed) *Ageing and intergenerational relations: Family reciprocity from a global perspective*, Bristol: The Policy Press.

Ribbens, J. (1994) *Mothers and their children: A feminist sociology of childrearing*, London: Sage Publications.

Robertson, J. (1976) 'Significance of grandparents perceptions of young adult grandchildren', *The Gerontologist*, vol 16, no 2, pp 137-40.

Szinovacz, M.E. (ed) (1998) *Handbook on grandparenthood*, Westport, CT: Greenwood Press.

Wheelock, J. and Jones, K. (2002) '"Grandparents are the next best thing": informal childcare for working parents in urban Britain', *Journal of Social Policy*, vol 31, no 3, pp 441-63.

Index

Page references for notes are followed by n

G

gender 1–2, 3, 8–9, 248, 258, 261
  childcare 36–7
  custodial grandparenting 67–8
  and demography 31
  and grandparental agency 178
  and lineage 10, 229, 232, 237
  role expectations and role
    enactment 34–5, 36–7
  see also grandfathers; grandmothers;
    mothers; women
Generations and Gender Survey (GGS)
  33
geographical proximity 12, 230, 233, 237,
  250–1
Germany
  grandparent–grandchild interaction
    232–42, 260
  role expectations and role
    enactment 34, 35, 36, 37, 38, 39
Geurts, T. 242
Giarrusso, R. 12–13
grandchild care 6–7, 28–9, 38, 42–3,
  143–4, 153–4, 250, 253–6
  Asia 113
  by foreign domestic workers and
    grandparents 115–18
  mother savers and family savers
    41–2
  Norway 32, 33
  role expectations and enactment
    35–7, 39–40
  Singapore 119–33
  substitution versus complementarity
    40–1
  and work 71–87
grandchild sets 10–11, 30
grandchildren 10–11
  influence on grandparents 203–5,
    207–21, 252–3, 259–60
  social contact with grandparents
    225–6, 232–42
grandfathers 8, 31, 181–2, 196–9, 258
  and adult children's divorce 164,
    192–4, 198–9
  ambivalence 14–15, 108
  China 104–5
  conceptual framework and method
    183–6
  custodial grandparenting 67–8
  divorce 3, 9, 190–2, 194–5, 198
  financial support 33, 34
  grandchild care 32, 33, 35, 36–7, 71

and grandchildren 186–90, 229,
  230, 232, 236–7
technology 195–6
see also maternal grandfathers;
  paternal grandfathers
grandmothers 8, 31, 248
  and adult children's divorce 160,
    164
  being there 33
  custodial grandparenting 6, 54, 64,
    67–8
  grandchild care 4, 32, 33, 35, 36–7,
    41, 54, 255
  grandchild sets 30
  and grandchildren 11, 213–14,
    220–1, 229, 230, 232, 236–7
  longevity 3
  work and grandchildren 71–87
  see also maternal grandmothers;
    paternal grandmothers
grandparent caregiver tax relief 119
grandparents 1–2, 27–9, 247–9, 260–2
  and adult children's divorce 159–62,
    163–78
  being there yet not interfering
    141–55
  cultural and generational changes
    251–3
  demography 2–3, 30–1
  depressive symptoms 62–5
  divorce 249–50
  gender and generation 8–12
  influence on grandchildren 203,
    204–5, 259
  influence of grandchildren 203–5,
    207–21, 259
  and intergenerational solidarity
    227–32
  norms 15–18, 139–41, 189, 257–8
  Norway 31–3
  research 4–7
  role expectations and role
    enactment 31–40
  rural China 60–2
  and social change 249–51
  social contact with older
    grandchildren 225–6, 235–42
  societal and cultural contexts 12–15
  typologies of styles 7
  see also custodial grandparenting;
    grandchild care; maternal
    grandparents; paternal
    grandparents
Grandparents Plus 254
great-grandparents 261

Understanding family meanings

A reflective text

Jane Ribbens McCarthy, Megan Doolittle, Shelley Day Sclater

Family Studies is a key area of policy, professional and personal debate. Perhaps precisely because of this, teaching texts have struggled with how to approach this area, which is both 'familiar' and also contentious and value laden. This innovative and reflective book deals with such dilemmas head-on, through its focus on family meanings in diverse contexts in order to enhance our understanding of everyday social lives and professional practices.

Drawing on extracts and research by leading authors in the field of family studies, *Understanding Family Meanings* provides the reader with an overview of the basic concepts and theories related to families using readings with questions and analysis to encourage reflection and learning. Published in association with The Open University, the book centralises the question what is 'family' and focuses on family meanings as the key underpinnings for academic study and professional training.

March 2012 • 296 Pages • **Paperback** £21.99 ISBN 978 1 44730 112 7
Hardback £60.00 ISBN 978 1 44730 113 4

To order copies of these publications or any other Policy Press titles please visit www.policypress.co.uk or contact:

In the UK and Europe:
Marston Book Services, PO Box 269,
Abingdon, Oxon, OX14 4YN, UK
Tel: +44 (0)1235 465500
Fax: +44 (0)1235 465556
Email: direct.orders@marston.co.uk

In Australia and New Zealand:
DA Information Services,
648 Whitehorse Road Mitcham,
Victoria 3132, Australia
Tel: +61 (3) 9210 7777
Fax: +61 (3) 9210 7788
E-mail: service@dadirect.com.au

In the USA and Canada:
ISBS, 920 NE 58th Street, Suite
300, Portland, OR 97213-3786,
USA
Tel: +1 800 944 6190
(toll free)
Fax: +1 503 280 8832
Email: info@isbs.com